QUALITY THROUGH

STATISTICAL THINKING

Improving Process Control

and Capability

GORDON H. ROBERTSON

Published by the ASI Press, a division of the American Supplier Institute.

Printed in the United States of America.

Library of Congress Cataloging-in-Publication Data

Robertson, Gordon H., 1927-
    Quality through statistical thinking: improving process control and capability / Gordon H. Robertson.
       p.   cm.
    Includes index.
    ISBN 0-9412343-08-7
    1. Process control—Statistical methods. I. Title.
TS156.8.R62   1989   89-14902
658.5—dc20   CIP

CONTENTS

FIGURES

CHAPTER 8   Other Control Charts for Variables

CHAPTER 9   Control Charts for Attributes

TABLES

PREFACE

Today there is a new definition of quality. It requires a new philosophy, a new perspective on who is involved in maintaining quality and tools that address the problem of variation. Statistical thinking, as a way of thinking and communicating about cost and quality, is a key aspect of this new philosophy. Statistical Process Control (SPC) is a system for providing a company with information on the ability of its manufacturing processes to produce high quality products.

SPC is one in a series of technologies that must be integrated into a company's total quality management system. Today's design technologies are based on the assumption that a system exists to provide information on the capabilities of existing processes. SPC is the basis for such a system.

In 1988 John Kennedy, of the ASI Press, asked if I would consider writing a book on the practical aspects of SPC. The book was to provide an immediately useful text for manufacturing technicians and managers. No matter how sophisticated a technology may be, it will be of little value to a company if management and employees do not readily understand how to use it in their environment.

This book is not intended for statisticians. Nor is it the final word on SPC. Small liberties have been taken with respect to pure statistical theory. However, the techniques used in the book are practical, simple and they work. The book is intended to enable manufacturing engineers and process operators to implement the techniques of SPC. At the same time, the book provides managers with the understanding necessary to give informed support for such implementation.

There have been many books written about improving productivity and product quality, as well as SPC, and there will be more. I believe that each can provide important benefits. This book is based on my quality control experience with the Ford Motor Company and as an independent instructor and consultant. It focuses on those fundamental techniques and attitudes that form the foundation for quality improvement.

The purpose of the book is twofold: (1) to provide a basic introduction to statistical thinking in manufacturing problem solving, and (2) to emphasize management's vital role in effectively introducing such thinking, and providing the opportunity, leadership and motivation for successful implementation.

Chapter 1 defines quality and introduces statistical thinking as part of the philosophy of continuous improvement. Chapters 2 and 3 introduce SPC and the basic concepts needed to apply the tools for process control. Chapter 4 deals with data collection as an integral part of control charting. Chapters 5 through 9 cover the construction and use of control charts and process capability assessment and improvement. Chapter 10 deals with measurement system evaluation. Operators must know what to chart and how to follow up on problems. Chapter 11, therefore, discusses the tools for problem solving: tools for deciding where to begin a process control study and tools for identifying the causes of process variation. It also discusses some practical considerations in sampling, the recording of effective data and adjusting a process. Chapter 12 stresses the crucial role of management in the success of an SPC program.

SPC has been adopted by many companies, but its full potential has often been ignored. Informational gains are often negated by failure to take advantage of the opportunities that such a system creates. Its real potential should not be obscured by an overemphasis on technique to the exclusion of a well managed program that takes the needs of the people involved into account. As an integral part of a program for continuous improvement it must be grounded in the idea that a company should examine itself objectively, base its decisions on data, and encourage participation.

Statistical information is no longer simply the province of quality assurance specialists. If a company is to remain competitive it must understand the capabilities of its processes. Every employee needs to be able to deal with statistical information at an appropriate level.

Today manufacturers operate in a world of better educated and increasingly value minded consumers who have a wider range of choices. The dictum "Buyer Beware" is rapidly changing to "Seller Beware". The companies that survive will be those that are able to use statistical information in order to provide customers with high quality products at the least cost.

Bringing out a new book on a quality technology is neither a simple nor a straightforward task. It requires cooperation with individuals with vision as well as organizational, communication and production skills. I have been extremely fortunate to have had access to individuals with these attributes and wish to acknowledge their contributions to this effort.

I would like to thank John Kennedy, of the ASI Press, for initiating this project. He was the first to suggest that I write a book on SPC, and he provided the resources and encouragement to see the project through.

I am grateful to ASI's staff and instructors for their insightful reviews of the manuscript. The various drafts benefited greatly from the suggestions of Robert Clark, Tom Kazmierski, Tom Scripps, Al Woodell, Kerry Kouvelas and Jim Wilkins.

Additional thanks go to Duane Orlowski who served as technical editor in the development of the manuscript and the production of the book.

Lastly, I should thank Fred Metzler for executing the control chart graphics and Kiya Sibley for her professional efforts in the typing and formatting of this work.

Gordon H. Robertson
March 22, 1989

THE NEW QUALITY CHALLENGE

CONTENTS

KEY CONCEPTS

In this chapter you will learn about the following key items and concepts:

Quality
Voice of the customer
Cost of quality
Costs vs. control
Internal failure costs
External failure costs
Continuous quality improvement
Quality Loss Function (QLF)
Dr. W. Edwards Deming Fourteen Points for Management
Quality Function Deployment (QFD)
Taguchi Methods™
Statistical Process Control (SPC)

THE NEW QUALITY CHALLENGE

1.1 INTRODUCTION

Major changes in the world manufacturing climate have made it important for American industry to produce quality products. The reasons for these changes are many and varied. They include changes in this post World War II economy, the rise of the new information technology, and the growth of worldwide competition. They have resulted in a new type of consumer—better informed, more objective, with a wider range of choices. Today's consumer is primarily interested in one thing—a sense of value. We cannot count on the American consumer's loyalty to company or country in the marketplace. Increased consumer income has created a demand for more diversified and sophisticated products, and Americans have begun to find that the products they want are not always manufactured in the United States. For some 30 years now, they have been actively shopping in the world marketplace (*Table 1.1*).

Table 1.1. *We are changing from a national to a world economy. SOURCE: Megatrends by John Naisbitt (1982).*

1950-1970	1970-1985
U.S. productivity up 3% per year.	Decreased to 0.4% per year
U.S. accounts for 25% of world manufacturing.	Slipped to 17%
In U.S. market, companies produce 95% of autos, steel, and electronics.	Dropped to: 70% of autos 86% of steel 50% of electronics

THE WORLD MARKETPLACE

World competition is growing. During the 1950s, American manufacturers stocked 25% of the world market and 95% of the domestic market. Since that time, foreign manufacturers have taken more than 8% of the world market, 30% of domestic automobiles, 14% of domestic steel, and 50% of domestic electronics.

Fighting for survival after World War II, Japanese manufacturers set out to upgrade the cheap, low-quality goods they were known to produce. Many an American line supervisor can tell stories of Japanese in dark suits and narrow ties roaming U.S. factories, studying the technology to take home those concepts that would work for them. Today, the Japanese manufacture high-quality products by using once-successful American methods (*Figure 1.1*).

QUALITY LEVEL

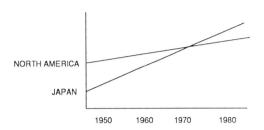

Figure 1.1 *Quality level of Japanese vs. American products, 1950-80. SOURCE: "Product Quality—A Prescription For The West," Management Review, 1981.*

The Japanese are most often named in this situation. But there are other nations already taking the place of the Japanese. The Pacific Rim nations—Korea, the Philippines, Singapore, China, Hong Kong, etc.—are rapidly entering the world marketplace. It is not simply the flood of Japanese products that has caused the problem. American companies must close the gap and provide quality goods if they are to survive (*Table 1.2*).

Table 1.2 *Comparison of U.S. and imported automobiles. SOURCE: Business Week, June 8, 1987.*

Problems reported per 100 cars	
DOMESTIC	
Ford	162
General Motors	179
Chrysler	180
IMPORTED	
Japanese	129
Imports sold by Detroit producers	152
German	152
Swedish	200
Other European	344

American manufacturers need not copy Japanese cultural practices. We have our own history, traditions, and resources. What we must find is a new way of thinking that provides an effective common perspective, language, values, objectives, and tools regarding quality. Some American companies have already begun to do this.

Eastman Kodak Co., for instance, has eliminated product inspection and made each worker responsible for quality before passing work on. Ford Motor Co. upper-level executives are reviewed on their contributions to quality throughout the corporation. General Motors Corp. has divided Lansing factory workers into small teams that define their own jobs and monitor their quality output by conducting daily audits and using stop-line cords to shut down a line with problems. And a company called W.L. Gore and Associates now employs sponsors. There, employees are responsible for one another's skill development, raises, promotions, and project involvement.

A new philosophy and approach to quality is necessary if American manufacturers are to maintain a competitive edge in today's world economy.

1.2 DEFINING QUALITY

While most popular definitions of quality are vague, quality really isn't hard to define. In today's competitive marketplace it means that our goods and services satisfy our customers' needs and expectations at a reasonable cost. This is achieved only by continually improving the performance and consistency of our products.

QUALITY AND CUSTOMER REQUIREMENTS

Customers will continue to purchase products that strike a perceived balance between cost and selected elements of quality—appearance, style, and utility. These ingredients of quality will vary in importance. A manufacturer of components may be less concerned about appearance or style than utility or function. They represent a balance for the customer in terms of his particular needs and expectations. A list price has relative worth. Whatever customers actually pay for products, they insist on receiving some sense of value for the money spent.

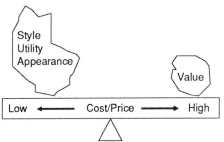

Figure 1.2 *Customers demand value: a balance between price and aspects of quality.*

In the past, quality-improvement efforts focused heavily on reducing waste, scrap, rework, downtime, etc. Manufacturers also tried to react to field service problems that came to their attention. While such efforts were important, they failed to recognize that something larger was at stake—the customer's demand for value.

A manufacturer's task is to find that level of quality, balanced by costs, to meet a market niche, where the greatest number of customers sense value. In this way he can make a profit. In a competitive situation, however, others are pressing for the same niche. For long-term success, the manufacturer must continually improve his product, reduce his costs, and eliminate his problems. If he is to remain competitive, a philosophy of continuous improvement must become a natural part of his operating culture.

QUALITY OF DESIGN AND MANUFACTURE

To fulfill this definition of value, at least two types of quality must be present:

- Quality of design

- Quality of manufacture.

Quality of design means that the design of a product or process correctly takes customer needs and expectations into account. The designer's task is not easy. He must find ways to determine customers' perceptions of value, translate them into a component design, and assign dimensions and other criteria to develop a blueprint. He may know that tighter tolerances or more stringent standards would improve quality, but he must also recognize the limitations of production processes and their variability. Design staff must avoid producing designs that look good on paper but cannot be built correctly with the available equipment.

Quality of manufacture is the principal subject discussed in this book. It means that as a minimum, all products must be within specification limits, and the smaller the variation around a target, the better the quality.

The definition "made to specification" is a bare minimum. It begins with the premise that if the designer has done his job, the best product is the one whose dimensional quality coincides with the designer's target values. Any deviation from the target value results in something less than intended—less utility, a compromise in appearance, or, at worst, waste in the form of scrap or rework. It establishes the worst conditions we are willing to accept. A part that is just barely within specification is hardly better than one that is slightly out of specification.

On the other hand, a part that is exactly on target is much better than one that is barely within tolerance limits.

PROBLEMS IN MANUFACTURE

As we have said, customer needs and expectations are transferred, in technical terms, to blueprints. This is the designer's way of expressing **the voice of the customer**. The rest of the company is expected to be able to produce the design intent. Downstream, however, this does not always occur.

1. The design intent may be second-guessed in production. Manufacturing supervisors may make their own decisions regarding production and customer value expectations.

2. Variation is inherent in mass production, and this can create products that vary significantly from design targets. The whole manufacturing process, including the purchase of machinery, equipment,

raw materials, tools, and supply components, as well as the training of people to operate equipment, are potential sources of variability.

3. Industry recognizes variability in manufacturing with tolerances and specifications that identify permissible levels of variation. Conformance to specification is thought to be an effective way of eliminating defects.

    This has led to an operating philosophy of detection, a view of quality control in which production produces the product followed by inspection, which is responsible for its quality. It has also resulted in widespread use of go/no-go inspection equipment. Go/no-go inspection cannot determine how close a product is to its target.

    Under this operating philosophy, the responsibility for quality is improperly assigned. The production operator deals with the process on a day-to-day basis. He must be given an adequate system and tools to monitor his own performance before defective parts are produced.

Designers test products during development using prototypes and pilot models. These usually function well. But this tells them little about how a product will behave when it confronts the many sources of variation on the factory floor. Production must have a clear understanding of the effect of sources of variation and the designer's intent. Design and manufacturing must have a good communicative relationship if quality goods are to be produced.

1.3 THE COST OF QUALITY

Manufacturers cannot be expected to commit to a program of continuous quality improvement without a clear understanding of the relationship between cost and quality. Here again, traditional notions about cost and quality must be reconsidered.

Dr. Joseph M. Juran cites three categories of costs in manufacturing:

1. **Standard costs** include inherent operational costs, such as rent, utilities, equipment, and labor. They occur no matter what the quality of the product.

2. **Costs of control** are discretionary costs that management decides to incur. They are dollars spent preventing product defects and nonconformities. Training, preproduction design review, quality planning, and Statistical Process Control are examples of prevention costs. Currently, American manufacturers spend only 0.5 to 5.0% of their total quality dollars on preventive activities.

3. **Costs of failure to control** occur because preventive measures are inadequate or nonexistent. There are two types:

   Internal failure costs include scrap, rework, downtime, spoilage, yield losses, etc. Here defects are found in unshipped products. These costs account for 25 to 40% of manufacturing expenditures.

   External failure costs include warranty charges, complaint adjustments, loss of business, etc. These costs occur because faulty products reach customers. They account for 25 to 40% of manufacturing expenditures.

Table 1.3 *The cost of prevention decreases over time. SOURCE: J.M. Juran, Management of Quality, 4th Edition, Juran Institute, Inc., 1981.*

Cost of Failure	Savings	Cumulative Savings	Year
$1,000,000			0
500,000	$500,000	$500,000	2
250,000	250,000	750,000	4
125,000	125,000	875,000	6
62,500	62,500	937,500	8
31,250	31,250	968,750	10

Preventive spending minimizes failure costs. But in most American companies the emphasis of quality expenditure is on appraisal or detection. Preventive dollars should be much more than 0.5 to 5% of total expenditure for quality.

The Japanese improved quality by realizing that spending on preventive activities was money spent in the most critical quality area. **The gains are achieved over the long run**. When preventive spending is first increased, the total cost of quality increases. Then, as fewer defective products are shipped, costs shift from external to internal failure. On the whole, the cost of quality goes down. *Table 1.3* illustrates this point. Spending 10 to 20% of the cost of failure in prevention reduced this failure cost 50% every one to three years. Quality improvement is something like a ten-year trip with 75% of the miles travelled during the first four years.

CONTINUOUS IMPROVEMENT DOLLARS

Dr. Genichi Taguchi, a Japanese statistical engineer, has developed the Quality Loss Function (QLF), a concept that relates cost, quality, and variation. Taguchi defines quality in terms of the loss that results when a product or process does not function as specified by its target, or "the loss imparted to the society from the time a product is shipped." This loss includes costs associated with customer complaints and dissatisfaction, time and money spent by customers for repair and replacement, warranty costs, returns, poor reputation for quality, and, eventually, loss of market share. The customer initially incurs these losses, but over time, it is the manufacturer who absorbs the losses.

LOSS FUNCTION CURVE

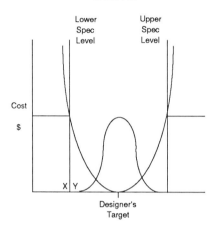

Figure 1.3 *American manufacturers consider quality products to be any that fall within a specification range. Therefore, y is a good product and x is a bad product. But Dr. Taguchi points out that there is almost no difference between a product barely in specifications and one barely out of specification. The Japanese continue to spend money improving a product even though it meets specification. They attempt to reduce the variation around the target value.*

The QLF captures the costs of failure to control, as well as such costs as loss of reputation for quality, noted by Juran. Viewing quality in this way is a great incentive for continuous improvement. It has allowed the Japanese to invest money to continue to improve products, an investment that would not be made in most American companies (*Figure 1.3*). The QLF encompasses the concepts of control, uniformity around a target, and continuous improvement. It expresses the relationship between cost and quality and relates it to the voice of the customer.

The QLF leads us to rethink some of our traditional notions regarding cost and quality. **Quality does not necessarily cost more. In the long run it costs less by reducing costs of failure to control.** It says that quality must be continually improved to meet customer expectations and that the most effective strategy for improving quality at minimal cost is a strategy of prevention.

1.4 A STRATEGY FOR IMPROVEMENT

Implementing a strategy of prevention means a change in attitudes, methods of management, and methods for production. American manufacturers have good reason to change some of their operational philosophy and procedures. What is needed is a strategy for improvement. Dr. W. Edwards Deming has provided 14 points for management that could well be called a blueprint for quality management and manufacture.

Deming's 14 points, shown on the next page, view many current American practices, such as inspection, short-term goals, personnel reviews with short-term objectives, and outsourcing to multiple suppliers, as costly and unproductive. The effort to change necessitates a different management philosophy, a permanent commitment to the production of quality goods, and a major overhaul of some company cultures. Of the many factors that manufacturers might consider in effecting a strategy for improvement, five of the most important are:

• Understanding the role of top management

• Adopting a philosophy of continuous improvement

• Deciding who is responsible for quality

• Involving everyone in the quality effort

• Changing some existing practices.

14 Points for Management
By Dr. W. Edwards Deming

The 14 points apply anywhere—to small organizations as well as large ones. The management of a service industry has the same obligation and the same problems as management in manufacturing.

1. Create constancy of purpose toward improvement of product and service with a plan to become competitive and to stay in business.

2. Adopt the new philosophy. We are in a new economic age. We can no longer live with commonly accepted levels of delays, mistakes, defective materials, or defective workmanship.

3. Cease dependence on mass inspection. Require instead, statistical evidence that quality is built in, to eliminate need for inspection on a mass basis. Purchasing managers have a new job, and must learn it.

4. End the practice of awarding business on the basis of price tag. Instead, depend on meaningful measures of quality along with price. Eliminate suppliers that cannot qualify with statistical evidence of quality.

5. Find problems. It is management's job to work continually on the system (design, incoming materials, composition of material, maintenance, improvement of machine, training, supervision, retraining).

6. Institute modern methods of training on the job.

7. Institute modern methods of supervision of production workers. The responsibility of foremen must be changed from sheer numbers to quality. Improvement of quality will automatically improve productivity. Management must prepare to take immediate action on reports from foremen concerning barriers, such as inherited defects, machines not maintained, poor tools, and fuzzy operational definitions.

8. Drive out fear so that everyone may work effectively for the company.

9. Break down barriers between departments. People in research, design, sales and production must work as a team to foresee problems of production that may be encountered with various materials and specifications.

10. Eliminate numerical goals, posters, and slogans for the work force asking for new levels of productivity without providing methods.

11. Eliminate work standards that prescribe numerical quotes.

12. Remove barriers that stand between the hourly worker and his right to pride of workmanship.

13. Institute a vigorous program of education and retraining.

14. Create a structure on top management that will push every day on the above 13 points.

Reprinted with permission from W. Edwards Deming, Quality, Productivity and Competitive Position, Massachusetts Institute of Technology, Center for Advanced Engineering Study, 1982.

UNDERSTANDING THE ROLE OF TOP MANAGEMENT

The role of top management is critical to the success of any improvement program. The commitment of top executives must be real and visible. It involves providing an awareness of new tools and new ways of thinking and an opportunity to implement them. It involves the training of many levels of employees. And it requires leadership, recognition, and reward.

In our society, new ideas come and go, often all too quickly. Workers tend to see training as the latest short-term fad, unless top executives and their entire management team put time, money, physical presence, and unconditional support into a program.

ADOPTING A PHILOSOPHY OF CONTINUOUS IMPROVEMENT

Continuous improvement means that quality is evaluated with respect to a target value. Quality then becomes consistency and uniformity requiring a long-term commitment to continually approximate the target value.

In order to do this, employees need to understand variation and be trained in statistical thinking. Management must institute improvement practices that reduce the variability that has made manufacturing products to specification so difficult in the first place.

DECIDING WHO IS RESPONSIBLE FOR QUALITY

Most American companies have separate quality control or quality assurance departments. Their job is to ensure product quality by applying the necessary inspection and statistical techniques after a product has been made.

The primary reason for this is that deadlines are a priority in manufacturing. This makes it reasonable to inspect after production—production tables are not interfered with. Production has priority over quality, and quality control is a separate, nonproduction job.

But quality control can only be ensured when every area in the manufacturing process understands its own role in the final quality of a product. Everyone is responsible for his own quality.

Statistical thinking and analysis provides the means for everyone to evaluate, discuss, and work toward maintaining and improving product quality. With the proper tools, personnel can react to control and capability problems as they occur.

INVOLVING EVERYONE IN THE QUALITY EFFORT

Producing quality goods demands that everyone in the manufacturing process be involved in the effort. It demands a level of teamwork that does not exist in most of American manufacturing. Teamwork is fundamental, and this requires better horizontal and vertical communication.

Vertical communication must come from the bottom up as well as top down. First-line supervisors and operators know the most about on-line difficulties, but they are often excluded from problem-solving efforts. Good horizontal communication is also important. Companies should take Deming's advice and tear down the barriers that exist between departments and allow communication to flow freely.

A consistent approach to quality and the application of statistical methods can improve constructive horizontal communication. But this will not be effective unless company management provides the opportunity, training, support, and visible leadership to develop the company's own tradition of continuous improvement.

CHANGING SOME EXISTING PRACTICES

Manufacturing policies can inhibit efforts toward quality improvement. Some practices, common in most American companies, should be changed.

1. **Quality standards**. There should be clear and constant application of consistent quality standards in a company. Management should know what standards are being used, if they express design intent, whether they meet the realities of production, and whether they adequately meet the needs of the customer. Changing standards to expedite shipment of parts will quickly negate any efforts toward continuous improvement.

2. **Incentives and merit review.** Over the years, manufacturers have believed that production incentives were important while they ignored the consequences of incentives for quality. If workers receive payment for the production of numbers—good and bad part—how can quality improve?

   Merit reviews can also have negative effects. Merit reviews potentially reward isolated behavior rather than team effort. Deming suggests that it leads workers toward meeting the short-term specifications of the review rather than the long-term objective of continuous improvement.

3. **Purchasing and sourcing.** Purchase decisions based primarily on price do not evaluate the quality aspects of alternative sourcing. Is the cheapest tool always the one that will produce the best part? Is the least expensive supplier the one who reliably meets the manufacturer's production schedule? Purchasing and sourcing need to be evaluated with respect to performance, control, and capability, as well as price.

1.5 TOOLS FOR QUALITY IMPROVEMENT

The purpose of this book is to provide the user with a working knowledge of one of the tools for the control and improvement of manufacturing quality that is finding wide acceptance in many American companies—Statistical Process Control (SPC).

Figure 1.4 shows the place of three major tools for quality improvement in the product development and production cycle.

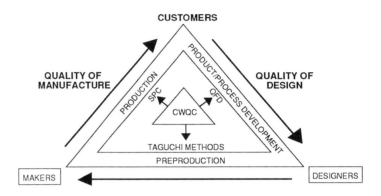

Figure 1.4 *Tools for quality improvement.*

- **Quality Function Deployment (QFD)** is a method for translating customer requirements into the appropriate technical requirements for each stage of product development and production. The voice of the customer is deployed horizontally throughout the organization—into marketing strategies, product design and engineering, prototype evaluation, process development, production, and sales. All activities of the company are driven by the voice of the customer.

- **Taguchi Methods** provide off-line quality control techniques for evaluating and improving quality before putting a product or process into production. The performance of a system is optimized through efficient, designed experimentation. Both a product's level of performance and "robustness" (the ability to overcome the many uncontrollable conditions experienced during production and use) are improved. When the key phase (parameter design) is completed, a product or process is at its highest level of performance at the lowest cost. This requires the need for much on-line quality control activity.

- **SPC** is a method for understanding the control of a manufacturing process through the statistical evaluation of data. It uses charts and other statistical tools to alert personnel to the occurrence of any abnormality in a process; aspects of variability requiring operator action and those requiring management action. This allows workers to take appropriate action based on objective, timely information. It allows them to take responsibility for their own quality.

  SPC helps control costs by reducing variability and increasing product life. It provides a common language for discussing product performance. It is a tool for prevention that can be applied whenever important areas of cost and quality have been identified.

1.6 THE STATISTICAL APPROACH TO QUALITY CONTROL

Since the beginning of the 1980s, there has been a growing emphasis on the use of SPC as a means of improving quality and productivity. The techniques have become standard practice in manufacturing operations and a precondition of doing business in some customer-supplier contracts. Although many people are still unfamiliar with SPC, it isn't a new or untried concept, nor was it invented by the Japanese.

We have learned from past errors and must now be fully committed to a vision of the future in which such tools as SPC supplant wasted labor, defective products, and squandered resources. For this reason, statistical thinking will become part of the mindset we work from; it will become a part of the language for continuous quality improvement that we think in. Therefore, it is crucial that every employee of a company—from the machine operator to the chief executive officer—and every supplier learn to view manufacturing from this new quality perspective.

INTRODUCTION TO STATISTICAL PROCESS CONTROL

CONTENTS

KEY CONCEPTS

In this chapter you will learn about the following key items and concepts:

Statistical Process Control (SPC)
Detection
Prevention
100% inspection
Go/no-go inspection
Action on the process
Action on the output
Basic tools for SPC

INTRODUCTION TO STATISTICAL PROCESS CONTROL

2.1 INTRODUCTION

The concept of quality control is as old as industry. Since man first began to manufacture items, there has been interest in product quality. Medieval guilds, as far back as the Middle Ages, insisted on a long training period for apprentices, and those who sought to become master craftsmen had to offer evidence of their ability to produce a quality product.

When production was carried on in small owner-managed shops, usually by hand methods, few quality control problems existed. This does not mean there were no quality problems; handmade does not automatically produce good quality. Rather, there were no control problems; management always knew what had to be corrected to make a quality product. The owner had personal, physical contact with practically every shoe, glove, or violin produced in his shop. No reports of any kind were maintained, since he lived in the midst of his enterprise.

With the advent of the mass production of thousands of products, this type of personal contact became impossible. Control of the production process became critically important, and in the first half of this century quantitative techniques were developed to ensure control of quality. These quantitative approaches to quality control were applied sporadically prior to the 1980s. The increasing international competition of the 1980s has made the use of these new ways of measuring and monitoring the manufacturing process a necessity. Statistical Process Control (SPC) is one of these methods. Once put into effect, such methods will enable American industry to improve product quality while decreasing product cost.

STATISTICAL QUALITY CONTROL

Western Electric Co. pioneered much of the early work in applying statistics to quality control, because manufacturing large numbers of identical telephones required the company to sample. Early issues of the *Bell System Technical Journal*, started in 1922, contained numerous papers on inspection and quality control. However, the real breakthrough in a well-structured approach to the subject came in 1924, when Dr. Walter A. Shewhart presented his initial thoughts on control of quality during manufacture, and in 1929, when Harold F. Dodge and Harry G. Romig formulated sampling inspection theory. Shewhart published his classical book on Statistical Quality Control (SQC), titled *Economic Control of Quality of Manufactured Product*, in 1931. (Reprints are available through the American Society for Quality Control, 230 West Wells Street, Milwaukee, Wisconsin 52303).

During the 1930s, quality control techniques were adopted very slowly. Professor H. A. Freeman, who was promoting SQC at the Massachusetts Institute of Technology, ascribed the slow response to two factors. The first was a deep-seated conviction of American production engineers that their principal function is to improve technical methods so that no important quality variations remain, and that of chance have no proper place among 'scientific' production methods. The second factor was "the difficulty of obtaining statisticians who are adequately trained in this fairly complicated field."

World War II provided impetus to the application of quality control techniques with the introduction of scientifically designed sampling plans. Books and publications during this period were General Leslie E. Simon's book, *An Engineer's Manual of Statistical Methods*, 1094; the American Standards Association's American war standards Z1.1-1941 and Z1.2-1941, "Guide for Quality Control and Control Chart Method of Analyzing Data," and American war standard Z1.3 - 1942, "Control Chart Method of Controlling Quality During Production."

Among the earliest SQC programs was an intensive ten-day course conducted at Stanford University in July 1942. This course, which was planned by Professors Eugene L. Grant and Holbrook Waring of Stanford University and Dr. W. Edwards Deming, was attended by war industry representatives and procurement agencies of the Armed Services.

It would be an impossible task to mention every individual who has contributed to developing and applying SQC methods. The one person given the most recognition in recent years, however, is Deming, who was one of the initial reviewers of Shewhart's work. He is best known for the educational campaign he initiated in 1950 to promote the "quality" concept to the Japanese, with the result that many Japanese products are now synonymous with quality.

2.2 STATISTICAL PROCESS CONTROL

SPC is a method for monitoring and understanding the behavior of manufacturing processes. It uses statistics to provide feedback about the abilities and limitations of a process. Thus, SPC assists a manufacturer in making economically sound decisions about the causes affecting his processes. Let us look at the meaning of each of these words separately in relation to their meaning together.

STATISTICAL

Statistics are numerical facts systematically collected and classified regarding a large group of people or things. The term "statistical" has to do with obtaining an understanding of something through the collection and analysis of measurements or data.

PROCESS

A process is a system of causes that interact to produce a given result. It is the entire combination of people, equipment, materials, methods, and environment that work together to produce a manufacturing output.

CONTROL

By controlling a process, the manufacturer makes it behave the way he wants it to behave. A process in "control" is stable and produces the same range of a product characteristic (size, weight, color, etc.) today as it did yesterday or the day before, and it can be expected to do the same tomorrow.

A SIMPLIFIED EXAMPLE

Let us look at a hole-boring process as a simplified example. How can we accurately and objectively learn about a boring process to see whether it is in control?

We might measure the bored diameters of 50 of every 250 items produced each hour—write down the measurements noting the time, the machine they were produced on, and the shift on which they were made. At the end of the month we would have some statistical data—a sample of the diameters produced by the boring process.

But this alone won't tell us much about how the boring process is operating. To find out more we need to perform some fairly simple arithmetic on the data. For example, of the 50 items, we could add all of the diameters together and divide by 50, the number of units measured in the sample. This would give the average or mean diameter of items in the sample. Over the course of a month we could learn something about the mean diameter of items that month. By recording the maximum size difference in each sample of 50 pieces we can obtain a measure of average spread of the hole sizes produced.

All of the items produced that month constitute a population. By carefully following specific rules and procedures, we can reach objective, unbiased, and correct conclusions about the boring process. This would include whether the process is producing defectives, whether a batch of material should be shipped, etc. The key concept here is that we can analyze the nature of the interaction of causes when the results are not those that we want. The techniques of SPC allow us to do this in a refined and efficient way.

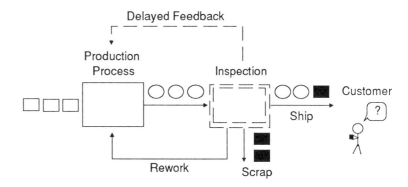

Figure 2.1a *Defect detection system.*

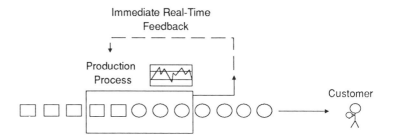

Figure 2.1b *Defect prevention system.*

2.3 PREVENTION VERSUS DETECTION

A traditional approach to manufacturing is to depend on production to make the product and on quality control to inspect the final product and screen out defects. In administrative situations, work is often checked and rechecked in efforts to catch errors. Both cases involve a strategy of detection. It is wasteful, because it allows time and materials to be invested in products or services that are not always usable.

LIMITATIONS OF 100% INSPECTION

In the first place, 100% inspection is too expensive. It is an activity that costs money but that does not bring in any additional revenue from customers. Or, to put it another way, customers pay for the parts shipped, but inspection does not result in any additional good parts being shipped.

One-hundred percent inspection is also limited in usefulness because it cannot contribute to defect prevention and productivity improvement. Inspection activities are always limited to reacting to the past and can find defective parts only after they have been produced. As shown in *Figure 2.1a*, this technique is basically a coarse safety net to screen out defective products after they have been made.

Finally, 100% inspection is never entirely effective. A motivated inspector working under good conditions doing repetitive industrial measurement will typically fail to take notice of 20% of the defective products inspected.

The comment is sometimes made that inspection could be made more dependable through automation. There is truth in this, since an automatic inspection device will be more consistent than a human. Nevertheless, even if inspection is automated, 100% inspection is not directed toward controlling the process to prevent defects. As an example, completely automatic inspection is frequently used in the area of electronics, because components and circuits are easily tested by computer. In these fields it is not uncommon to find that the rejects at automatic inspection stations reach 5 to 10%.

PREVENTION

A quality product can be produced only when the machine or process involved can maintain the specified tolerance. The concept of prevention presupposes that:

- The manufacturing engineer provides machines and fixtures that are more than capable of meeting tolerances.

- Purchasing obtains materials that are demonstrably manufactured to their target values with minimum variability.

- Operators are trained in specific methods of operation and are given the means to monitor the quality of their output.

- Quality standards are clear, and a philosophy of continuous improvement prevails.

A prevention strategy sounds sensible (*Figure 2.1b*) to most people. It is much more effective to avoid waste by not producing unusable output in the first place. It is easily captured in such slogans as, "do it right the first time." However, these kinds of slogans are in themselves not enough. What is needed is a more efficient system that provides manufacturing personnel with immediate feedback so that corrective action can be taken before a defective product is made.

INFORMATION ABOUT PROCESS PERFORMANCE

Process performance depends on the way the process is designed and built, and on the way it is operated.

A process control system is a feedback system that provides information to show whether action is needed to correct the process. If information is gathered and interpreted correctly, timely and appropriate action can be taken to correct and control a process.

Action on a process is future-oriented. It is taken on a process to prevent the production of out-of-specification products. Action might consist of change in operations, operator training, change in incoming materials, change in equipment, redesign of the process, etc.

Action on the output of a process is past-oriented. It involves detecting out-of-specification output already produced. It may entail sorting and scrap or rework of nonconforming items. Inspection followed only by action on the output is a poor substitute for monitoring and maintaining effective first-time performance.

APPLYING STATISTICS TO UNDERSTAND A PROCESS

There are three basic steps in applying statistics to help us understand a process:

1. **Data collection**. After a problem is defined, data is collected in numerical form. Data must be relevant, timely, accurate, and complete. Data collection is an important step in statistical analysis. Results will be no better than the quality of the data itself.

2. **Presentation and analysis.** This data is summarized, organized, and presented in a way that is easily understood. Statistical measures, charts, and graphs can be used to summarize thousands of pieces of data.

3. **Inference and action.** Following specific rules and procedures, we can consistently reach objective, unbiased conclusions about a process. We can then take informed corrective action when results are not those we desire.

2.4 THE CONCEPT OF SPC

The goal of a process control system is to make economically sound decisions about the causes affecting a process. Process control is a system of prevention.

LIMITATIONS OF GO/NO-GO INSPECTION

Go/no-go inspection is a widespread form of inspection frequently performed using checking fixtures, plug gages, or other devices that do not give a numerical readout. The widespread use of go/no-go techniques dates from a time when quality was viewed differently than it is today. The aim was to minimize the costs associated with measuring quality.

However, go/no-go inspection is no better a method of prevention than 100% inspection. The technique isn't sensitive enough to provide quality data. This can be seen in the following example.

Twenty percent of the parts coming off a machine are out of specification. An inspector checking a sample of ten pieces per hour with a go/no-go gage would probably find some defective parts on the first try. The probability of finding defective parts in a sample of ten pieces is given in *Table 2.1*.

Table 2.1 *Probability of finding defective parts in a sample of ten pieces.*

True Defect Rate	Probability of Finding No Defective Parts in Sample of 10 Pieces
20%	11/100
10%	35/100
5%	60/100
1%	90/100
0.27%	97/100

We can see that the lower the defective rate, the greater the chance that the sample will contain no defective parts. For a machine producing 1% defectives, an inspector would not find defects nine out of ten times. On the basis of this information, we would continue that machine with an unacceptable defect rate.

To make better decisions we need information that shows us patterns of variation in the process. We can compare these patterns to the target and the specifications in order to control the process and prevent defects. To do this we need to use instruments that provide us with numerical measurement readings.

EXAMPLE—COMPARISON USING NUMERICAL DATA

Suppose that three machines are set up to produce the same part. First, the setup operator checks the 25 pieces off each machine with a go/no-go gage (a plug gage for hole diameter). The operator records the following results:

Machine A	**Machine B**	**Machine C**
All 25 pieces in spec.	All 25 pieces in spec.	All 25 pieces in spec.

On the basis of this information, the setup operator would naturally put all three machines into production, perhaps only to find some hours later that two of the machines were making defective parts.

Suppose, however, that the setup operator had taken actual measurements with a vernier and had plotted the results for each machine on a histogram (*Figure 2.2*). The results are consistent with the go/no-go evaluation.

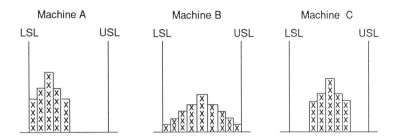

Figure 2.2 *Machine comparison histograms.*

Histograms are more fully described in Chapter 3. For now, let each "X" represent a measurement. The histogram simply displays the measurements of each number of values described on the horizontal scale. The picture that emerges gives us a quick look at the variation of each machine.

The outputs of the machines are in fact quite different. Machine A and Machine B look like they are going to produce at least a few parts out of spec (even though all the sample parts happen to be good). Machine C, on the other hand, looks like it is capable of producing all good parts so long as it is kept operating properly. Here we can see the tremendous power of using numerical measurement data and examining patterns.

Most of us have a go/no-go device on our cars to measure oil pressure. A better device would be an oil gage that monitors oil pressure in relation to a range of normal pressure. This type of device allows us to take action before engine damage might occur.

The histogram is a statistical tool that performs a similar function as the oil pressure gage—it shows us the actual industrial process operation zone in relation to the normal operating zone (*Figures 2.3a* and *2.3b*).

New Method

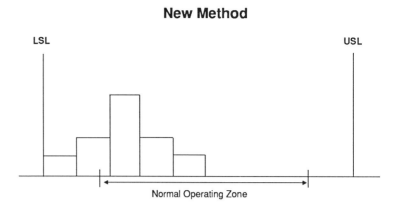

Figure 2.3a *Marginal conditions.*

New Method

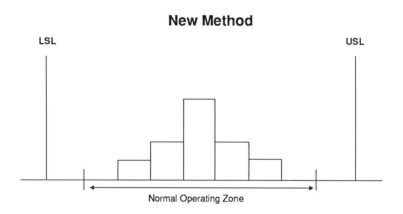

Figure 2.3b *Preferred operation.*

If the process continued to operate as in *Figure 2.3a*, go/no-go inspection might show no sign of trouble. A histogram reveals the process to be operating abnormally and that corrective action is needed to prevent it from making defective parts.

In actual practice, the histogram is generally used for troubleshooting and diagnosis. For hour-by-hour process control, other techniques, called control charts, are used. Both the histogram and control charts will be covered in detail in subsequent chapters.

2.5 BASIC TOOLS FOR SPC

There are a number of tools that can be applied in SPC. Those listed below generally provide the greatest benefit, especially in the early stages of a quality improvement program. Here they are simply introduced. The techniques are discussed in detail in subsequent chapters.

1. **Pareto analysis.** This technique allows us to identify and prioritize problems, to decide where to concentrate our quality control efforts. If we concentrate our efforts on the "vital few" rather than the "trivial many," we get a better return on our efforts.

2. **Check sheets.** These are simplified data collection sheets that help ensure that data is collected easily, accurately, and completely.

3. **Flow diagrams.** This is a chart that depicts the steps or activities of a process in the order that they occur. It can be used to identify points in the process where control activities should be initiated.

4. **Histograms.** Histograms are bar charts of a distribution. They help us to picture the distribution, to determine whether a process is operating the way we would like, and to identify some causal factors.

5. **Cause-and-effect diagrams.** This technique helps us to use the collective knowledge of many people to identify cause-and-effect relationships. Identifying a potential cause can help us find a solution.

6. **Scatter diagrams.** Scatter diagrams help to evaluate possible causal relationships. They help verify the presence of a relationship and determine its strength and direction.

7. **Control charts.** These are probably the most valuable tools for process control. They allow us to distinguish between desirable and undesirable operating conditions. Control charts will be discussed later in more detail.

8. **Other techniques**. There are other useful tools, such as probability paper, special graphs, cost-of-quality reports, and design of experiments. The basic tools mentioned above have proven to be the most useful in beginning an SPC program. They are the topics of the following chapters.

2.6 SUMMARY

This book provides a brief introduction to the concept and application of SPC. It covers some basic statistical concepts fundamental to understanding the control of a manufacturing process, issues in the collection of data, and some basic tools for beginning the program. The application of the fundamental tool of SPC, control charting, is covered step by step—control charts for variables and control charts for attributes. Lastly, measurement system evaluation is discussed and some key points in implementing a successful SPC program are emphasized.

The next chapter discusses some statistical concepts necessary for understanding process control.

BASIC
STATISTICAL CONCEPTS

CONTENTS

KEY CONCEPTS

In this chapter you will learn about the following key items and concepts:

Frequency distribution
Grouping
Class size
Histogram
Measures of central tendency: (mean, median, mode)
Measures of dispersion: (range, standard deviation)
Population
Sample
Probability distribution
Normal distribution curve
Non-normal distribution
Skewness
Kurtosis
Central Limit Theorem
Sample average
Distribution of sample averages
Mirror-image technique
Statistical inference
Type I error (alpha risk)
Type II error (beta risk)

BASIC STATISTICAL CONCEPTS

3.1 INTRODUCTION

Variation has been defined as "the difference between things that arc produced under conditions that are as nearly alike as it is possible to make them." However, knowing that variation exists is helpful to us only if we can organize the data we record into patterns that can tell us how a process is currently functioning with respect to past performance and in what direction it is headed.

UNDERSTANDING VARIATION

Here are some general **principles of variation**.

1. **No two things are exactly alike.** No two parts are precisely identical. Tolerances result from engineers recognizing this fact and our need to keep variations as small as possible.

2. **Variation in a product or process can be measured.** If the measurement unit is small enough, each part can be shown to be different from the next. This difference or variation is important when it has some effect on the functioning of the part being produced.

3. **Individual outcomes are not predictable.** Can it be reliably predicted whether the next flip of a coin will turn up heads or tails? Mistakes in decisions can be made where only one or two items are examined.

4. **Groups of things form patterns with definite characteristics.** Pour out a cupful of sugar on the table. Can an accurate prediction be made concerning where a particular grain will fall? No!

Yet if this procedure was repeated again and again, the same pattern, or the same representative mound, would appear each time.

If parts from a process are carefully measured for a given dimension and are counted and arranged in order of size, a definite pattern will be revealed, as illustrated in the shaft diameter tally in *Figure 3.1*. This general pattern will also repeat with another group from the same production process. A variation pattern is also obtained by throwing two dice 50 times and recording the results in a tally form (*Figure 3.1*).

	Inches		Face Sum	
	1.03-1.07	II	12	I
	.98-1.02	ЖHI I	11	I
	.93-.97	ЖHI IIIII-HIII	10	IIII
Shaft	.88-.92	IHI IHI IHI IHI III	Two	9	IIII
Diameters	.83-.87	IHI IHI IHI IHI IHI II	Dice	8	IHI III
	.78-.82	IHI IHI IHI IHI IIII	Values	7	IHI IHI I
	.73-.77	IHI IIII	6	IHI II
	.68-.72	IHI I	5	IHI I
	.63-.67	III	4	IIII
			3	II
			2	I

Figure 3.1   *Variation patterns.*

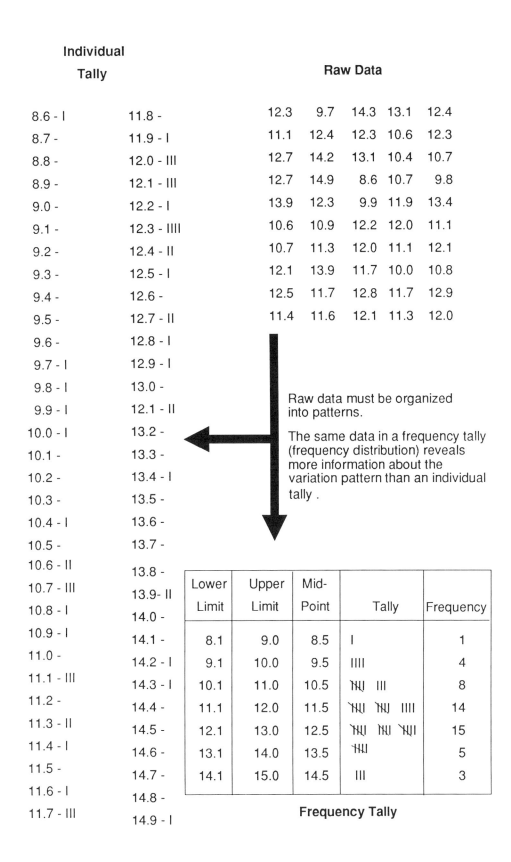

Individual

Tally

8.6 - I	11.8 -				
8.7 -	11.9 - I				
8.8 -	12.0 - III				
8.9 -	12.1 - III				
9.0 -	12.2 - I				
9.1 -	12.3 - IIII				
9.2 -	12.4 - II				
9.3 -	12.5 - I				
9.4 -	12.6 -				
9.5 -	12.7 - II				
9.6 -	12.8 - I				
9.7 - I	12.9 - I				
9.8 - I	13.0 -				
9.9 - I	12.1 - II				
10.0 - I	13.2 -				
10.1 -	13.3 -				
10.2 -	13.4 - I				
10.3 -	13.5 -				
10.4 - I	13.6 -				
10.5 -	13.7 -				
10.6 - II	13.8 -				
10.7 - III	13.9- II				
10.8 - I	14.0 -				
10.9 - I	14.1 -				
11.0 -	14.2 - I				
11.1 - III	14.3 - I				
11.2 -	14.4 -				
11.3 - II	14.5 -				
11.4 - I	14.6 -				
11.5 -	14.7 -				
11.6 - I	14.8 -				
11.7 - III	14.9 - I				

Raw Data

12.3	9.7	14.3	13.1	12.4
11.1	12.4	12.3	10.6	12.3
12.7	14.2	13.1	10.4	10.7
12.7	14.9	8.6	10.7	9.8
13.9	12.3	9.9	11.9	13.4
10.6	10.9	12.2	12.0	11.1
10.7	11.3	12.0	11.1	12.1
12.1	13.9	11.7	10.0	10.8
12.5	11.7	12.8	11.7	12.9
11.4	11.6	12.1	11.3	12.0

Raw data must be organized into patterns.

The same data in a frequency tally (frequency distribution) reveals more information about the variation pattern than an individual tally .

Lower Limit	Upper Limit	Mid-Point	Tally	Frequency
8.1	9.0	8.5	I	1
9.1	10.0	9.5	IIII	4
10.1	11.0	10.5	ЖЦ III	8
11.1	12.0	11.5	ЖЦ ЖЦ IIII	14
12.1	13.0	12.5	ЖЦ ЖЦ ЖЦ	15
13.1	14.0	13.5	ЖЦ	5
14.1	15.0	14.5	III	3

Frequency Tally

Figure 3.2 *A frequency tally.*

3.2 CONSTRUCTING A FREQUENCY TALLY

When recording a series of measurements, it is common practice to tabulate successive readings. This method is useful only when production order is important. By comparing this kind of individual tally with the tally sheet in *Figure 3.2*, it is immediately apparent that the same data in a **frequency tally** or **frequency distribution** reveals much more information about the variation pattern than the tabular information does.

The frequency tally is constructed by:

- Determining the largest and the smallest readings

- Tabulating in a column all values sequentially, from the smallest to the largest

- Tallying beside each of these values the number of observations for each value.

The frequency tally (*Figure 3.2*) provides a picture of the variation pattern. A **histogram**, or **bar chart**, is a special frequency distribution form that shows the same information as the frequency tally. If the sample is large with low frequencies for some values, or if the sample is small with a large spread, the pattern may be distorted. It is essential that some method for grouping the data be devised to provide a more compact variation pattern.

Table 3.1 *Continuous frequency distribution — pipefitting thread pitch diameter—grouped by ones.*

Pitch Diameter (X 0.0001 inch)	Actual Frequency	Relative Frequency
21	0	0
22	0	0
23	1	0.01
24	1	0.01
25	0	0
26	1	0.01
27	3	0.03
28	2	0.02
29	2	0.02
30	7	0.07
31	6	0.06
32	11	0.11
33	17	0.17
34	8	0.08
35	14	0.14
36	12	0.12
37	4	0.04
38	3	0.03
39	3	0.03
40	2	0.02
41	2	0.02
42	0	0
43	1	0.01
TOTAL	100	1.00

Table 3.2 *Continuous frequency distribution— pipefitting thread pitch diameter—grouped by twos.*

(a)		(b)	
Pitch Diameter (X 0.0001 inch)	Actual Frequency	Pitch Diameter (X 0.0001 inch)	Actual Frequency
22-23	1	23-24	2
24-25	1	25-26	1
26-27	4	27-28	5
28-29	4	29-30	9
30-31	13	31-32	17
32-33	28	33-34	25
34-35	22	35-36	26
36-37	16	37-38	7
38-39	6	39-40	5
40-41	4	41-42	2
42-43	1	43-44	1
TOTAL	100	**TOTAL**	100

GROUPING

Arranging raw data into ordered classes to show corresponding frequencies is called **grouping**. Sometimes, a grouping into cells may show few or no frequencies for some cells due to the large spread of the data. It may be desirable to further group into cells containing two, three, five, ten, or more measurements, in order to show a better general picture of this parent universe. Groupings should have a constant interval size.

Problems can arise in choosing interval size and location. Different guides suggest anywhere from 8 to 20 cells. It is best to try several different interval sizes and locations to select the one giving the most appropriate picture.

EXAMPLE—SAME DATA, DIFFERENT GROUPINGS

Table 3.1 shows a distribution for 100 observations grouped by ones and having 23 cells. *Table 3.2* shows the groupings by two into 11 cells. The first grouping, *Table 3.2a*, is more symmetrical about the middle cell, with the highest frequency 28. *Table 3.3* shows three different groupings by three into seven and eight cells. The second grouping, *Table 3.3b*, seems the most symmetrical with the two middle cells each having a frequency of 34. *Table 3.4* shows the cell midpoints and cell boundaries for this symmetrical grouping by three into eight cells (*Table 3.3b*). The midpoint is easier to locate when the cell contains an odd multiple of units.

Table 3.3 *Continuous frequency distribution— pipefitting thread pitch diameter—grouped by threes.*

(a)			(b)	
Pitch Diameter (X 0.0001 inch)	Actual Frequency		Pitch Diameter (X 0.0001 inch)	Actual Frequency
21-23	1		22-24	2
24-26	2		25-27	4
27-29	7		28-30	11
30-32	24		31-33	34
33-35	39		34-36	34
36-38	19		37-39	10
39-41	7		40-42	4
42-44	1		43-45	1
TOTAL	100		TOTAL	100

(c)	
Pitch Diameter (X 0.0001 inch)	Actual Frequency
23-25	2
26-28	6
29-31	15
32-34	36
35-37	30
38-40	8
41-43	3
TOTAL	100

Table 3.4 *Continuous frequency distribution—cell midpoints and boundaries—grouped by threes.*

Pitch Diameter (X 0.0001 inch)	Cell Midpoint	Cell Boundary	Actual Frequency
		21.5	--
22-24	23		2
		24.5	--
25-27	26		4
		27.5	--
28-30	29		11
		30.5	--
31-33	32		34
		33.5	--
34-36	35		34
		36.5	--
37-39	38		10
		39.5	--
40-42	41		4
		42.5	--
43-45	44		1
		45.5	--
		TOTAL	100

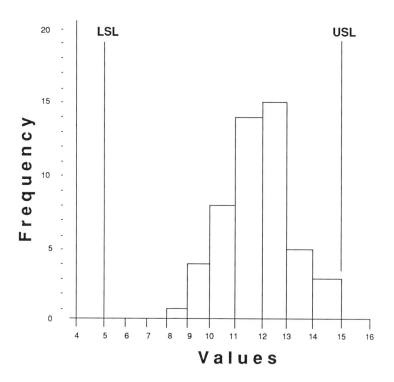

Figure 3.3 *Histogram constructed from the data in Figure 3.2.*

3.3 CONSTRUCTING A HISTOGRAM

A histogram is one method for grouping data so that the shape of a distribution can be revealed (*Figure 3.3*). A histogram can be constructed by using the following procedure:

1. **Determine the number of class intervals in the histogram.** The number of class intervals in the histogram is the number of groups into which our data must be divided. This must be selected carefully. If the number is too small or too large, the true shape may be obscured. The appropriate number of classes depends upon the number of measurements in the sample. One method is to take the square root of the number of data $(\sqrt{n})$ as an approximation of the number of classes.

The following table is typical:

Number of Data	Number of Classes
Less than 50	5 to 7
50 to 99	6 to 10
100 to 250	7 to 12
250 plus	10 to 20

2. **Estimate the size of each class.** First determine the range of the data collected. The range is the difference between the largest and the smallest data readings. From the individual tally in *Figure 3.2*, we can see that: Range = 14.9 - 8.6 = 6.3

The **class size** is based upon the range divided by the number of classes. The number of data in *Figure 3.2* is 50. We can use seven classes.

$$\text{Class size} = \frac{\text{Range}}{\text{No. of classes}}$$

$$= \frac{6.3}{7} = 0.9$$

Since 0.9 is not a convenient value to work with, round it off to 1.0.

3. **Make certain that the lowest class includes your smallest measurement.** In *Figure 3.2*, the smallest measurement was 8.6. The lowest class does not necessarily have to begin with 8.6. Use values that fit in with the specifications and gaging numbers. In our example, the first class should be 8.0 or 8.1. Once the lowest class limit is set at 8.0, we simply add 1 to the other measurements, as shown in the tally sheet and frequency distribution in *Figure 3.3*.

Notice that in *Figure 3.2*, the upper limit for any one class is not the same as the lower limit for the next class. Measurements should not fall into more than one class.

4. Count the frequency (number of measurements) in each class. This gives you the frequency for each class. All of the class frequencies for all of the recorded measurements constitute a **frequency distribution**.

5. Plot the histogram. The bases of the histogram rectangles are always equal and one class interval wide. All measurements are characterized by the midpoint of that class interval. Each class height is proportional to the class frequency, and the histogram total area is proportional to the total frequency (*Figure 3.3*).

SHORTCUT METHODS

It is often possible to simplify this procedure by using such shortcuts as a check sheet. A check sheet can be used when the range of typical measurement values expected for a given process are known from past experience. A standard set of classes for that process can be calculated and reproduced on a form for use at the time of data collection. If graph paper is used to make up the check sheet, a histogram can be obtained directly (*Figure 3.4*).

Another shortcut can be taken when the sample range is small. If the number of units in the sample range is equal to or less than the suggested number of classes, no further grouping is required.

CHECK SHEET

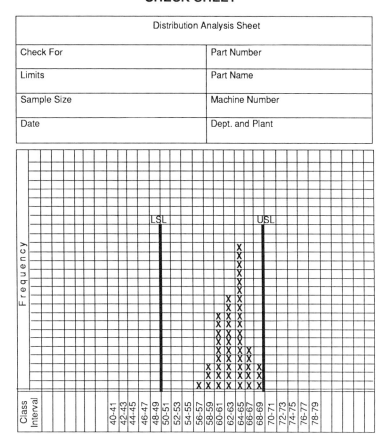

Distribution Analysis Sheet	
Check For	Part Number
Limits	Part Name
Sample Size	Machine Number
Date	Dept. and Plant

Figure 3.4 *Obtaining a histogram from a check sheet.*

	1:00	2:00	3:00	4:00	5:00	Total
35 - 39	Low Spec.					
40 - 44						
45 - 49	I					I
50 - 54	II	I				III
55 - 59	ⅣH III	III	II			ⅣH ⅣH III
60 - 64	ⅣH ⅣHI	ⅣH III	ⅣH	II		ⅣH ⅣHⅣHⅣHⅣHII
65 - 69	IIII	ⅣH III	ⅣH III	ⅣH I	I	ⅣH ⅣHⅣHⅣHⅣHIIII
70 - 74		IIII	ⅣH I	ⅣH IIII	ⅣH I	ⅣH ⅣHⅣHⅣHⅣHⅣHI
75 - 79		I	III	ⅣH I	ⅣH IIII	ⅣH ⅣHⅣHIII IIII
80 - 84	High Spec.	I	II	ⅣH II	ⅣH ⅣHI	
85 - 89				II	II	

Figure 3.5 *A histogram summing the day's run does not reveal the shift in the process over time.*

3.4 ANALYSIS WITH A HISTOGRAM

After constructing the histogram we draw in the specification limits. We can then compare the histogram distribution with the specification limits. This allows us to ask such questions as the following:

- Is the distribution consistent with previous checks?

- Is the distribution meeting specifications?

- Is the histogram roughly symmetrical (indicating that the process output distribution is normal)?

- Is the average close to the specification midpoint (indicating a centered process)?

- Is the spread greater than the specification limits (indicating that the process needs to be improved)?

USES FOR HISTOGRAMS

Histograms reveal much information about the process and are easily understood by operating personnel. The histogram may be used for such purposes as:

- Assessing material strengths

- Estimating process capabilities

- Indicating the necessity for corrective action

- Measuring the effects of corrective action

- Estimating machine capability

- Portraying life characteristics

- Comparing operators, materials, vendors, and products.

LIMITATIONS OF HISTOGRAMS

Histograms do have limitations. Histogram use is limited because:

- It requires many measurements.

- It does not take time into consideration.

- It does not separate the two kinds of variation factors (common or special causes).

- It does not show trends.

A histogram portrays a situation that has already occurred. A histogram may also hide more than it reveals, if care is not taken. For example, a frequency distribution or histogram summing the day's run fails to reveal the shift in the process over the time period shown (*Figure 3.5*). A control chart, on the other hand, gives a measure of process output shifts over time, using relatively small samples taken on a repetitive basis.

HISTOGRAM VARIATION

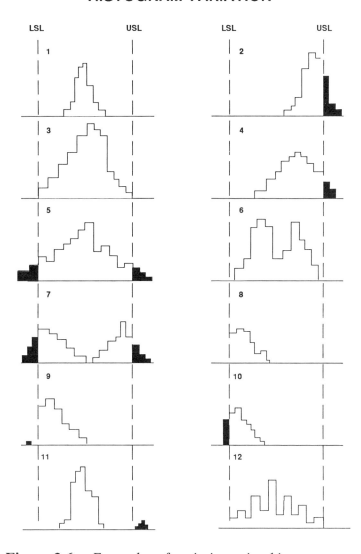

Figure 3.6 *Examples of variation using histograms.*

EXAMPLES OF VARIATION USING HISTOGRAMS

Examples of typical variation are shown (*Figure 3.6*) using histograms.

1. Well-centered and well within specification

2. Off-center with parts outside the upper limit

3. Well-centered with maximum variation

4. Off-center with parts beyond specification

5. Variation greater than the specification limits

6. Bimodal distribution, two different machines, materials, or products, or two separate distributions

7. Bimodal distribution is two separate distributions

8. Process off-center, 100 percent inspection is effective

9. Process off-center, 100 percent inspection not effective

10. Process off-center with a gage set up incorrectly (zero on gage actually reads -1)

11. Well-centered distribution, setup pieces not removed

12. Gaging inadequate or operator not trained

3.5 MEASURES OF CENTRAL TENDENCY

A frequency distribution provides an overall view of the variation in a data set—whether the data is concentrated at one or more peaks, the degree of variability or dispersion, the degree of symmetry, and the relative concentration in the center and in the tails of the distribution. Numerical tools provide a better basis for decision making. They concisely summarize distribution characteristics. This permits us to make more direct comparisons and to make inferences from sample data about a process.

The two principal numerical tools used are:

- Measures of central tendency

- Measures of dispersion or variability.

One of our major concerns is with the **center** or **central tendency** of a frequency distribution. The center of a distribution tells us **where the process is aimed.** Three commonly used measures for locating the center of a distribution are the **mean** (also called the **average** or more properly, the **arithmetic mean**), the **median**, and the **mode**.

FINDING THE MEAN

The arithmetic mean is the most commonly used central measure. It is usually represented by a bar over the symbol for a variable, such as $\overline{X}$ *(called "X bar")*. *The mean is* the sum of all numerical values represented in the distribution divided by the total number of values in the distribution (the total frequency).

Example:

1	3	5	6	10
1	3	5	6	11
2	3	5	6	12
2	3	5	6	13
2	5	6	7	14

$$\overline{X} = \frac{1 + 1 + 2 + 3 + \ldots + 14}{25}$$

$$= \frac{142}{25} = 5.68$$

The mean for this group of samples is 5.68.

FINDING THE MEDIAN

The median is **the middle value of the data, such that half the values are below it and half the values are above it.** It is sometimes defined as the central value in ordered data. The median is probably the next most common measure of central tendency. It is indicated by a tilde (a wavy bar) over the variable, $\tilde{X}$. The median is found by arranging all the data in order of magnitude and selecting the middle value as the median.

When there is an odd number of data, the median will be one of the data points. To find the median, add 1 to the total number of samples and divide that sum by 2. In the example below, the 13th sample is the **middlemost sample.** In this case, 5 is the median.

Example:

1	1	2	2	2
3	3	3	3	5
5	5 →	5	5	6
6	6	6	6	7
10	11	12	13	14

$$\text{Median} = \frac{25 + 1}{2} = \frac{26}{2} = 13\text{th value, which is } 5$$

When there is an even number of data, the median is the average of the two middle values. In the example below, the median would be the average of the fifth and sixth observations.

Example:

$$\downarrow \quad \downarrow$$

49, 50, 51, 52, **52, 52,** 53, 53, 54, 54

Median $\dfrac{52 + 52}{2} = 52$

From a practical standpoint, as used in Statistical Process Control, the median is always determined from an odd numerical sample.

Although the median is easy to calculate, it is less sensitive to process changes that affect only the extreme values. For this reason, the mean rather than the median is used more frequently to measure the process center.

FINDING THE MODE

The mode is a much less commonly used central measure. It is **the value that occurs most often in the sample**. A tally of the sample of 25 measurements is shown below. The mode is the measurement value with the highest frequency. In our example, the mode is 5.

FREQUENCY TABLE

Measurements	Frequency
1	I
2	III
3	IIII
→ 5	HH
6	IIII
7	II
10	I
11	I
12	I
13	I
14	I

3.6 SIGNIFICANCE OF DISPERSION

In order to evaluate a process, it is essential to know the center, but this by itself is not enough. We must also have some way to measure the **spread** or **variation.**

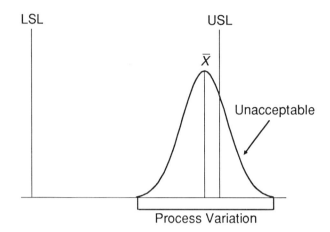

Figure 3.7a *Small variation, improperly centered.*

Figure 3.7a shows the distribution for a process that is producing much of its output above the upper specification. In this case, we can see that the variation is small compared to the size of the specification "doorway." The problem is that the process is aimed too high. If the aim could be adjusted, the result shown in *Figure 3.7b* could be obtained: small variation and good aim. Such changes in aim or operating level can often be achieved by adjustment. They may not require modification of the basic process itself.

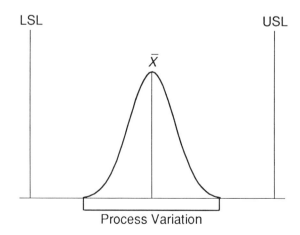

Figure 3.7b *Small variation, properly centered.*

Now, consider the case shown in *Figure 3.8a*, which contains the distributions for two processes on the same chart. Both processes have exactly the same mean, but one process is "tight" and the other is "sloppy." They have different variation. The process with small variation has all production well within specification, while the process with large variation has a large amount of production out of specification, despite the fact that both have the same center.

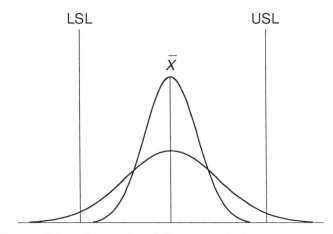

Figure 3.8a *Same aim, different variation.*

Adjustments to the process that change the aim will not make the process better but worse (*Figure 3.8b*). If the variation is excessive, then the process itself must be changed to bring about improvement.

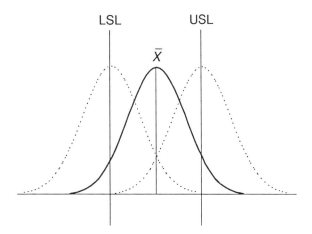

Figure 3.8b *Effect of inappropriate adjustment.*

3.7 MEASURES OF DISPERSION

Having calculated the center of a distribution, the next step is to determine the amount of variability or dispersion of the data.

Variation or variability of a distribution can be expressed in two useful ways—the **range** and the **standard deviation**.

RANGE

The range (R) is simply determined by subtracting the lowest value from the highest value of the data.

Example: 52, 50, 54, 52, 52, 51, 54, 49, 53, 53

Range = 54 - 49 = 5

Since the range is determined from only two values, it is very easy to compute. We will use it, therefore, for operation control purposes in developing control charts.

The range is a perfectly satisfactory measure of dispersion for small samples (say ten or less) but since it ignores all but two values in the sample, a more efficient measure of dispersion is required for larger samples for predicting behavior.

STANDARD DEVIATION

The more efficient measure of dispersion is variously called the standard deviation or the **root-mean-square deviation (RMS)**. It is efficient because it uses all of the data in the sample.

The serious student may recognize that it corresponds in engineering and physics to the concept in mechanics of the radius of gyration about a centroidal axis. When squared, it corresponds to the moment of inertia about the same axis. This is unimportant to our present understanding, but it does illustrate that this measure of dispersion has a parallel in any approach to measuring bulk or mass, which, of course, is what dispersion is.

More advanced textbooks make a careful distinction between the standard deviation of the universe (designated σ, the Greek letter sigma) and the standard deviation of a finite sample (*s*). The formula for each is as shown:

$$\sigma = \sqrt{\frac{\sum (X_i - \mu)^2}{N}}$$

$$s = \sqrt{\frac{\sum (X_i - \overline{X})^2}{n - 1}}$$

Where:

$\sum$ = the Greek letter *S* meaning summation

X_i = an individual reading

$\overline{X}$ = the calculated average

n = sample size

μ = the mean of the population

N = population size

The major distinction can be seen to be in the denominator, whether to use N or n - 1. An explanation for this difference becomes extremely complicated and unnecessary for our basic understanding. When applying these techniques to problem solving, we most often use samples, so the second formula will be almost universally used. Because the concept of sigma (σ) is becoming so well-entrenched as an expression of standard deviation, in this book we take the liberty of using the symbol σ for *s* (contrary to best academic practice). Thus:

$$\sigma = \sqrt{\frac{\sum (X_i - \overline{X})^2}{n - 1}}$$

and this is the formula for use in nearly all our statistical analysis and predictions from samples.

Another way of looking at the meaning of the standard deviation is to use its alternative description, the RMS, by reading that in reverse.

1. It (σ) is first of all an analysis of data noting the **deviation** of each individual measurement from the average.

   Thus, $(X_i - \overline{X})$ will calculate the deviation of each X_i from $\overline{X}$.

2. Each is next **squared**:

   Thus, $(X_i - \overline{X})^2$

3. The **mean** or average of the squared deviations may be obtained by using the traditional averaging technique:

   Thus, $\dfrac{\sum (X_i - \overline{X})^2}{n}$

4. Finally, the **square root** of this value will determine σ.

   Thus, $\sigma = \sqrt{\dfrac{\sum (X_i - \overline{X})^2}{n}}$

   and to correct for the use of samples rather than having universe data we will restate as previously mentioned:

   $$\sigma = \sqrt{\frac{\sum (X_i - \overline{X})^2}{n - 1}}$$

CALCULATING STANDARD DEVIATION

To illustrate calculation of standard deviation for the following five numbers, 130, 110, 120, 125, 105, we first compute the average:

$$\overline{X} = \frac{130 + 110 + 120 + 125 + 105}{5} = \frac{590}{5} = 118$$

Next, we subtract $\overline{X}$ from each value, square the results, and get the sum of the squares:

$(X - \overline{X})$	$(X - \overline{X})^2$
130 - 118 = 12	$12^2 = 144$
110 - 118 = -8	$-8^2 = 64$
120 - 118 = 2	$2^2 = 4$
125 - 118 = 7	$7^2 = \mathbf{49}$
105 - 118 = -13	$-13^2 = 169$
	Total: 430

Then, divide the total of the squares by the number of values minus one, i.e., $(n - 1)$, and determine the square root:

$$\frac{430}{4} = 107.5 \text{ and } \sqrt{107.5} = 10.37 \text{ (standard deviation)}$$

Today, with the convenience of affordable, handheld calculators and the availability of computer software, the calculation of standard deviation is quite simple.

CALCULATING THE MEAN AND STANDARD DEVIATION FOR GROUPED DATA

Formulas have been derived for calculating the mean and standard deviation for grouped data. The first formula shown below is used for ungrouped raw data. The second formula in each case is the long method used for grouped data; the third formula is a short method for grouped data.

The Mean

Ungrouped Data:

$$\bar{X} = \sum X / n$$

Grouped Data—Long Method:

$$\bar{X} = \sum fX / n$$

Grouped Data—Short Method:

$$\bar{X} = \text{ARBITRARY ORIGIN} + \text{CELL INTERVAL}$$
$$(\sum fd / n) = AO + (CI)\left(\sum fd / n\right)$$

Standard Deviation

Ungrouped Data:

$$s = \left[\frac{\sum (X - \bar{X})^2}{n-1}\right]^{\frac{1}{2}} = \left[\frac{n \sum X^2 - (\sum X)^2}{n(n-1)}\right]^{\frac{1}{2}}$$

Grouped Data—Long Method:

$$s = \left[\frac{n \sum fX^2 - (\sum fX)^2}{n(n-1)}\right]^{\frac{1}{2}}$$

Grouped Data—Short Method

$$s = (CI)\left[\frac{n \sum fd^2 - (\sum fd)^2}{n(n-1)}\right]^{\frac{1}{2}}$$

The following tables show the computations for grouped data. This data is grouped in measurement intervals by ones.

Table 3.5 *Pitch diameter grouped by ones.*

Pitch Diameter (X 0.0001 inch) Cell Midpoint X	f	fX	f(X^2)
23	1	23	529
24	1	24	576
25	0	0	0
26	1	26	676
27	3	81	2187
28	2	56	1568
29	2	58	1682
30	7	210	6300
31	6	186	5766
32	11	352	11264
33	17	561	18513
34	8	272	9248
35	14	490	17150
36	12	432	15552
37	4	148	5476
38	3	114	4332
39	3	117	4563
40	2	80	3200
41	2	82	3362
42	0	0	0
43	1	43	1849
TOTALS	**100**	**3355**	**113793**

$$\overline{X} = \sum fX \, / \, n = 3355 \, / \, 100 = 33.55$$

$$s = \left[\frac{n \sum fX^2 - (\sum fX)^2}{n(n-1)} \right]^{\frac{1}{2}}$$

$$= \left[\frac{100\,(113793) - (3355)^2}{100\,(99)} \right]^{\frac{1}{2}} = 3.53$$

Table 3.6 shows the calculations for the pitch diameter data grouped by three (the most symmetrical grouping of the groupings previously shown in Table 3.3b).

Table 3.6 *Pitch diameter, grouped by threes.*

Pitch Diameter (X 0.0001 inch) Cell Midpoint X	Frequency f	Deviation in Cell from Assumed Origin (AO) d	fd	$f(d^2)$
23	2	-3	-6	18
26	4	-2	-8	16
29	11	-1	-11	11
AO=32	34	0	0	0
35	34	1	34	34
38	10	2	20	40
41	4	3	12	36
44	1	4	4	16
TOTALS	100		45	171

$$\overline{X} = \text{ASSUMED ORIGIN } (AO) + \text{CELL INTERVAL } (CI) \left(\sum fd / n \right)$$
$$= 32 + (3)(45 / 100) = 33.35$$

$$s = (CI) \left[\frac{n \sum fd^2 - \left(\sum fd \right)^2}{n(n-1)} \right]^{\frac{1}{2}}$$

$$= (3) \left[\frac{100(171) - (45)^2}{100(99)} \right]^{\frac{1}{2}} = 3.70$$

Notice that there are obvious differences between the calculated mean and standard deviations calculated in the two tables. This always exists with continuous measurement data—measurements always coexist with cells having midpoints and boundaries. Calculations for the mean and standard deviation assume that cell values lie right at the midpoint. Examining Table 3.6, we can see that the assumption is not always valid. Grouping to show a better overall generalization of the distribution to the parent universe usually introduces some degree of unknown distortion in the calculated mean and standard deviation. Efforts to be more precise have disadvantages as well as advantages.

3.8 FREQUENCY AND PROBABILITY DISTRIBUTIONS

Statistics is concerned with drawing inferences and making decisions based on sample data. Frequency distributions express probabilities. Relative frequencies are, in effect, ratios expressing probabilities.

Whether a distribution is considered to be a frequency distribution or a probability distribution depends on one's point of view. A frequency distribution simply describes how a given data set is distributed. A **probability distribution** can be used to forecast how a given data set from the same parent universe will be distributed. A "smoothing process" can be applied mathematically to provide a generalization from the sample to the universe.

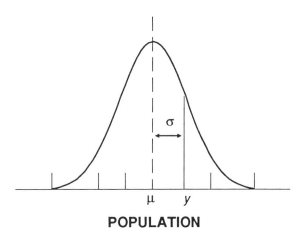

POPULATION

Figure 3.9   *The role of parameters in the normal distribution curve.*

POPULATIONS AND SAMPLES

Conclusions about an unknown universe or population depend on samples drawn from a particular universe. Sample values are used to estimate corresponding unknown universe measures, called **universe parameters**. A universe parameter is a special constant that defines the probability distribution, just as measures of central tendency and spread defined frequency distributions.

For example, *Figure 3.9* shows two parameters that define the normal distribution curve (the population mean, μ, and the population standard deviation, σ).

To draw conclusions about a population:

1. Samples are drawn from the population.

2. Sample values (the sample mean, $\overline{X}$, and sample range, R, or sample standard deviation, s) can be used to estimate corresponding universe parameters (population mean, μ, and population standard deviation, σ).

If variation in our industrial processes can be assumed to follow a particular kind of distribution, we can use samples drawn from the process to make inferences and decisions about the nature of variation in that process. The sample parameters for that distribution (i.e., the mean and the standard deviation) can be used to estimate the percentages of a product that are likely to fall within certain limits.

3.9 THE NORMAL DISTRIBUTION CURVE

The natural behavior and variation of many of our industrial processes are truly random. Although the distributions of many processes may assume a variety of shapes, many random variables observed in nature have a frequency distribution that comes very close to a well-known statistical model—the **normal probability distribution**.

The normal distribution is completely described by two characteristics, the average (or mean) and the standard deviation. Since the normal curve is the distribution of a continuous random variable, the probability of any particular given values can be predicted based on the area under the curve, which is the **probability density function** (*Figure 3.10*).

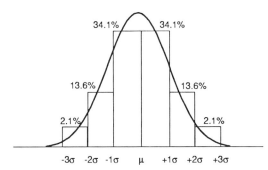

Figure 3.10 *A normal curve percentage of product in different zones.*

A normal distribution is perfectly symmetrical about its mean and has the familiar bell shape.

This distribution has a number of important characteristics:

1. The areas on either side of the mean are equal.

2. About 68.26% of the total area is included within a distance of $\pm \sigma$ from the mean.

3. About 95.44% of the total area is included within a distance of $\pm 2\sigma$ from the mean.

4. About 99.73% (or virtually all) of the area is included within a distance of $\pm 3\sigma$ from the mean.

The normal distribution is important in quality control for two reasons:

• Many distributions of quality characteristics of a product are reasonably similar to the normal distribution. This makes it possible to use the normal distribution for estimating percentages of products that are likely to fall within certain limits (*Figure 3.10*).

• Even when the distribution of a product is quite far from normal, many distributions of statistical quantities, such as averages, tend to distribute themselves in accordance with the normal curve. For this reason, the normal distribution has important uses in statistical theory, including some of the theory that underlies control charts.

3.10 NON-NORMAL DISTRIBUTIONS

Some process characteristics will inherently produce data that will have a non-normal distribution. For example, ovality and eccentricity have a minimum value of zero. As the process average is moved toward zero, the majority of data points are compacted into a narrow band close to zero, while larger values are spread out to the right in a positive direction resulting in a skewed (positive) distribution (*Figure 3.11*). Non-normal distributions require more advanced statistical techniques and should be referred to a specialist for evaluation. One technique, referred to as the **mirror-image technique** is described in section 3.12.

MEASURES OF SHAPE

In addition to central tendencies and the characteristics of dispersion, distributions can exhibit characteristics with respect to shape. These include measures of symmetry and measures of the relative concentration at the center and in the tails of a distribution as compared to a normal bell curve.

Skewness

A distribution departing from the symmetrical is said to be lopsided or **skewed**. Whether the skewness is positive or negative refers to the algebraic direction of the longer tail, to the right (higher values) or to the left (lower values).

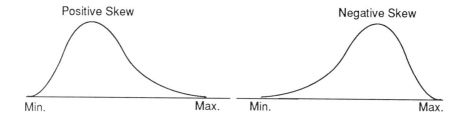

Figure 3.11 *A frequency distribution characteristic—skewness.*

Kurtosis

Kurtosis refers to the relative concentration at the center and in the tails of the distribution compared to a bell curve. Kurtosis is a measure of the size of the combined weight of the two tails relative to the rest of the distribution. High kurtosis, a **leptokurtic** distribution, has high concentration in the middle and out in the tails. In other words, it has a high, thin peak and fat tails. Low kurtosis, a **platykurtic** distribution, is flat in the middle and low in the tails. Expressed otherwise, it has a low, fat peak and thin tails.

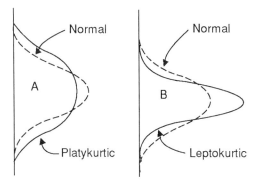

Figure 3.12 *A frequency distribution characteristic—kurtosis.*

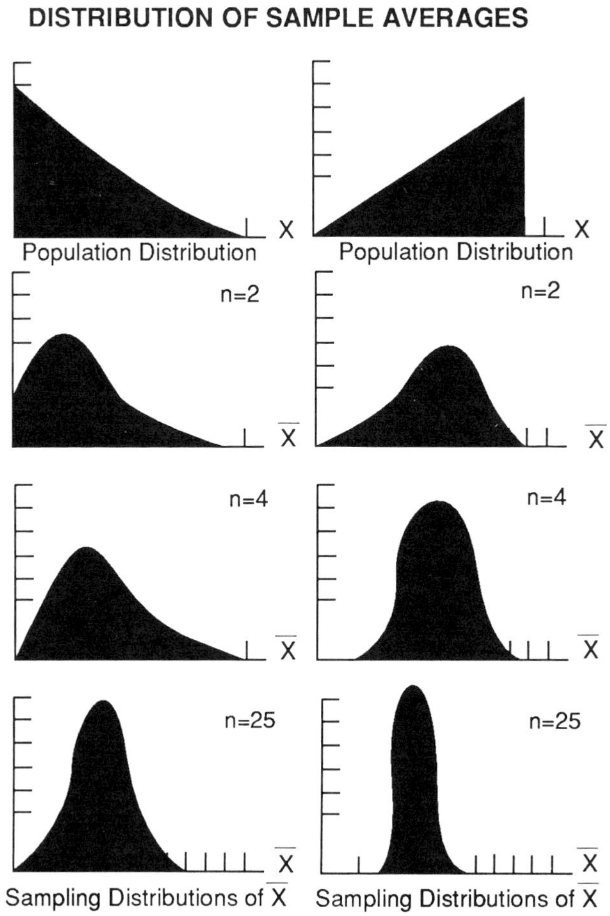

DISTRIBUTION OF SAMPLE AVERAGES

Figure 3.13 *Illustration of the Central Limit Theorem.*

3.11 THE CENTRAL LIMIT THEOREM

Universe parameters will take on different values in different situations. Discrete probability distributions used for industrial decisions are the hypergeometric, the binomial, and the Poisson. Continuous probability distributions employed in industry are the exponential, the Normal, and the Weibull.

The normal probability distribution is undoubtedly the most widely used of them all. It is possible to compute the mean and standard deviation for almost any conceivable set of sample data in industry or nature. Many measured qualities of manufactured products and many distributions follow the normal probability distribution. Process control charts use statistics that have universes corresponding to the normal by virtue of the Central Limit Theorem rationale or as a practical approximation.

Figure 3.13 illustrates an important theorem in mathematical statistics, the **Central Limit Theorem.** This states:

Irrespective of how the universe distribution is shaped, average values $(\overline{X})$ computed from samples of size n drawn from that universe, will tend toward a normal distribution as the sample size n increases.

Additionally, the dispersion (spread) of the sample average's distribution decreases in proportion to the square root of n. Specifically, if the original standard deviation is σ, the distribution of sample means $(\overline{X})$, from samples of size n will have a standard deviation equal to $\frac{\sigma}{\sqrt{n}}$. This standard deviation is referred to as the **standard error of the mean.**

The Central Limit Theorem is one of the most powerful statistical concepts in process control. It is the underlying basis for control charting.

Typically, information about the actual distribution of the population from which our data is taken is not available. Industrial processes may not be normal because of frequent adjustments (the tendency to turn control knobs).

The Central Limit Theorem permits us to move ahead with a method of making process control decisions without worrying about the underlying distribution. Sample averages are used. The sample averages will tend to become normal as the number of samples increases (*Figure 3.13*). This allows us to use the fundamental relationships of the normal curve—the mean, median, mode, and standard deviation of the distribution of averages.

3.12 THE MIRROR-IMAGE TECHNIQUE

The determination of process capability following demonstration of a process in statistical control is usually based on the assumption that product measurements follow a normal probability distribution. There are, however, product measurements that, by their inherent nature, cannot have a normal distribution. Flatness, squareness, out-of-roundness, taper, full indicator movement, runout, and out-of-balance are examples of truncated measurements where zero indicates perfection. The closer the distribution is to zero, the more non-normal it will appear.

Over the years, different techniques have been used to accommodate such non-normal data in order to make predictions about a process. However, these techniques have neither been simple to understand nor easy to use. The mirror-image method does meet these requirements for simplicity and ease of use.

The mirror-image method simply divides a skewed distribution into two parts at its mode and reflects the right and/or left side into one or two symmetrical distributions, depending upon the intent of the analysis.

EXAMPLE—APPLYING THE MIRROR-IMAGE TECHNIQUE

The illustrative example in *Table 3.7* applies the method for each of the two directions. In *Table 3.7, (a)* shows the original data, (b) demonstrates the reflection about the mode for the high side, and (c) exhibits the reflection about the mode for the low side. *Table 3.8* provides the computations for the mean and standard deviation of the original data. *Table 3.9* provides for the mean and standard deviation of the high side, *Table 3.10* for the low side. Note that the computed mean in *Table 3.9* and in *Table 3.10* lies exactly at the mode, as it should. Furthermore, the standard deviation for the wider mirror image (*Table 3.9*) is larger than for the original data, while in the narrower mirror image (*Table 3.10*) it is smaller than for the original.

Table 3.7 *Mirror-image method. The skewed distribution is divided into two parts at its mode and reflected in one or two symmetrical distributions.*

Skewed Original Data (a)		Reflect High Side (b)		Reflect Low Side (c)	
x	f	x	f	x	f
		-2.0	1		
		-1.5	1		
		-1.0	2		
		-0.5	1		
0.0	0	0.0	2		
0.5	0	0.5	2		
1.0	0	1.0	5		
1.5	4	1.5	6	1.5	4
2.0	8	2.0	8	2.0	8
2.5	10	2.5	10	2.5	10
3.0	8	3.0	8	3.0	8
3.5	6	3.5	6	3.5	4
4.0	5	4.0	5		
4.5	2	4.5	2		
5.0	2	5.0	2		
5.5	1	5.5	1		
6.0	2	6.0	2		
6.5	1	6.5	1		
7.0	1	7.0	1		
TOTAL	50	**TOTAL**	66	**TOTAL**	34

Table 3.8 *Computation of mean and standard deviation—skewed original data in Table 3.7.*

Cell Midpoint x	Frequency f	Deviation d	fd	f(d²)
1.5	4	- 3	-12	36
2.0	8	- 2	-16	32
2.5	10	- 1	-10	10
AO=3.0	8	0	0	0
3.5	6	1	6	6
4.0	5	2	10	20
4.5	2	3	6	18
5.0	2	4	8	32
5.5	1	5	5	25
6.0	2	6	6	72
6.5	1	7	7	49
7.0	1	8	8	64
	50		24	364

$$\overline{X} = AO + (CI) \left(\sum fd / n \right)$$
$$= 3.0 + (0.5)\ 24 / 50) = 3.24$$

$$s = (CI) \left[\frac{n \sum fd^2 - \left(\sum fd \right)^2}{n\,(n-1)} \right]^{\frac{1}{2}}$$

$$= (0.5) \left[\frac{50\,(364) - (24)^2}{50\,(49)} \right]^{\frac{1}{2}} = 1.34$$

Table 3.9 *Computation of mean and standard deviation—reflect high side in Table 3.7.*

Cell Midpoint x	Frequency f	Deviation d	fd	$f(d^2)$
-2.0	1	-9	-9	81
-1.5	1	-8	-8	64
-1.0	2	-7	-14	98
-0.5	1	-6	-6	36
0.0	2	-5	-10	50
0.5	2	-4	-8	32
1.0	5	-3	-15	45
1.5	6	-2	-12	24
2.0	8	-1	-8	8
AO=2.5	10	0	0	0
3.0	8	1	8	8
3.5	6	2	12	24
4.0	5	3	15	45
4.5	2	4	8	32
5.0	2	5	10	50
5.5	1	6	6	36
6.0	2	7	14	98
6.5	1	8	8	64
7.0	1	9	9	81
	66		0	876

$$\overline{X} = AO + (CI) \left(\sum fd \, / \, n \right)$$
$$= 2.5 + (0.5) \, (0 \, / \, 66) = 2.5$$

$$s = (CI) \left[\frac{n \sum fd^2 - \left(\sum fd \right)^2}{n \, (n-1)} \right]^{\frac{1}{2}}$$

$$= (0.5) \left[\frac{66 \, (876) - (0)^2}{66 \, (65)} \right]^{\frac{1}{2}} = 1.84$$

Table 3.10 *Computation of mean and standard deviation—reflect low side in Table 3.7.*

Cell Midpoint x	Frequency f	Deviation d	fd	f(d²)
1.5	4	-2	-8	16
2.0	8	-1	-8	8
AO=2.5	10	0	0	0
3.0	8	1	8	8
3.5	4	2	8	16
	34		0	48

$$\overline{X} = AO + (CI) \left(\sum fd\ /\ n \right)$$

$$= 2.5 + (0.5)\ (0\ /\ 34) = 2.5$$

$$s = (CI) \left[\frac{n \sum fd^2 - (\sum fd)^2}{n\ (n-1)} \right]^{\frac{1}{2}}$$

$$= (0.5) \left[\frac{34\ (68) - (0)^2}{34\ (33)} \right]^{\frac{1}{2}} = 0.60$$

3.13 STATISTICAL ERROR

Decisions must be made regarding whether to take action on a process. Such decisions are based on whether or not a process is out of control. There is always a risk of statistical error in making these decisions. How can we minimize such error?

Statistical inference is basically a prediction of what we can know about the characteristics of a population or universe from studying sample results. It is a prediction of what we could know if the process were completely analyzed. One form of this is called **hypothesis testing**. Such a test is useful in telling us what course of action to take when corrective action is indicated.

EXAMPLE—TYPE I AND TYPE II ERROR

Consider the following game to illustrate the two kinds of error involved in making decisions. A die is shaken in a box and rolled on the table by Umpire C. An even number turning up will cause Player A to pay a dollar to Player B. An odd number turning up will cause B to pay a dollar to A.

By the theory of probability, a balanced die rolled in a random manner is 50-50 with respect to even and odd numbers. Such conditions would provide a fair game. How can we tell if the game is fair? The fundamental hypothesis of balance and randomness should be tested before the game begins. We therefore agree to roll the die 100 times prior to starting to ensure a fair game. The crucial question is how close to 50-50 will establish fairness. The two potential errors are to say the odds are not 50-50 when they are, or to say they are 50-50 when they actually are not.

A **Type I error** is to reject a true hypothesis with probability alpha, and a **Type II error** is to accept a false hypothesis with probability beta. The **alpha risk** is always specified when the statistical test is designed and is called the **significance level**. The **beta risk** will vary depending on the actual existing conditions, which are unknown (subject to estimation). It is thus a function of those conditions. The chance of accepting a game as unbiased when false must depend on the degree of unsymmetry and bias. There is less chance of accepting balance and unbias if the true odds for an even number are 75-25 as compared to true odds of 55-45 or possibly 51-49. When such risks are specified numerically, statistical techniques can determine the appropriate sample size.

Type I (Also Known As Alpha Error, Or "Producer's Risk")

A Type I error occurs when we interpret a sample as being outside the limits of randomness when it actually represents how the process is functioning. If we make this error, then we interpret a process as being out of control when it is not. This must be investigated.

Type II (Also Known As Beta Error, Or "Consumer's Risk")

This is the opposite of a Type I error. It occurs when we interpret a sample as being in control when the process is actually out of control or a change has taken place. In making the error, we assume that a process is in control when it is not.

When we begin working with control charts, our goal will be to reduce our chances of making a Type I error, and to minimize the risk of making Type II errors. We can minimize the problems we might encounter in making Type II errors by collecting a large enough sample before we measure whether the process is in control.

3.14 SUMMARY

This chapter covered some basic statistical concepts necessary for making decisions in process control.

Variation is inherent in manufacturing. Managing variation is important to manufacturing quality. SPC provides tools for describing variation and distinguishing different kinds of causes of variation.

To be useful, data must be structured. Frequency distributions provide informative pictures of variation. Numerical measures allow us to compare distributions more efficiently. Measures of central tendency and dispersions let us describe the location and spread of a distribution.

Frequency distributions can be used both to describe how data is distributed and to predict how a parent universe is distributed. If variation in a process can be assumed to follow a particular type of distribution, we can make inferences and decisions about the nature of variation in that process. The distributions of many quality characteristics of products and processes follow a normal distribution. Once a process is shown to be in statistical control, process capability calculations are based on the assumption that product measurements will follow a normal distribution.

The Central Limit Theorem allows us to assume a normal distribution by using sample averages and a large enough sample. We can then move ahead and make process control decisions without worrying about the underlying distribution.

The goal of SPC is to help make informed decisions on whether to take action on a process. **Control charts** let us monitor a process and reduce the chances of interpreting a process as out of control when it is actually in control (Type I error). **Taking a large enough sample** before deciding whether a process is in control minimizes the chances of interpreting a process as in control when it is actually out of control (Type II error).

The first step in applying statistics is to collect data. The next chapter discusses some important issues in the collection of data. Subsequent chapters cover the use of control charting in assessing and maintaining control and capability of manufacturing processes.

COLLECTION OF DATA

CONTENTS

KEY CONCEPTS

In this chapter you will learn about the following key items and concepts:

Attribute (discrete) data
Variable (continuous) data
Cumulative distribution
Cumulative relative frequency
Continuous cumulative frequency distribution
Discrete cumulative frequency distribution
Sampling
Rational subgrouping
Measurement error
Purposes of data collection
Checksheets

COLLECTION OF DATA

4.1 INTRODUCTION

Having the right data is critical if we are to determine whether a process is in control, prevent defects, and improve quality. Data is collected in numerical form. In Statistical Process Control (SPC), this involves measuring quality characteristics or counting the number of defects or defectives. The importance of this first step is often underestimated. The data collected must be timely, complete, and accurate. Untimely or incomplete data can be useless. Inaccurate data is worse than useless—it is dangerous in that it leads to wrong conclusions. These are points that must be understood by everyone involved in the SPC program.

4.2 PURPOSES OF DATA COLLECTION

A process is a system of causes leading to an effect or outcome. For a manufacturing process, the main causes that affect product quality are:

- People

- Machines

- Materials

- Methods

- Environment

- Measurement.

If any of these elements are changed in an important way, the process system will be changed, and there will be a corresponding change in product quality.

Keeping in mind that quality means uniformity, consider what would happen if the following changes were made to some of the causes listed below:

People: A change from a poorly trained operator to a well-trained operator.

Machine: A change from a well-maintained machine to a poorly maintained, sloppy machine.

Material: Replacing inconsistent raw materials with raw materials of consistent quality.

Method: Using the same man, machine, and material, but changing the speed or temperature setting on the machine.

Environment: Allowing the dust or humidity to increase where painting is done.

Measurement: Measuring good parts with an erratic measuring device.

These elements must be considered when we begin making decisions about what data to collect. How can you be sure the operator is at fault if you haven't checked the accuracy of the measurement system? Or, how do you know you're working with low-quality raw materials if you haven't made sure that different methods, such as a change in the temperature or speed of the machine, might not solve the problem?

Our basis for action on a process is **data** from **samples** systematically chosen from a **population**. Based on measurements of items from the lot where our sample was selected, we can make inferences about the population and then decide whether to take action on the production process (*Figure 4.1*).

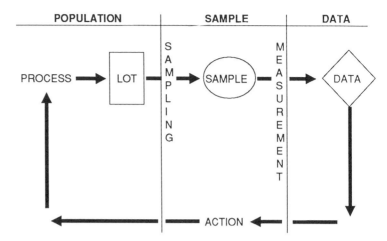

Figure 4.1   *Goal of data collection: action on the process.*

Data can be collected for a number of purposes. Here's a list of some of the most common purposes:

1. To understand the actual situation.

Example: measure dispersion of parts, estimate percent of defects.

2. To analyze a process or operation.

Example: analyze a product or process to identify and eliminate defects.

3. To improve process control.

Example: collect data for control charts.

4. To regulate components of a process.

Example: collect data to determine ideal operating conditions.

Table 4.1 *Attribute data: vehicle errors at final inspection.*

Vehicle Number	Number of Errors	Vehicle Number	Number of Errors
1	7	14	9
2	6	15	8
3	6	16	15
4	7	17	6
5	4	18	4
6	7	19	13
7	8	20	7
8	12	21	8
9	9	22	15
10	9	23	6
11	8	24	6
12	5	25	10
13	5	**TOTAL**	**200**

Table 4.2 *Variable data: thread pitch diameter measurements (expressed in units of 0.0001 inch above 0.4000).*

Group Number	a	b	c	d	e
1	36	35	34	33	32
2	31	31	34	32	30
3	30	30	32	30	32
4	32	33	33	32	35
5	32	34	37	37	35
6	32	32	31	33	33
7	33	33	36	32	31
8	23	33	36	35	36
9	43	36	35	24	31
10	36	35	36	41	41
11	34	38	35	34	38
12	36	38	39	39	40
13	36	40	35	26	33
14	36	35	37	34	33
15	30	37	33	34	35
16	28	31	33	33	33
17	33	30	34	33	35
18	27	28	29	27	30
19	35	36	29	27	32
20	33	35	35	39	36

4.3 TYPES OF DATA

There are two general types of data: **attribute** and **variable.** The purpose of collecting and analyzing data is to control and improve the process. The ultimate use of the data should determine how it is collected and the form that it takes. It should be used to identify the causes of variation or to measure changes in a process.

ATTRIBUTE DATA

Data that comes from counting and is expressed as integers or whole numbers is called attribute or **discrete** data. *Table 4.1* shows the number of errors observed at final inspection in each of 25 vehicles. An **error** is an integral unit that either exists or does not. Only in referring to an average can there be a fractional error. The errors for each vehicle must be whole numbers and must vary by units of one from vehicle to vehicle.

VARIABLE DATA

Variable data can potentially take on any value within a given range with no natural restriction. It is also called **continuous** data. A confusing aspect is that measurement equipment limitations on least count necessarily cause the observations to be recorded in jumps. It must be remembered, however, that inherently the data are continuous, and the jumps are artificial measuring instrument constraints. *Table 4.2* contains thread pitch diameter measurements. The values were originally expressed in ten-thousandths of an inch but are shown coded as whole numbers beyond the gage zero setting. The highest is 43 and the lowest is 23, measured to the nearest ten-thousandth of an inch. Thus, each measurement ends on an integral one ten-thousandth, a limitation imposed by the measuring instrument.

Table 4.3 *Discrete cumulative frequency distribution —tractor errors at final inspection.*

	Tractors with Designated Number of Errors	
Number of Errors	Cumulative Actual Frequency	Cumulative Relative Frequency
0	0	0
1	0	0
2	0	0
3	0	0
4	2	0.08
5	4	0.16
6	9	0.36
7	13	0.52
8	17	0.68
9	20	0.80
10	21	0.84
11	21	0.84
12	22	0.88
13	23	0.92
14	23	0.92
15	25	1.00

Table 4.4 *Continuous cumulative frequency distribution—pipefitting thread diameter.*

Cell Midpoint	Cell Boundary	Cumulative Actual Frequency	Cumulative Relative Frequency
	21.5		
23		2	0.02
	24.5		
26		6	0.06
	27.5		
29		17	0.17
	30.5		
32		51	0.51
	33.5		
35		85	0.85
	36.5		
38		95	0.95
	39.5		
41		99	0.99
	42.5		
44		100	1.00
	45.5		

CUMULATIVE DISTRIBUTION FOR CONTINUOUS AND DISCRETE DATA

A cumulative distribution is generated when frequencies are accumulated, usually from the lower end to the higher end. *Table 4.3* shows a discrete cumulative frequency distribution constructed from *Table 4.1*. *Table 4.4* shows a continuous cumulative frequency distribution generated from *Table 4.2*.

Notice that the cumulative relative frequency for any value below the distribution's lower limit is zero, and the cumulative relative frequency for any value above the distribution limit is 1 (unity). *Figure 4.2a* and *4.2b*, respectively, show graphs for these discrete and continuous cumulative distributions.

The graph for a discrete distribution will always be a step function, as shown in *Figure 4.2a*. The graph for a continuous distribution will initially be a step function. However, its steps can be smoothed by a superimposed curve called an **ogive**. This gives a better representation of the universe from which the sample was drawn. The curve approximates a continuous function for extremely small cell intervals with an extremely large sample. A bell curve can likewise be superimposed on a noncumulative histogram.

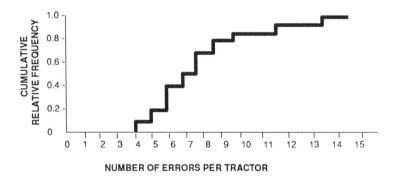

Figure 4.2a *Discrete cumulative frequency distribution (data from Table 4.3).*

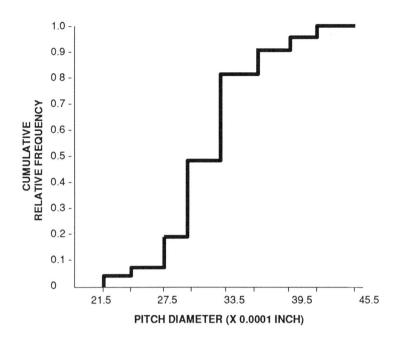

Figure 4.2b *Continuous cumulative frequency distribution (data from Table 4.4).*

4.4 MISTAKES IN DATA COLLECTION

Everything in life varies. Where industrial processes are concerned, variation can be expected. Individual events or variations are not predictable, but large groups of items are predictable. We do not have to measure every item produced in a population, but we do have to sample and measure.

There are two sources of mistakes in data collection:

1. Mistakes in selection of the sample

2. Measurement error

SAMPLE SELECTION—RATIONAL SUBGROUPING

Prediction of variation in large groups is based on the data collected from samples. The type of sample selected and the method used to select the sample are extremely important. A sample should be representative—it should truly reflect the overall characteristics of the process you are sampling. A random sample is selected by a method that demands that every unit and every combination of units from the population has an equal chance of being chosen. You must ensure that there aren't any conditions that would make it more likely for you to pick some items over others that would bias your sample.

There are two techniques that can help you to do this: One has to do with timing; the other has to do with location. By carefully determining the times to measure the sample items, you can help ensure a random reading of the entire lot or process.

If we take samples between 8:00 a.m. and 4:00 p.m., to ensure we have a random sample, we might set up the following schedule: collect samples each hour, but time our selection of samples so that we take them at sequential quarter hours. If you simply took the readings at the beginning of each hour, you might pick up readings that were cyclical.

In addition to selecting samples at random time intervals, we also want to ensure that we select sample units randomly. Suppose that widgets are deposited in a bin. A sample wouldn't be truly random if we always took the 25 widgets off the top of the bin. It's better to take some from the top, some from the middle, and others from the bottom.

SAMPLING CONSIDERATIONS

Process operators are the individuals responsible for the control of a process. They may or may not be the machine operators, but they should be individuals directly involved in the process on a day-by-day basis (e.g., taking samples, measuring parts, making statistical charts, reacting to statistical signals, and making corrections, as necessary).

Table 4.5 *Considerations in selecting samples and sampling frequency.*

- Select samples early and know the operator's limitations.

- Select separate samples for separate sources of variation.

- Minimize changes within the samples.

- Decide on sampling frequency:

  — How critical is the characteristic?

  — What is the control and capability history of the process?

The following considerations should be observed in sample selection:

1. Sample early and know the process operator's limitations.

   Sampling should occur upstream in the production process in order to allow maximum opportunity to analyze and correct process difficulties. A sampling plan should be developed that takes into account what an operator can and cannot do with a process.

2. Select separate samples for separate sources of variation.

   For example, two machines are producing parts that are sent to the shipping container if good and to scrap and rework if rejected. A process operator is concerned with the control of the machine. If he samples from the end of the line, the characteristic he is measuring will have two sources of variation mixed into his samples. He should sample separately from each machine.

3. Sampling should minimize the change that can occur within the sample itself.

In other words, samples should be selected consistently. Inconsistent sampling may lead to artificially high ranges that incorrectly indicate poor process uniformity. The best way to avoid inconsistent sampling is to take consecutive sample pieces directly from a machine having a known order of production.

4. Sampling frequency should be based on the history of the process characteristic, process control, uniformity, and economics.

SAMPLING FREQUENCY

Sampling frequency has to do with how often an operator should take his samples. A well-controlled process may only need to be sampled twice per day. Or, control may be so poor that sampling needs to occur every ten minutes.

The following questions should be asked regarding frequency of sampling:

1. How critical is the dimensional characteristic? If the characteristic is critical, it needs to be sampled more often.

2. What is the control history of the process? Those that are out of control require the most frequent sampling.

3. How capable is the process? Less capable processes require more frequent sampling.

4. How captive is the process? Some processes, once set up, run the same part for long periods. Others are almost in a routine state of changeover, running only a few pieces and setup again. Sample frequency should be increased for processes in a high state of changeover to accommodate the variety of conditions.

5. What is the cost of the part? Frequency may need to be increased for high-cost parts in order to avoid producing large numbers of expensive, inferior parts.

Decisions regarding sampling should be flexible. Conditions can change over time—a process that was in control can go out of control.

Remember that the frequency prescribed on a control chart is a minimum requirement. If something goes wrong in a process, frequency of sampling may need to be increased.

MEASUREMENT ERROR

In collecting data, we also have to consider the possibility of **measurement error**. This can be caused by several factors, including differences in measuring devices, differences in the way people use measuring devices, or differences in the way one person measures a unit from one time to the next. (See Chapter 10 for further explanation of measurement error.)

4.5 GUIDELINES FOR DATA COLLECTION

Data that is collected and not used is a wasted expense. Before wasting manpower and effort, and possibly coming to erroneous conclusions, it's a good idea to spend time focusing on why the data needs collecting, who will collect it, etc.

A planning session for data collection is an excellent opportunity to improve communication among everyone involved. Line operators, maintenance personnel, anyone familiar with the machinery, materials, and operation will have insights. It would be a serious loss of information to ignore the insights that hourly workers can share with supervisors and foremen when planning data collection.

Here are some questions that could be brought up for discussion during planning sessions:

1. What is the purpose of collecting the data?

2. Have the specific data parameters been identified?

3. Will this effort duplicate something that's already been done?

4. Have you coordinated data collection with other organizations that might be affected?

5. Who will collect the data?

6. How will the data be collected?

7. When should it be collected?

8. Where should the data originate?

9. What forms should be used to collect the data?

10. Where will the data be kept?

11. How long will the records be kept?

12. Who coordinates the effort?

13. Is any training required?

14. Does everyone involved clearly understand the purpose for collecting the data?

15. Who prepares the final report?

16. Who will the report be addressed to?

17. Has budget authorization for the project been coordinated?

4.6 CHECK SHEETS

There are several ways that data can be collected. A specific form for data collection can make both the collection and analysis easier. Check sheets make it easier for us to compile data and put it into a format so that it can be readily analyzed.

Some of the more common types of check sheets are:

- Check sheets for process distributions

- Check sheets for defective items

- Check sheets for location of defects

- Check sheets for cause and effect.

PROCESS DISTRIBUTION CHECK SHEETS

In evaluating a production process, we need to determine the shape of the distribution and relationships to specification limits. The data collection for capability analysis form (*Figure 4.3*) is an example of a frequency distribution format. All the operator needs to do is make checkmarks in the tally columns of the form. The frequency distribution is developed as the data is collected.

When using this format:

- There must be no time lapses in the data.

- All the data must be recorded. Missing data will not be obvious.

- When machines, materials, or people change, it is best to use a separate check sheet for each change, and review them later.

- On a single check sheet, it is best to use different colors or types of marks for different data sources.

When the check sheet is completed:

- It can be analyzed for the shape of the distribution. Is it bell-shaped, or is there more than one peak? Is it skewed?, etc.

- It can be analyzed for the relationship between the distribution and specification limits. Is the spread within the specification limits? Is the center of the distribution near the center of the specification limits?

DATA COLLECTION FOR CAPABILITY ANALYSIS

Part No. & Name		Char. Measured
Operation No. & Desc.		Date

SAMPLE DATA

No.	Value	No.	Value	No.	Value	No.	Value	No.	Value
1		21		41		61		81	
2		22		42		62		82	
3		23		43		63		83	
4		24		44		64		84	
5		25		45		65		85	
6		26		46		66		86	
7		27		47		67		87	
8		28		48		68		88	
9		29		49		69		89	
10		30		50		70		90	
11		31		51		71		91	
12		32		52		72		92	
13		33		53		73		93	
14		34		54		74		94	
15		35		55		75		95	
16		36		56		76		96	
17		37		57		77		97	
18		38		58		78		98	
19		39		59		79		99	
20		40		60		80		100	
Remarks									

TALLY SHEET

VALUE																	
TALLY																	
FREQUENCY																	

Figure 4.3 *Data collection for capability analysis form.*

DEFECTIVE ITEM CHECK SHEETS

The defective item check sheet shows the kind of defects and their percentages. When a worker finds a defect, a mark is made in the appropriate column. At the end of the day, you can see the total number of defects and the items on which the defects occurred (*Figure 4.4*).

This type of check sheet will not show changes in values over time on an individual sheet. It may be necessary to view several sheets in chronological order to determine trends (e.g., some defects may be produced mainly at start-up time). This type of information is important in improving a process.

When the frequency of a major defect shows a decline, your actions were successful, and your overall control has improved. Such information can be used in developing a Pareto analysis.

Defective Item Check Sheet

Product _____

Part No. _____   Date _____

Operation Name _____   Dept. _____

Purpose _____   No. _____

Instructions/Procedure_____

_____

Time/Check _____   Total Insp. _____

Remarks _____   Operator _____

Defect	Tally	Subtotal
Scratches		
Cracks		
Misformed		
Incomplete		
Other		
Total Pieces		

Figure 4.4   *Check sheet—defective items.*

DEFECT LOCATION CHECK SHEETS

The defect location check sheet is extremely useful and will include a sketch or drawing of the product so that the location of defects can be identified on the sketch. *Figure 4.5* is a check sheet used to examine bubbles in laminated glass. The location and form of the bubble defects might indicate that one side of the glass is receiving less pressure during lamination. Action can be taken (equalization of pressure) to reduce the frequency of bubbles.

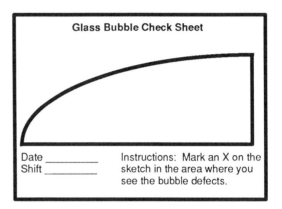

Glass Bubble Check Sheet

Date _____   Instructions: Mark an X on the
Shift _____   sketch in the area where you
                              see the bubble defects.

Figure 4.5   *Glass bubble check sheet.*

DEFECT CAUSE CHECK SHEETS

To investigate defect causes, data concerning causes and corresponding data on defects (percent defectives, yield, etc.) are arranged so that the relationship between cause and effect is clear.

Figure 4.6 is an example of a defect cause check sheet. Defects in molded knobs are recorded and the occurrence of defects are recorded separately by category: workers, machines, dates, and type of defect.

Process operations produce defects. As seen in *Figure 4.6*, on Wednesday all workers had more defects. A new employee, Operator B, was not rotating his stock of parts, and the materials used on Wednesday were defective. Once the cause was detected, the situation was easily remedied.

This type of check sheet helps to link cause and effect. It can become quite complex.

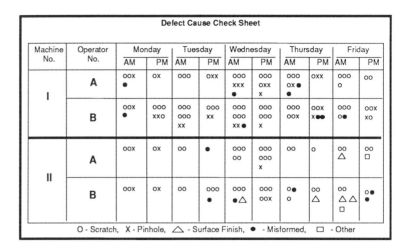

Figure 4.6 *Defect cause check sheet.*

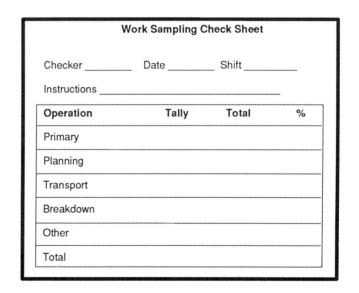

Figure 4.7 *Work sampling check sheet.*

OTHER TYPES OF CHECK SHEETS

Other types of check sheets can be developed. Work sampling is a method of analyzing working time. Total work is divided into primary work, preparatory work, allowance time, etc. (*Figure 4.7*). The percentage devoted to each is evaluated by observing work content at randomly selected times; the number of workers engaged in each category can be checked and the percentages determined.

In selecting or developing a check sheet:

* Keep the purpose of your data collection in mind.

* Use the simplest check sheet that will meet your needs.

CONTROL CHARTS

CONTENTS

KEY CONCEPTS

In this chapter you will learn about the following key items and concepts:

Dr. Walter A. Shewhart
Common causes
Special causes
Process control
Process capability
Control charts for variables
Control charts for attributes
Averages and range chart
Subgroup: (size, frequency)
Process average
Process range
Control limits
Center line
Control chart analysis
Statistical signal
Points out of control limits
Runs and trends
Under control (Type II error)
Over control (Type I error)
Problem solving (finding and correcting special causes)

CONTROL CHARTS

5.1 INTRODUCTION

Dr. Walter A. Shewhart of AT&T Bell Laboratories, while studying process data in the 1920s, first made the distinction between controlled and uncontrolled variation due to common and special causes. He developed a simple but powerful tool to dynamically separate the two—the control chart. Since that time, control charts have been successfully used in a wide variety of process control situations, both in the United States and other countries, notably Japan.

Several types of control charts have been developed to analyze both variables and attributes. However, all control charts have the same two primary functions and are prepared and analyzed according to the same basic outline. The functions are:

1. To signal the presence of special causes of variation, so that corrective action can be taken to bring the process into a state of statistical control.

2. To give evidence whether a process has been operating in a state of statistical control, so that a meaningful assessment of its capability to meet engineering specifications can be made.

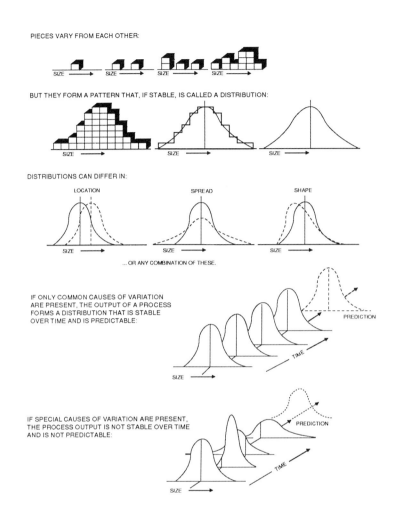

Figure 5.1 *Variation: common and special causes. SOURCE: Ford Motor Co., <u>Continuous Process Control and Process Capability Improvement</u>, Statistical Method, Office, Operations Support, 1985.*

5.2 VARIATION: COMMON AND SPECIAL CAUSES

No two products or characteristics are exactly alike, because any process contains many sources of variation. The diameter of a machined shaft would be susceptible to variation from the machine, tool, material, operator, maintenance, and environment.

Some sources of variation in the process cause very short-run, piece-to-piece differences (e.g., backlash and clearances within a machine and its fixturing). Other sources of variation tend to cause changes in output only over a longer period of time, either gradually, as with tool or machine wear, or irregularly, as with such environmental changes as power surges. Both the time period and conditions during the production run affect variation. **To manage and reduce variation, the variation must be traced back to its source**.

A process is said to be in a state of statistical control when it can be demonstrated over time that the process is not changing—i.e., not, on average, deviating from its intended target or deteriorating in any way.

Common causes refer to many sources of measurable variation within a process that is in statistical control. They behave like a constant system of chance causes. While individual measured values are all different, as a group they tend to form a pattern that can be described as a distribution. This distribution can be characterized by specific measures: location, spread, and shape.

Special causes, often called **assignable causes**, refer to any factors causing variation in measurements that cannot be adequately explained by any single distribution of the process output, as would be the case if the process were in statistical control. They are considered unusual and can be eliminated. Until all the special causes of variation are identified and corrected, they will continue to affect the process output in unpredictable ways (*Figure 5.1*).

Special causes of variation can be detected by statistical techniques for evaluating process variation. The discovery of a special cause of variation, and its removal, is usually the responsibility of personnel who are directly connected with the operation. The resolution of a special cause of variation usually requires local action.

The extent of common causes of variation can be indicated by statistical techniques, but the causes themselves need more detailed analysis in order to be isolated. These common causes of variation are usually the responsibility of management to correct. The resolution of common causes of variation usually requires actions on the system: machinery, material, methods, people, environment, or measuring equipment.

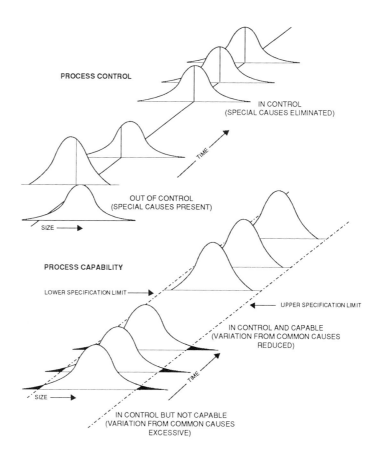

Figure 5.2 *Process control and process capability. SOURCE: Ford Motor Co., <u>Continuous Process Capability Improvement</u>, Statistical Method, Office, Operations Support, 1985.*

5.3 PROCESS CONTROL AND PROCESS CAPABILITY

The goal of a process control system is to make economically sound decisions about actions affecting the process. This means balancing the risks of taking action when action is not necessary (over control or Type I error) versus failing to take action when action is necessary (under control or Type II error). These risks must be handled, however, in the context of the two sources of variation previously mentioned —special causes and common causes (*Figure 5.2*).

A process is said to be operating in statistical control when the only source of variation is due to common causes. According to Dr. W. Edwards Deming, "... a state of statistical control is not a natural state for a manufacturing process. It is instead an achievement, arrived at by elimination, one by one, of special causes of excessive variation." The initial function of a process control system, then, is to provide a statistical signal when special causes of variation are present and to avoid giving false signals when they are not present. This will enable appropriate action that can eliminate those special causes and prevent their reappearance.

Process capability is determined by the total variation that comes only from common causes—the minimum variation that can be achieved after all special causes have been eliminated. Thus, capability represents the best performance of the process itself, as demonstrated when the process is operating in a state of statistical control. Capability is often thought of in terms of the proportion of output that will be within product specification tolerances. Since a process in statistical control can be described by a predictable distribution, the proportion of out-of-specification parts can be estimated from this distribution. As long as the process remains in statistical control, it will continue to produce the same proportion of out-of-specification parts. Management action to reduce variation from common causes is required to improve the ability to meet specifications consistently.

In short, the process must first be brought into statistical control by detecting and eliminating special causes of variation. Then its performance is predictable, and its capability to meet customer expectations can be assessed. This is the basis for continuous improvement. This chapter will focus primarily on the concept and techniques for determining control. The topic of process capability is reviewed in greater detail in Chapter 7.

5.4 WHAT CONTROL CHARTS CAN DO

Histograms and similar techniques allow us to analyze a distribution using a large number of data. These methods, however, have inherent limitations. First, the large number of data required makes them too expensive to be utilized for on-line quality control on an hour-by-hour basis. Second, the histogram does not allow us to recognize the different sources of variation that may be present in the process. In a histogram, a large sample is analyzed all at one time. These limitations can be overcome using control charts. A control chart deals with small samples taken periodically, not just an accumulation of individual measurements. It allows us to track the critical characteristics of a process over time. Control limits can be calculated and used to distinguish between special and common causes of variation.

BENEFITS OF CONTROL CHARTS

Properly used, control charts can:

- Be used by operators for ongoing control of a process.

- Help the process perform consistently and predictably for quality and cost.

- Allow the process to achieve:

  — Higher quality

  — Lower unit cost

  — Higher effective capacity

- Provide a common language for discussing process performance.

- Distinguish between special and common causes of variation, as a guide to local or management action.

- Control charts, by distinguishing special from common causes of variation, give a good indication of whether any problems are due to local faults (the way the process is being operated) or system faults (the process as it was designed, built, and maintained). This minimizes the confusion, frustration, and excessive cost of misdirected problem-solving efforts.

- Control charts are simple to use—especially for ongoing process control—so they lend themselves to being maintained at the job station by the operator. This gives the operator almost immediate information on when to take action or when not to take action.

- Control charts can provide a common language for communication about the performance of a process—between the two or three shifts that operate a process; between line production (operator, foreman) and support activities (maintenance, material control, process engineering, quality control, etc.); between different stations in the process; between the supplier and the user; and between the manufacturing/assembly plant and the design engineering activity.

- As long as a process is in statistical control, its performance to process specification will remain consistent over time.

- Only a process in statistical control can be assessed for capability.

- Only a process that is in statistical control can achieve its best performance. Process control provides the ability to:

  — Increase the percentage of parts within specification (improved quality).

  — Decrease the out-of-specification parts requiring scrap or rework (improved cost per good unit produced).

  — Increase the total yield of good parts through the process (improved first time through capability).

- When a process is in statistical control but still needs improvement in total performance (is not yet capable), the expected effects of proposed improvements in the system can be clearly quantified, and the actual effects of even relatively small changes can be identified through the control-chart data.

5.5 TYPES OF CONTROL CHARTS

There are basically two general types of control charts:

1. Control charts for variables

2. Control charts for attributes.

Table 5.1 *Definitions of the most commonly used types of control charts.*

ATTRIBUTE

Symbol	Description	Sample Size
p	The proportion of nonconforming units in a sample	May change
np	The number of nonconforming units in a sample	Must be consistent
c	The number of nonconformities in a sample	Must be consistent
u	The number of nonconformities per unit	May change

VARIABLE

Symbol	Description	Sample Size
$\overline{X}$	The average (mean) measurements in a sample	Must be consistent
R	The range of measurements in a sample	Must be consistent
s	The standard deviation of measurements in a sample	Must be consistent
$\tilde{X}$	The median (middle) measurement in a sample	Must be consistent (Is usually an odd numbered sample)
X	The individual value in a sample	One

Attributes are simply judgments as to whether a part is good or bad. Control charts for attributes are used when parts are judged by appearance and can be classified only as meeting or not meeting standards. **Variables** are specific measurements of a given product or process characteristic along a continuous scale, such as temperature, weight, length, width, dimension, etc. *Table 5.2* lists the kinds of control charts most commonly used for specific types of data collection.

As you can see from *Table 5.2*, control charts are referred to by symbols. *Table 5.1* gives a slightly more detailed description of some of these control charts, along with the symbols associated with them. It also provides information about the sample size for each type.

Table 5.2 *Types of data and control charts.*

	Types of Data	Control Chart Used
Variable	Measurements	$\bar{X}$ and R
	Volume (cc)	$\bar{X}$ and s
	Product weight (g)	*Median* and R
	Power consumed (kwh)	Individuals and moving range
Attribute	Number of defectives	np
	Fraction defective (Second-class product rate)	p
	Number of pinholes in pieces of plated sheet metal, differing in area	u
	Number of foreign particles in pharmaceutical compounds, differing in volume (when the range in which the defects are possible, such as length, area, volume, etc., is not fixed)	
	Number of pinholes in a specified area; number of foreign particles in a specified volume (when the length, area volume, etc., is fixed)	c

5.6 OUTLINE FOR PREPARING TO USE CONTROL CHARTS

The basic outline for preparation and analysis of control charts is described in *Figure 5.3*.

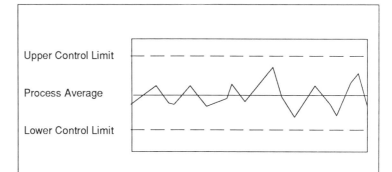

Upper Control Limit

Process Average

Lower Control Limit

1. **Collection**. Gather data and plot on a chart.

2. **Control**. Calculate control limits from process data, using simple formulas.

3. **Interpretation**. Identify special causes of variation; take local action to correct.

4. **Capability**. Quantify common cause variation; take action on the system.

Figure 5.3 *Control chart phases.*

These four phases are repeated for continuous process improvement.

1. **Gather data and plot the chart.** The process is run, and data for the characteristic being studied are gathered and converted to a form that can be plotted on a graph. These data might be the measured values of a dimension of a machined piece, the number of flaws in a bolt of vinyl, the percent of nonconforming parts produced per day, etc.

2. **Calculate control limits.** Trial control limits are calculated based on the data from the output of the process; they reflect the amount of period-to-period variation that could be expected from only common causes. They are drawn on the chart as a guide to analysis. Control limits are not specification limits or objectives, but are reflections of the natural variability of the process.

3. **Interpret for process control.** The data are compared against the control limits to see whether the variation is stable and appears to come only from common causes. If special causes of variation are evident, operation of the process is studied to determine what is affecting the process. After the faults are corrected, the process continues running; further data are collected, control limits are recalculated if necessary, and any additional special causes are studied and corrected.

4. **Interpret for process capability.** After all special causes have been corrected and the process is running in a reasonable state of statistical control, the process capability can be assessed. If the variation from common causes is excessive, the process, at its best, cannot produce parts that consistently conform to specification. The process itself must be investigated, and action must be taken to identify and correct the significant faults of the system.

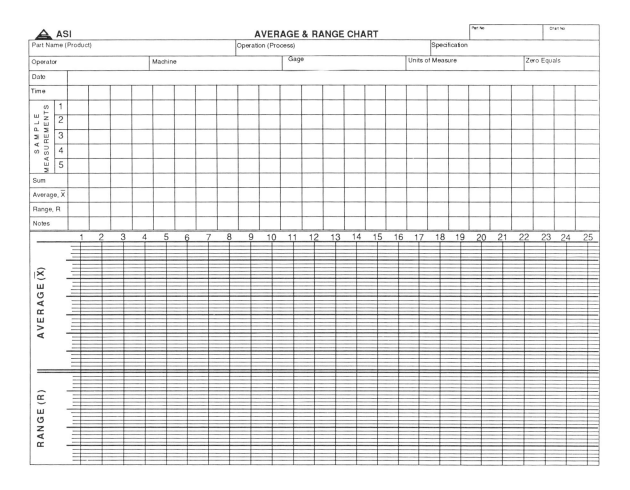

Figure 5.4 *Average and range chart ($\overline{X}$ and R).*

5.7 USING CONTROL CHARTS FOR VARIABLES: $\overline{X}$ AND R CHARTS

A simple run chart, in which data are plotted in order of time of production together with a center line, can help us to identify major disruptions in a process. However, it does not give us much information hour-by-hour on changes in the process center and process spread. Nor does it provide an exact method for distinguishing between common and special causes of variation.

These limitations are overcome with control charts for sample averages and ranges (also called $\overline{X}$ and R charts). In $\overline{X}$ and R charts, the centering and spread of a distribution are continually tested by the sample averages and ranges. Control limits for $\overline{X}$ and R are used to distinguish between special and common variation (*Figure 5.4*).

5.8 PREPARATORY STEPS

Before $\overline{X}$ and R charts can be used, several preparatory steps must be taken:

1. **Establish an environment suitable for action.** Any quality improvement will fail unless management has prepared a responsive environment. People should be certain that their candid opinions are welcome. People who do not know their jobs must be trained. People must be evaluated on quality, not just quantity. Management must provide resources to support improvement actions.

2. **Define the process.** The process must be understood in terms of its relationship to other operations/users both upstream and downstream, and in terms of the process elements (people, equipment, material, measurement, methods, and environment) that affect it at each stage. Such techniques as the cause-and-effect diagram help make these relationships visible and allow the pooling of experience from people who understand different aspects of the process.

3. **Determine characteristics to be managed.**
Efforts should be concentrated on those characteristics that are most promising for process improvement (an application of the Pareto principle). Several considerations are appropriate:

Customer needs. This includes both any subsequent processes that use the product or service as an input and the final end-item customer. Communication of the needs of both types of customer to the point in the process where improvement can occur takes teamwork and understanding.

Current and potential problem areas. Consider existing evidence of waste or poor performance (e.g., scrap, rework, excessive overtime, missed targets) where operators seem to have difficulty in achieving requirements and areas of risk (e.g., upcoming changes to the design of the product or service or to any elements of the process). These are opportunities for improvement, requiring application of all the disciplines involved in running the business.

Correlation between characteristics. For an efficient and effective study, take advantage of relationships among characteristics. For instance, if the characteristic of concern is difficult to measure (volume, for example), track a correlated characteristic that is easier to measure (e.g., weight). Also, if several individual characteristics on an item tend to vary together (e.g., correlation), it may be sufficient to chart only one of them.

4. **Define the measurement system.** The characteristic must be operationally defined so that findings can be communicated to all concerned in ways that have a common, consistent meaning. This involves specifying what information is to be gathered, where, how, and under what conditions. The measurement equipment itself must be predictable for both accuracy and precision. Periodic calibration is not enough. The definition

of the characteristic will affect the type of control chart to be used—a variables data chart, such as $\overline{X}$ and R, or an attributes data chart.

5. **Minimize unnecessary variation.** Unnecessary external causes of variation should be reduced before the study begins. This could simply mean watching that the process is being operated as intended, or it could mean conducting a controlled study with known input materials, constant control settings, and so on. The purpose is to avoid obvious problems that could and should be corrected even without use of control charts; this includes excessive process adjustment or over control. In all cases, a process log should be kept noting all relevant events, such as tool changes, new raw material lots, and other items. This will aid in subsequent problem analysis.

6. **Consider the operator.** The principal benefit of control charting results from providing information to the process operator on when lack of control occurs. It is important to set up control techniques recognizing what corrective measures are available to the operator. The chart should provide the operator with information he can react to directly.

5.9 STEP 1: GATHER DATA

An $\overline{X}$ chart and an R chart, as a pair, are developed from measurements of a particular single characteristic of the process output. These data are reported in small subgroups of constant size, usually including from three to nine consecutive pieces, with subgroups taken periodically (say once every 15 minutes, twice per shift, or some other appropriate time). A data-gathering plan must be developed and used as the basis for collecting, recording, and plotting the data on a chart.

1.A SELECT THE SIZE, FREQUENCY, AND NUMBER OF SUBGROUPS

Subgroup size. The first key step in variable control charting is the determination of **rational subgroups** —they will determine the effectiveness and efficiency of the control chart.

The subgroups should be chosen so that opportunities for variation among the units within a subgroup are small. If the variation within a subgroup represents the piece-to-piece variability over a very short period of time, then any unusual variation between subgroups would reflect changes in the process that should be investigated for appropriate action (*Figure 5.5*).

For an initial study of a process, the subgroups could typically consist of five consecutively produced pieces representing only a single tool, head, die cavity, or any single process stream. This means that the pieces within each subgroup would be produced under very similar production conditions over a very short time interval; hence, if in control, variation within each subgroup would primarily reflect only common causes. Sample sizes should remain constant for all subgroups.

Subgroup frequency. The goal is to detect changes in the process over time. Subgroups should be collected often enough, at appropriate time intervals, that they can reflect the potential opportunities for change. Such potential causes of change could be shift patterns or relief operators, warm-up trends, off-standard material lots, or other factors.

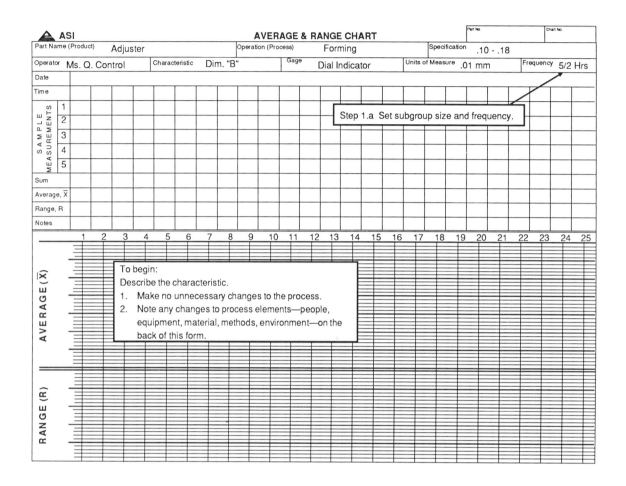

Figure 5.5 $\overline{X}$ *and R chart. Select the size, frequency, and number of subgroups.*

During an initial process study, the subgroups themselves are often taken consecutively or at short intervals to detect whether the process can shift or show other instability over brief time periods. As the process demonstrates stability (or as process improvements are made), the time period between subgroups can be increased. Subgroup frequencies for ongoing production monitoring could be hourly, twice per shift, or daily, depending on the process stability established over time.

There is no fixed rule for establishing frequency of sampling. Some considerations include: 1) how critical the characteristic is, 2) the history of control and capability, 3) whether the process is subject to changeover, 4) the value of the part. See Chapter 4 for details.

Number of subgroups. The number of subgroups for the initial study should satisfy two criteria. From a process standpoint, enough subgroups should be gathered to ensure that the major sources of variation have had an opportunity to appear. From a statistical standpoint, 25 or more subgroups containing about 100 or more individual readings give a good test for stability and, if stable, good estimates of the process location and spread.

1.B SET UP CONTROL CHARTS AND RECORD RAW DATA

$\overline{X}$ and R charts are normally drawn with the $\overline{X}$ chart above the R chart. The values of $\overline{X}$ and R will be the vertical scales, while the sequence of subgroups through time will be the horizontal scale. The data values and the plot points for the range and average should be aligned vertically.

The data block should include space for each of the individual readings. It should also include a space for the sum of the readings, the average ($\overline{X}$), the range (R), and the date/time or other identification of the subgroup.

Enter the individual raw values and the identification for each subgroup. (See *Figure 5.6,* step 1.b, for the first five subgroups).

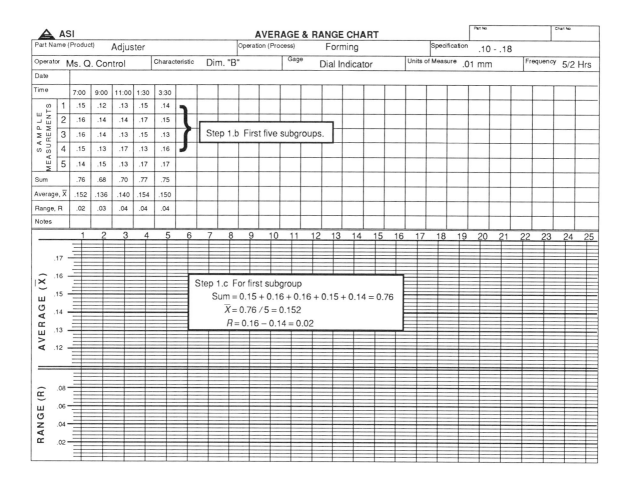

Figure 5.6 $\overline{X}$ *and R chart. Record raw data and calculate average* ($\overline{X}$) *and range* (R) *for each subgroup.*

1.C CALCULATE THE AVERAGE ($\overline{X}$) AND RANGE (R) OF EACH SUBGROUP

The characteristics to be plotted are the sample average ($\overline{X}$) and sample range (R) for each subgroup; these reflect the overall process average and its variability, respectively.

For each subgroup, calculate:

$$\overline{X} = \frac{X_1 + X_2 + \ldots + X_n}{n}$$

$$R = X_{\text{highest}} - X_{\text{lowest}}$$

where $X_1, X_2, \ldots$ are individual values within the subgroup and n is the subgroup sample size (*Figure 5.6,* step 1.c).

1.D SELECT SCALES FOR THE CONTROL CHARTS

The vertical scales for the two charts are the measured values of $\overline{X}$ and $R,$ respectively. Some general guidelines for determining the scales may be helpful, although they may have to be modified in particular circumstances. For the $\overline{X}$ chart, the difference between the highest and lowest values on the scale should be at least two times the difference between the highest and the lowest subgroup average $(\overline{X})$. For the R chart, values should extend from a lower value of zero to an upper value about two times the largest range (R) encountered during the initial period (*Figure 5.7*, step 1.d).

NOTE: One helpful guide is to set the scale spacing for the range chart to be double that of the averages chart (for example, if one scale unit equals .01 inch on the averages chart, one scale unit would equal .02 inch on the range chart). For typical subgroup sizes, the control limits for averages and ranges will be about the same width, a visual aid to analysis. The selection of scales should consider the needs of the operator. The scale should be developed in easy to use, uniform increments.

1.E PLOT THE AVERAGES AND RANGES ON THE CONTROL CHARTS

Plot the averages and ranges on their respective charts. Connect the points with lines to help visualize patterns and trends (*Figure 5.7.,* step 1.e).

Briefly scan the plot points to see if they look reasonable; if any points are substantially higher or lower than the others, confirm that the calculations and plots are correct. Make sure that the plot points for the corresponding $\overline{X}$ and R are vertically in line.

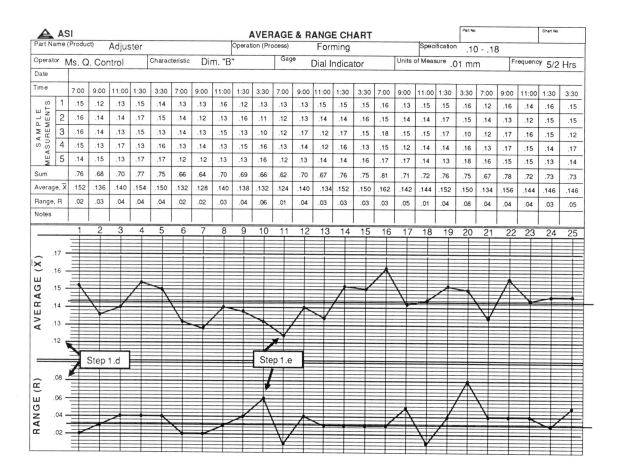

Figure 5.7 $\overline{X}$ and R chart. Select scales and plot averages and ranges.

5.10 STEP 2: CALCULATE CONTROL LIMITS

Control limits for the range chart are developed first, and then those for the chart for averages. The calculations for the control limits for variable charts use constants that appear as letters in the formulas that follow. These factors, which differ according to the subgroup size, n, are shown in brief tables, accompanying the respective formulas (*Figure 5.8*). More complete tables of constants and formulas for control charts are shown in Appendix B.

2.A CALCULATE THE AVERAGE RANGE ($\overline{R}$) AND THE PROCESS AVERAGE ($\overline{\overline{X}}$)

For the study period, calculate:

$$\overline{R} = \frac{R_1 + R_2 + \ldots + R_k}{k}$$

$$\overline{\overline{X}} = \frac{\overline{X}_1 + \overline{X}_2 + \ldots + \overline{X}_k}{k}$$

where k is the number of subgroups, R_1 and $\overline{X}_1$ are the range and average of the first subgroup, R_2 and $\overline{X}_2$ are from the second subgroup, and so on (*Figure 5.8*, step 2.a).

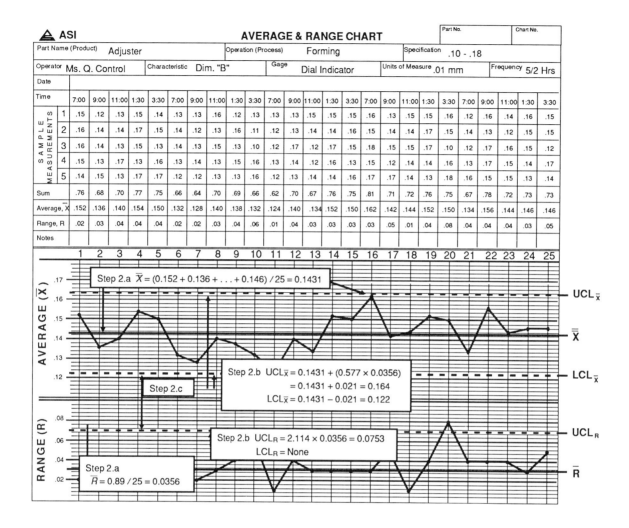

Figure 5.8 $\overline{X}$ and R chart. Calculate process average $(\overline{\overline{X}})$, average range $(\overline{R})$, and control limits.

2.B CALCULATE THE PRELIMINARY CONTROL LIMITS

When *k* equals 25, that is 25 subgroups have been collected and measured, control limits are calculated to show the extent by which the subgroup averages and ranges would vary if only common causes of variation were present. They are based on the subgroup sample size and the amount of within-subgroup variability reflected in the ranges. Calculate the **upper and lower control limits (UCL and LCL)** for ranges and for averages as in *Figure 5.8*, step 2.b.

$$UCL_R = D_4\overline{R}$$

$$LCL_R = D_3\overline{R}$$

$$UCL_{\overline{X}} = \overline{\overline{X}} + A_2\overline{R}$$

$$LCL_{\overline{X}} = \overline{\overline{X}} - A_2\overline{R}$$

where D_4, D_3, and A_2 are constants that vary with sample size, with values for sample sizes from two to ten as shown in the following partial table:

n	2	3	4	5	6
D_4	3.267	2.574	2.282	2.114	2.004
D_3	*	*	*	*	*
A_2	1.880	1.023	0.729	0.577	0.483

n	7	8	9	10
D_4	1.924	1.864	1.816	1.777
D_3	0.076	0.136	0.184	0.223
A_2	0.419	0.373	0.337	0.308

* For sample sizes below seven, the LCL_R would technically be a negative number; in those cases there is no lower control limit.

2.C DRAW LINES FOR THE AVERAGES AND THE CONTROL LIMITS ON THE CHARTS

Draw the average range ($\overline{R}$) and process average ($\overline{\overline{X}}$) as solid horizontal lines, the control limits (UCL_R, LCL_R, $UCL_{\overline{X}}$, $LCL_{\overline{X}}$) as dashed horizontal lines, and label the lines. During the initial study phase, these are considered trial (or preliminary) control limits (*Figure 5.8*, step 2.c).

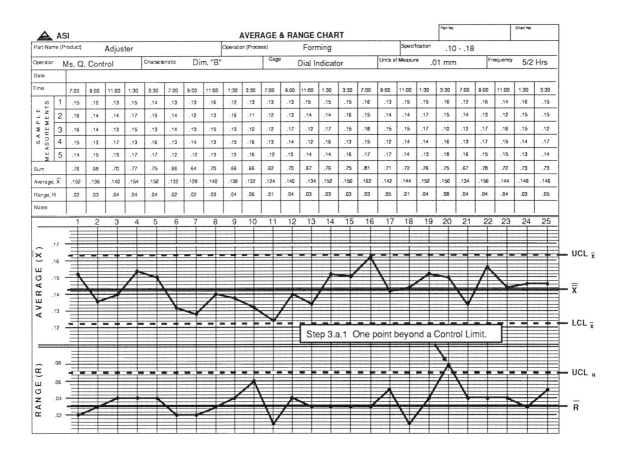

Figure 5.9 $\overline{X}$ *and R chart. Interpret for process control: points beyond control limits (range chart).*

5.11 STEP 3: INTERPRET FOR PROCESS CONTROL

The control limits can be interpreted as follows: if the process piece-to-piece variability and the process average were to remain constant at their present levels (as estimated by $\bar{R}$ and $\bar{X}$ respectively), the individual subgroup ranges (R) and averages (X) would vary by chance alone, but they would seldom go beyond the control limits (less than 1% of the time for ranges, and only 0.27% of the time for averages, for the $\pm 3\sigma$ limits calculated above). Likewise, there would be no obvious trends or patterns in the data beyond what would likely occur due to chance. The objective of control chart analysis is to identify any evidence that the process variability or the process average are not operating at a constant level—that one or both are out of statistical control—and to take appropriate action. The R and $\bar{X}$ charts are analyzed separately, but comparison of patterns between the two charts may sometimes give added insight into special causes affecting the process.

Chapter 6 provides the basis for pattern analysis and more complete understanding of expected patterns. Any number of unnatural (out-of-control) patterns may emerge.

In this chapter we will limit our analysis to what the operator will initially be asked to respond to:

- Any point outside of the control limits

- A run of seven points on one side of the line

- A run (trend) of seven consecutive points up or down.

3.A ANALYZE THE DATA PLOTS ON THE RANGE CHART

Since the ability to interpret either the subgroup ranges or the subgroup averages depends on the estimate of piece-to-piece variability, the R chart is analyzed first. The data points are compared with the control limits in order to observe any points that are out of control or unusual patterns or trends.

3.A.1 Points Beyond The Control Limits (Range Chart)

The presence of one or more points beyond either control limit is primary evidence of noncontrol at that point. Since points beyond the control limits would be very rare if only variation from common causes was present, we presume that a special cause has accounted for the extreme value. Therefore, any point beyond a control limit is the signal for immediate analysis of the operation for the special cause. Mark any data points that are beyond the control limits for further investigation and corrective action (*Figure 5.9*, step 3.a.1).

A point above the UCL for ranges is generally a sign that:

- The control limit or plot point has been miscalculated or misplotted

- The piece-to-piece variability or the spread of the distribution has increased or worsened, either at that one point in time or as part of a trend

- The measurement system has changed (for example, a different inspector or gage).

A point below the LCL (for sample sizes of seven or more) is generally a sign that:

- The control limit or plot point are in error

- The spread of the distribution has decreased or gotten better

- The measurement system has changed (including editing or alteration of the data).

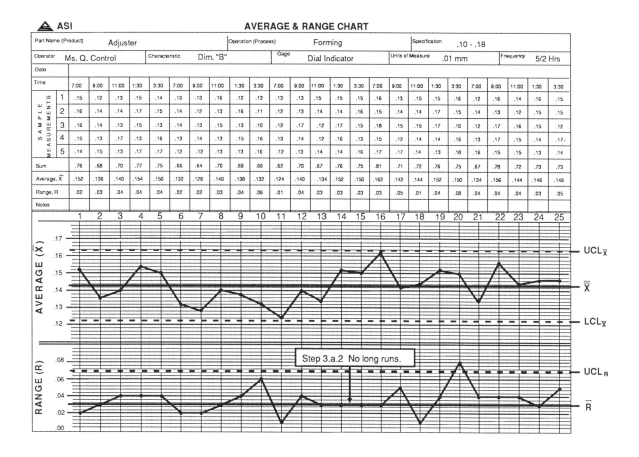

ASI							AVERAGE & RANGE CHART																	
Part Name (Product)		Adjuster					Operation (Process)		Forming					Specification		.10 - .18								
Operator	Ms. Q. Control		Characteristic	Dim. "B"			Gage	Dial Indicator					Units of Measure		.01 mm				Frequency		5/2 Hrs			
Date																								
Time	7:00	9:00	11:00	1:30	3:30	7:00	9:00	11:00	1:30	3:30	7:00	9:00	11:00	1:30	3:30	7:00	9:00	11:00	1:30	3:30	7:00	9:00	11:00	1:30	3:30

SAMPLE MEASUREMENTS	1	.15	.12	.13	.15	.14	.13	.13	.16	.12	.13	.13	.13	.15	.15	.15	.16	.13	.15	.15	.16	.12	.16	.14	.16	.15
	2	.16	.14	.14	.17	.15	.14	.12	.13	.16	.11	.12	.13	.14	.14	.16	.15	.14	.14	.17	.15	.14	.13	.12	.15	.15
	3	.16	.14	.13	.15	.13	.14	.13	.15	.13	.10	.12	.17	.12	.17	.15	.18	.15	.15	.17	.10	.12	.17	.16	.15	.12
	4	.15	.13	.17	.13	.16	.13	.14	.13	.15	.16	.13	.14	.12	.16	.13	.15	.12	.14	.14	.16	.13	.17	.15	.14	.17.
	5	.14	.15	.13	.17	.17	.12	.12	.13	.13	.16	.12	.13	.14	.14	.16	.17	.17	.14	.13	.18	.16	.15	.15	.13	.14
Sum		.76	.68	.70	.77	.75	.66	.64	.70	.69	.66	.62	.70	.67	.76	.75	.81	.71	.72	.76	.75	.67	.78	.72	.73	.73
Average, X̄		.152	.136	.140	.154	.150	.132	.128	.140	.138	.132	.124	.140	.134	.152	.150	.162	.142	.144	.152	.150	.134	.156	.144	.146	.146
Range, R		.02	.03	.04	.04	.04	.02	.02	.03	.04	.06	.01	.04	.03	.03	.03	.03	.05	.01	.04	.08	.04	.04	.04	.03	.05
Notes																										

Figure 5.10 $\overline{X}$ and R chart. Interpret for process control: runs or trends within control limits (range chart).

3.A.2 Runs Or Trends Within The Control Limits (Range Chart)

Even when all ranges are within the control limits, the presence of unusual runs or trends (seven points in a row consecutively on one side of the centerline or seven in a row in ascending or descending order) can be evidence of noncontrol or change in the process spread during the period of the pattern or trend. This could give the first warning of unfavorable conditions that should be corrected even before points are seen beyond the control limits. Conversely, certain patterns or trends could be favorable and should be studied for possible permanent improvement of the process. Comparison of patterns between the range and average charts may give added insight (*Figure 5.10*).

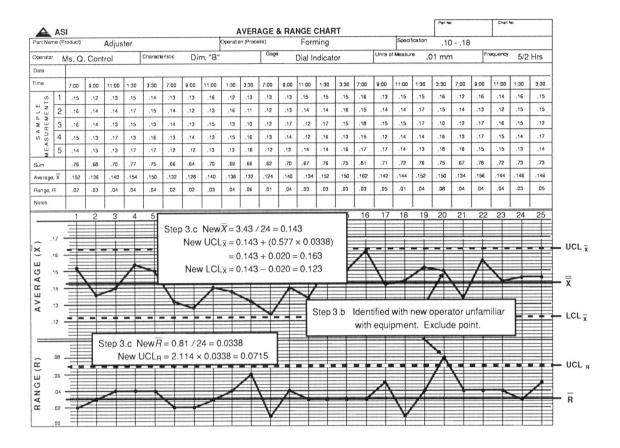

Figure 5.11 $\overline{X}$ *and R chart. Find and correct special causes (range chart). Recalculate control limits, if necessary.*

3.B FIND AND CORRECT SPECIAL CAUSES (RANGE CHART)

For each indication of a special cause in the range data, conduct an analysis of the operation of the process to determine the cause. Correct that condition to prevent it from recurring. The control chart itself should be a useful guide in problem analysis, suggesting when the condition began and how long it continued (*Figure 5.11*, step 3.b).

Timeliness is important in problem analysis, both in terms of minimizing the production of nonconforming output and of having fresh evidence for diagnosis. For instance, the appearance of a single point beyond the control limits is reason to begin an immediate analysis of the process.

It should be emphasized that problem solving is often the most difficult and time-consuming step. While statistical input from the control chart is used as a starting point, the explanations for behavior lie within the process and the people who are involved with it. Thoroughness, patience, insight, and understanding will be required to develop actions that will measurably improve performance.

3.C RECALCULATE CONTROL LIMITS (RANGE CHART)

When conducting an initial process study or a reassessment of process capability, the control limits should be recalculated to exclude the effects of out-of-control periods for which process causes have been found and corrected. Exclude all subgroups affected by the special causes that have been corrected, then recalculate and plot the new average range $(\bar{R})$ and control limits. Confirm that all range points show control when compared to the new limits, repeating the identification, correction, and recalculation sequence if necessary.

In the recalculation, if any subgroups were dropped from the R chart because of identified special causes, they should also be excluded from the $\bar{X}$ chart. Then, the revised $\bar{R}$ and $\bar{X}$ should be used to recalculate the trial control limits for averages, $\bar{X} \pm A_2\bar{R}$ *(Figure 5.11, step 3.c)*.

NOTE: The exclusion of subgroups representing unstable conditions is not just "throwing away bad data." Rather, by excluding the points affected by known special causes, we have a better estimate of the background level of variation due to common causes. This, in turn, gives the most appropriate basis for the control limits used to detect future occurrences of special causes of variation.

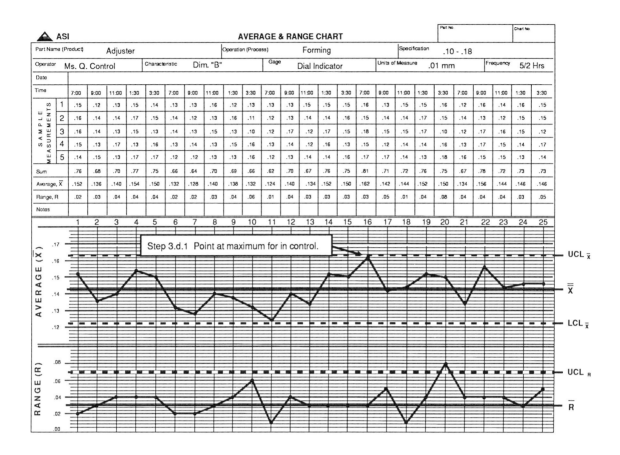

ASI					AVERAGE & RANGE CHART								Part No		Chart No									
Part Name (Product) Adjuster					Operation (Process) Forming								Specification .10 - .18											
Operator Ms. Q. Control				Characteristic Dim. "B"				Gage Dial Indicator						Units of Measure .01 mm					Frequency 5/2 Hrs					
Date																								
Time	7:00	9:00	11:00	1:30	3:30	7:00	9:00	11:00	1:30	3:30	7:00	9:00	11:00	1:30	3:30	7:00	9:00	11:00	1:30	3:30	7:00	9:00	11:00	1:30	3:30
1	.15	.12	.13	.15	.14	.13	.13	.16	.12	.13	.13	.13	.15	.15	.15	.16	.13	.15	.15	.16	.12	.16	.14	.16	.15
2	.16	.14	.14	.17	.15	.14	.12	.13	.16	.11	.12	.13	.14	.14	.16	.15	.14	.14	.17	.15	.14	.13	.12	.15	.15
3	.16	.14	.13	.15	.13	.14	.13	.15	.13	.10	.12	.17	.12	.17	.15	.18	.15	.15	.17	.10	.12	.17	.16	.15	.12
4	.15	.13	.17	.13	.16	.13	.14	.13	.15	.16	.13	.14	.12	.16	.13	.15	.12	.14	.14	.16	.13	.17	.15	.14	.17
5	.14	.15	.13	.17	.17	.12	.12	.13	.13	.16	.12	.13	.14	.14	.16	.17	.17	.14	.13	.18	.16	.15	.15	.13	.14
Sum	.76	.68	.70	.77	.75	.66	.64	.70	.69	.66	.62	.70	.67	.76	.75	.81	.71	.72	.76	.75	.67	.78	.72	.73	.73
Average, $\overline{X}$	.152	.136	.140	.154	.150	.132	.128	.140	.138	.132	.124	.140	.134	.152	.150	.162	.142	.144	.152	.150	.134	.156	.144	.146	.146
Range, R	.02	.03	.04	.04	.04	.02	.02	.03	.04	.06	.01	.04	.03	.03	.03	.03	.05	.01	.04	.08	.04	.04	.04	.03	.05
Notes																									

Step 3.d.1 Point at maximum for in control.

Figure 5.12 $\overline{X}$ *and R chart. Interpret for process control: points beyond control limits (averages chart).*

3.D ANALYZE THE DATA PLOTS ON THE AVERAGES CHART

When the ranges are in statistical control, the process spread or the variation within subgroups is considered to be stable. The averages can then be analyzed to see if the process location is changing over time. If the averages are in statistical control, they reflect only the amount of variation seen in the ranges, the common cause variation of the system. If the averages are not in control, some special causes of variation are making the process location unstable.

3.D.1 Points Beyond The Control Limits (Averages Chart)

The presence of one or more points beyond either control limit is primary evidence of the presence of special causes at that point. It is the signal for immediate analysis of the operation. Mark such data points on the chart. Notice that the point in *Figure 5.12*, step 3.d.1 is not out of control. A point beyond either control limits is generally a sign that:

- The control limit or plot point are in error

- The process has shifted, either at that one point in time (possibly an isolated incident) or as part of a trend

- The measurement system has changed (for example, different gage or inspector).

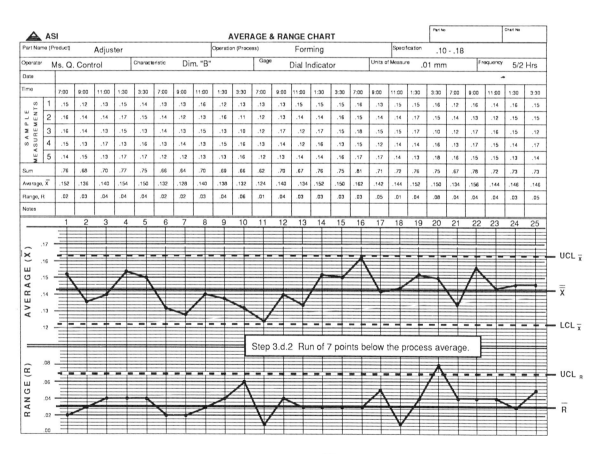

Figure 5.13 *$\overline{X}$ and R chart. Interpret for process control: patterns within control limits (averages chart).*

3.D.2 Runs Or Trends Within The Control Limits (Averages Chart)

The presence of unusual patterns or trends can be evidence of noncontrol or change in capability during the period of the pattern or trend. Comparison of patterns between the range and average charts may be helpful.

The following are signs that a process shift or trend has begun:

- Seven points in a row show on the one side of the average

- Seven points in a row that are consistently increasing or decreasing (*Figure 5.13*, step 3.d.2).

Mark the point that prompts the decision; it may help to extend a reference line to the point where the run began. Analysis should consider the time that the trend or shift appeared to begin.

A run relative to the process average is generally a sign that:

- The process average has changed, and may still be changing

- The measurement system has changed.

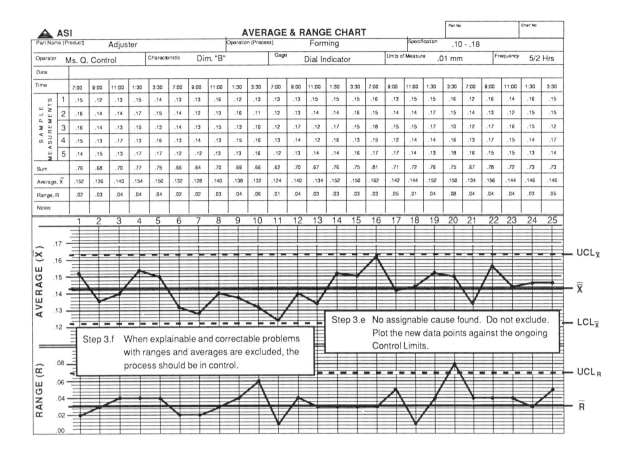

Figure 5.14 $\overline{X}$ *and R chart. Find and correct special causes (averages chart). Recalculate control limits, if necessary.*

3.E FIND AND CORRECT SPECIAL CAUSES (AVERAGES CHART)

For each indication of an out-of-control condition in the average data, conduct an analysis of the operation of the process to determine the reason for the special cause, and correct that condition, in order to prevent its recurrence. Use the chart data as a guide to when problem conditions began and how long they continued. Timeliness in analysis is important both for diagnosis and to minimize nonconforming output (*Figure 5.14*, step 3.e).

3.F RECALCULATE CONTROL LIMITS (AVERAGES CHART)

When conducting an initial process study or a reassessment of process capability, exclude any out-of-control points for which special causes have been found; recalculate and plot the process average and control limits. Confirm that all data points show control when compared to the new limits, repeating the identification/correction/recalculation sequence if necessary (*Figure 5.14*, step 3.f).

While it is wise to investigate all signaled events as possible evidence of special causes, it should be recognized that they may have been caused by the system, and that there may be no underlying local process problem. If no clear evidence of a process problem is found, any corrective action will probably serve to increase rather than decrease the total variability in the process output.

For further discussion of interpretation, tests for randomness in data, and problem solving, see background references.

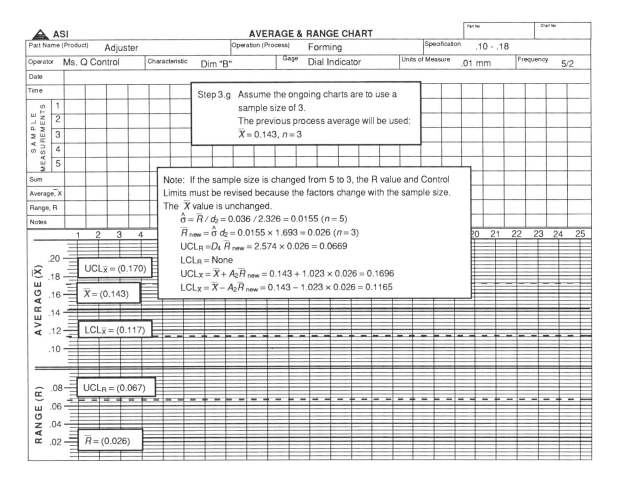

Figure 5.15 $\bar{X}$ *and R chart. Extend control limits for ongoing control.*

3.G EXTEND CONTROL LIMITS FOR ONGOING CONTROL

When the initial or historical data are consistently contained within the trial control limits, extend the limits to cover future periods. These limits would be used for ongoing control of the process, with the operator and local supervision responding to signs of out-of-control conditions on either the $\bar{X}$ or R chart with prompt action.

Control limits do not necessarily have to be recalculated at the completion of every 25 subgroups or finished charts. Rather, they require recalculation only when the subgroup sample size changes or there is evidence of process improvement:

- $\overline{X}$ has shifted closer to the initial target

- Range values are showing improved variability (at least seven points in a row below $\overline{R}$)

For example, control limits must be recalculated after improvement of process capability (see Chapter 7).

Recalculating Control Limits

A change in the subgroup sample size would affect the expected average range and the control limits for both ranges and averages. This situation could occur, for instance, if it was decided to take smaller samples more frequently, in order to detect large process shifts more quickly without increasing the total number of pieces sampled per day. To adjust central lines and control limits for a new subgroup sample size, the following steps should be taken (*Figure 5.15*):

1. Estimate the process standard deviation (the estimate is shown as $\hat{\sigma}$ — "sigma hat"). Using the existing sample size, calculate:

$$\hat{\sigma} = \overline{R} / d_2$$

where $\overline{R}$ is the average of the subgroup ranges (for periods with the ranges in control), and d_2 is a constant varying by sample size, as shown in the partial table below:

n	2	3	4	5	6
d_2	1.128	1.693	2.059	2.326	2.534

n	7	8	9	10
d_2	2.704	2.847	2.970	3.078

2. Using the tabled factors for d_2, D_3, D_4, and A_2 based on the new sample size, calculate the new range and control limits, following these worksheet formulas:

$$\overline{R}_{new} = \hat{\sigma}\, d_2$$

$$UCL_R = D_4\overline{R}_{new}$$

$$LCL_R = D_3\overline{R}_{new}$$

$$UCL_{\overline{X}} = \overline{X} + A_2\overline{R}_{new}$$

$$LCL_{\overline{X}} = \overline{X} - A_2\overline{R}_{new}$$

Plot these new control limits on the chart as the basis for ongoing process control (*Figure 5.15*).

As long as the process remains in control at constant levels for both averages and ranges, the ongoing limits can be extended for additional periods. If, however, there is evidence that the process average or range has changed (the process has improved), control limits should be recalculated based on current performance. Control limits should not be changed to accomodate a deteriorating process. Instead, the process should be corrected.

5.12 STEP 4: INTERPRET FOR PROCESS CAPABILITY

Having determined that a process is in statistical control, the question still remains whether the process is capable. Does its output meet customer needs? To understand and improve the capability of a process, an important shift in thinking must occur. Capability reflects variation from common causes, and management action on the system is almost always required for capability improvement.

Assessment of process capability begins after control issues in both the $\overline{X}$ and R charts have been resolved (special causes identified, analyzed, corrected, and prevented from recurring), and the ongoing control charts reflect a process that is in statistical control, preferably for 25 or more subgroups.

Process capability is discussed in detail in Chapter 7.

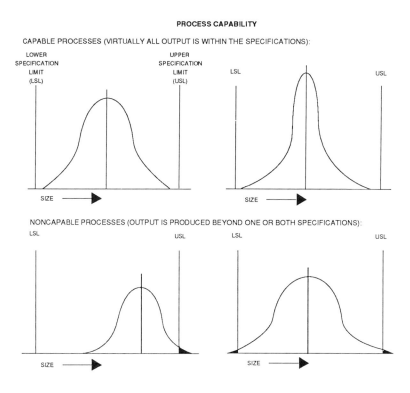

Figure 5.16 *Process Capability. SOURCE: Ford Motor Co., Continuous Process Control and Process Capability Improvement, Statistical Method, Office, Operations Support, 1985.*

Capability assessment begins when two conditions have been met:

1. $\overline{X}$ and R charts have been used to identify, analyze, and correct special causes of variation.

2. Ongoing control charts, using 25 or more subgroups, have shown that a process is in a reasonable state of statistical control.

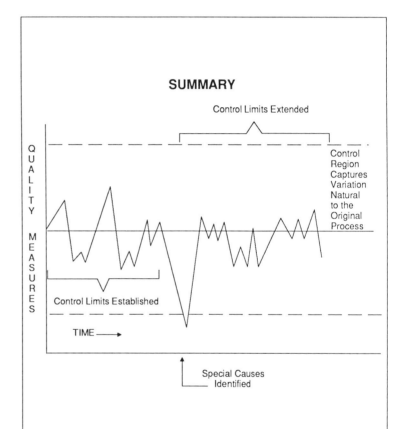

Control Charts:

- Identify nonrandom impacts to a process (**special causes**)

- Warn of system degradation **prior** to production of defects (**prevention**)

- Provide a basis for improving a process within the specifications (**control and capability improvement**).

Figure 5.17 *Control chart summary.*

PATTERN ANALYSIS
FOR CONTROL CHARTS

CONTENTS

KEY CONCEPTS

In this chapter you will learn about the following key items and concepts:

Pattern analysis
Natural pattern
Unnatural pattern
Tests for unnaturalness
Points outside control limits
Nonrandom patterns within control limits
Shifts
Trends
Runs
Cycles
Instability
Stratification
Mixtures
Freaks
Systematic variables

PATTERN ANALYSIS FOR CONTROL CHARTS

6.1 INTRODUCTION

Control charts are a powerful tool for determining the degree of stability and capability of a process. However, unless properly analyzed in a timely manner, by knowledgeable personnel, their power can be wasted. This chapter reviews some of the more common signals and patterns that emerge on control charts.

The Central Limit Theorem is the basis for the analysis and interpretation of control chart patterns. According to the theorem, a distribution of sample averages from any universe will tend toward a normal distribution as the size of subgroups increases. This means that if a process was in a state of statistical control we should see evidence of a normal distribution—a control chart demonstrating a situation other than that shown in *Figure 6.1* indicates an unstable, uncontrolled process.

In practical terms, this means that even skewed or other non-normal populations take on the characteristics of the normal model if we properly create a frequency distribution using sample averages.

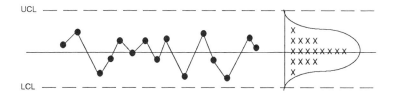

Figure 6.1 *If a process is stable, the plotted values on the control chart represent a normal distribution spanning the control limits.*

In control charting we assume that the normal model may be used to depict expected performance. Control limits can then be considered to be the ±3σ boundaries of the frequency distribution of sample averages in a controlled or stable situation. The formulas and constants used to calculate control limits in the previous chapter simply determine, from range data, what these ±3σ would be in a perfectly stable situation. Pattern analysis assumes that roughly two-thirds (68.26%) of plotted data will occur within the ± 1σ range of the control chart. Ninety-five percent will fall in the ± 2 σ range of the chart. More than 99% (99.73%) will fall within the ± 3 σ range. In other words, only 5% of the time will the points from a perfectly controlled process fall somewhere between the second and third sigma ranges on either side of the center line.

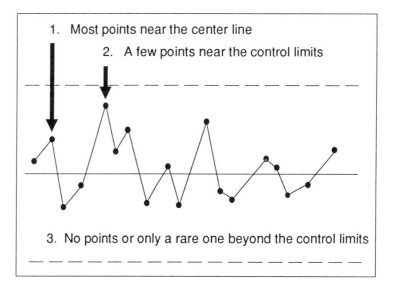

Figure 6.2 *Characteristics of a natural pattern.*

6.2 NATURAL AND UNNATURAL PATTERNS

The points plotted on a control chart form an irregular pattern that can be classified as natural or unnatural. Interpretation of the control chart depends on the ability to make this determination. If it is determined that the pattern is unnatural, the analyst, working with the operator, can attempt to identify and remove the special causes of variation that led to process instability. A visual check on each point must be made to determine if it is part of a natural or unnatural pattern. It is recommended that points that indicate an unnatural pattern be marked with an X to make chart interpretation easier.

Characteristics of a **natural pattern** can be summarized as follows (*Figure 6.2*):

1. Most of the points are near the center line.

2. A few of the points spread out and approach the control limits.

3. None of the points exceed the control limits.

Unnatural patterns always involve the absence of one or more of the characteristics of a natural pattern:

1. Absence of points near the center line.

2. Too many points near the control limits.

3. Presence of points outside the control limits.

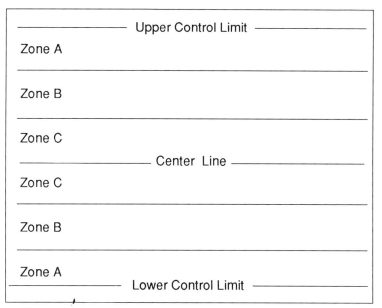

Figure 6.3   *Three zones for a control chart.*

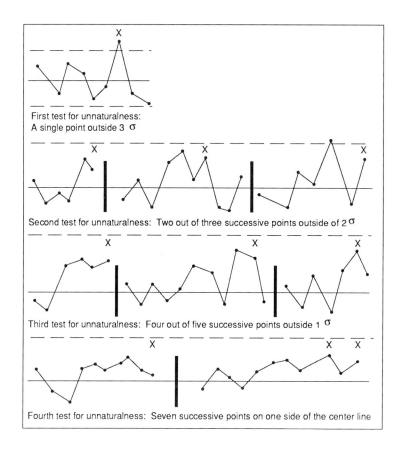

Figure 6.4   *Tests for unnaturalness.*

6.3 TESTS FOR UNNATURALNESS

In applying these tests, consider only one-half of the control band at a time; that is, consider only the area between the center line and one of the control limits. Divide this area mentally into three equal zones (*Figure 6.3*). Since the control limits represented are $\pm 3 \sigma$ process limits, each zone is one sigma in width. The pattern is unnatural if any of the following combinations are found in the various zones (*Figure 6.4*):

Test I: A single point falls outside of the $\pm 3\sigma$ limit. (beyond Zone A) Mark with an X.

Test II: Two out of three successive points fall in Zone A or beyond. (The odd point may be anywhere. Only two points count.) Mark only the second of the two points with an X.

Test III: Four out of five successive points fall in Zone B or beyond. (The odd points may be anywhere. Only the four points count.) Mark only the last of the four points with an X.

Test IV: Seven successive points fall in Zone C or beyond. (Mark only the seventh point with an X.) Apply the same tests to the opposite half of the control chart.

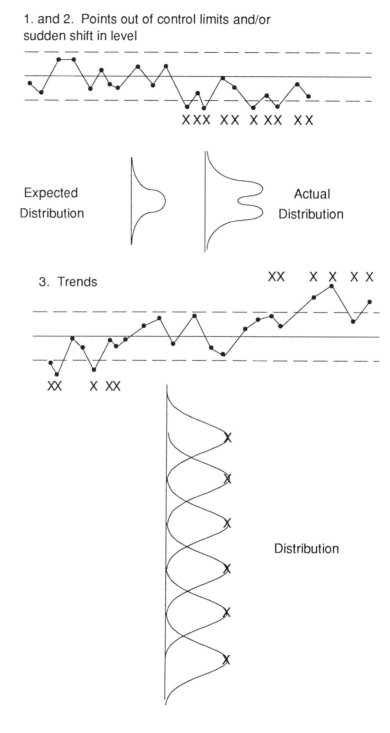

1. and 2. Points out of control limits and/or sudden shift in level

Expected Distribution   Actual Distribution

3. Trends

Distribution

Figure 6.5   *Indications of assignable causes: points outside of control limits, shifts, and trends. SOURCE: Ford Motor Co., Analysis of Control Chart Patterns, Body and Assembly, SQA, 1983.*

6.4 INDICATIONS OF ASSIGNABLE CAUSES

Some of the more obvious indications of the presence of assignable causes are the following (*Figure 6.5*):

Points outside control limits. Points located outside the control limits indicate a special cause. Whenever possible, the reason and corrective action should be recorded on the chart.

Shift. A shift is a sudden change in level. It indicates that the process has shifted, perhaps caused by a new lot of material, a new operator, or a new machine setting.

Trend. A trend is a gradual rise or fall of plot points (usually six, seven, or more consecutive points). It indicates that the process is drifting. Tool wear, wear or loosening of holding devices, operator fatigue, or production schedule changes may be the cause.

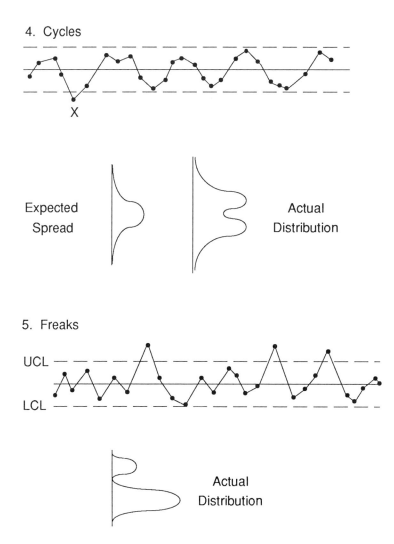

Figure 6.6 *Other patterns: cycles and freaks.*
SOURCE: Ford Motor Co., Analysis of
Control Chart Patterns, Body and
Assembly, SQA, 1983.

6.5 OTHER PATTERNS

When performing process capability studies, time, or the order of production, is a very important variable. As the process operates over a period of time, other patterns may be recognized (*Figure 6.6*).

Cycles. Consistent patterns of repeated high and low points that recur periodically (short trends in replicated patterns). Cycles may be caused by rotation of operators, shipping schedules, operator fatigue, warm-up, temperature variation during different shifts, roller eccentricity, voltage fluctuation, etc.

Freaks or outliers. Occasional points lie outside a control limit with no apparent consistent pattern or trend. Freaks are generally hard to replicate and analyze. They may result from a mistake in calculation or plotting error, an incomplete or omitted operation, or a damaged part or setup part, end rod, or strip.

6. Instability

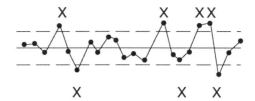

Distribution

7. Mixtures

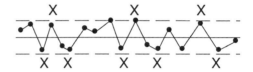

8. Stratification

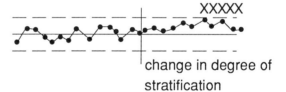

change in degree of
stratification

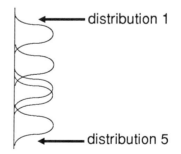

distribution 1

distribution 5

Figure 6.7 *Other patterns: instability, mixtures, and stratification. SOURCE: Ford Motor Co., Analysis of Control Chart Patterns, Body and Assembly, SQA, 1983.*

Instability. Unnaturally large fluctuations characterized by erratic ups and downs resulting from $\bar{X}$'s on both sides of the chart. Instability may be caused by erratic test equipment, an operator adjusting a machine on the basis of one or two measurements, different lots of material, or too much play in a holding fixture.

Mixtures. Too few points near the center line (absence of normal fluctuations near the middle) with unnaturally large lines joining the points give a seesaw effect. Mixtures may represent two different sources of material, two machines, or two operators.

Stratification. A form of stable mixture with an artificial consistency. The pattern appears to hug the center line instead of fluctuating naturally within control limits. This results when samples are consistently taken from widely different distributions in such a way that units in every sample come from each distribution (e.g., one from each operator in a group or one part from each machine or position on a machine (*Figure 6.7*).

Review of the sampling techniques used is vital to our analysis. A control chart works best when it represents the behavior of a single source of variation (one fixture, one cavity, etc.). Mixing several sources of variation in the sample data plotted on a control chart should be avoided, since it can cause the appearance of stratification or any of the other unnatural patterns.

9. Systematic Variable

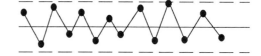

Expected
Distribution

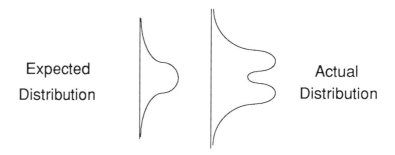

Actual
Distribution

10. Runs

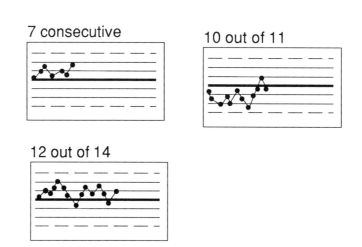

7 consecutive

10 out of 11

12 out of 14

Figure 6.8 *Other patterns: systematic variables and runs. SOURCE: Ford Motor Co., Analysis of Control Chart Patterns, Body and Assembly, SQA, 1983.*

Systematic variables. These variables are characterized by a predictable point-to-point pattern of variation; for example, a low point always followed by a high point. The most common systematic pattern is the sawtooth pattern. Cycles are another form, if they alternate on a regular basis (e.g., day shift always high, night shift always low) (*Figure 6.8*).

Runs. Runs indicate a shift in a process parameter. Several rules exist for too many points on one side of a center line.

NOTE: These rules are treated in Duncan and in Grant and Leavenworth in the Background References section.

6.6 PATTERN ANALYSIS

The *Statistical Quality Control Handbook* originally published by Western Electric Co. provides a comprehensive and useful treatment of control chart patterns. The chapter on analysis of patterns describes 15 common control chart patterns and should be considered mandatory reading for anyone wishing to study control chart interpretations further.

Cycles, freaks, gradual level changes, grouping/bunching, instability, interaction, mixtures, natural patterns, stable mixtures, stratified situations, level shifts, systematic variables, correlation, trends, and unstable mixtures are all discussed in some detail.

PATTERN ANALYSIS AND OPERATORS

Pattern analysis is important to the analyst for determining the degree of stability of a process characteristic or possible sampling difficulties. It may, however, be a subject beyond the understanding of the process operator. The operator needs to be trained in what to look for and what to react to.

Initially he may be instructed to react only to points outside the control limits. As his understanding matures, some of the other patterns may be brought to his attention for recognition and action.

PROCESS
CAPABILITY

KEY CONCEPTS

In this chapter you will learn about the following key items and concepts:

Process capability
Process standard deviation
Capability values
Z value
Percentage out-of-specification
Capability index (C_p, C_{pk})
Process potential
Process performance
Off-target condition
Short run capability
Long run capability
Capability analysis paper
Estimated Accumulated Frequency (EAF)
Line of best fit
Plot point percentage
Curve Fitting
Bilateral tolerance
Unilateral tolerance
Mirror-image technique

PROCESS CAPABILITY

7.1 INTRODUCTION

Process capability is the minimum variation that can be achieved after all special causes have been eliminated. Capability thus represents the best performance of the process itself, when the process is operating in a state of statistical control (*Table 7.1*).

A process in statistical control can be described by a predictable distribution. Therefore, the proportion of out-of-specification parts can be estimated from this distribution. As long as the process is in statistical control, it will continue to produce the same proportion of out-of-specification parts. In order to further improve the ability of a process to consistently meet specifications, management action to reduce variation from common causes is needed.

PROCESS CAPABILITY

Process capability is a comparison of the spread of the process output to specification limits under statistically stable conditions.

Process capability cannot be determined directly from the control chart. Specifications are not drawn on control charts. Nor are process averages and control limits compared to specification limits. Specification limits are compared to the process output **of individual pieces, not to sample averages**.

Using a control chart to demonstrate that a process is in statistical control means that our process is stable. But a stable process may be producing a repeatable pattern consistently and still yield defective products because:

- The pattern may not be acceptable

- The distribution may not be within specifications.

Thus, even if all points (sample averages) are within control limits and control limits are within specifications, this, by itself, does not guarantee that all of the process output will be within specifications. The spread of sample averages follows a normal curve, but the spread of individual pieces making up the process output is larger than the spread of sample averages.

It is the spread of individual units (process output) that is compared to specification limits. We must determine the process capability in order to establish whether the process can hold specifications. This will be valid **only** if the process is demonstrated to be in statistical control.

ASSESSING PROCESS CAPABILITY

There are many techniques for assessing the capability of a process that is in statistical control. Some assume that the process output follows the bell-shaped normal distribution. If it is not known whether the distribution is normal, a test for normality should be made. If non-normality is suspected or confirmed, more flexible techniques should be used, such as computerized curve-fitting or graphical analysis through the use of normal probability paper. When the distribution shape is normal, the techniques described below can be used. They involve simple calculations based on data from the control chart. The process average, $\overline{X}$, is used as the location of the distribution. As a measure of spread, the standard deviation is used, calculated from a simple formula involving the average range, $\overline{R}$.

Using $\overline{X}$ and R chart data to assess process capability involves four distinct phases of activity:

1. Calculating capability values

2. Evaluating process capability

3. Improving process capability

4. Recharting the improved process.

NOTE: Any capability analysis technique, no matter how precise it appears, can give only approximate results. This happens because 1) there is always some sampling variation, 2) no process is ever fully in statistical control, and 3) no actual output exactly follows the normal distribution (or any other simple distribution). Final results should always be used with caution and interpreted conservatively.

Table 7.1 *Capability and control. SOURCE: Ford Motor Co., Continuous Process Control and Process Capability Improvement, Statistical Methods, Office, Operations Support, 1985.*

By asking two questions :
- Is the process statistically stable (in control)?
- Is the process capable (of meeting specifications) ?

We can determine at which case (or what level) we are operating:

"Capability"	"Control"	
	Process is in control (Statistically stable) .	Process is out of control .
Process is capable of meeting specifications (centered) .	Case A Healthy situation .	Case C Situation is o.k. now, but not stable. Be alert until process can be stabilized.
Process is not capable of meeting specifications .	Case B Evaluate product requirements against the need for new process approach .	Case D Major process improvement is required .

7.2 CALCULATE CAPABILITY VALUES

Capability values are expressed in numbers that represent the ability of a controlled process to produce output that conforms to assigned tolerances or specifications. Two commonly used methods for calculating capability values are **the prediction of percent out of specification using Z values** and, alternatively, the use of a **capability index**.

Both methods assume a normal process distribution and use the process average ($\overline{\overline{X}}$) as a measure of location and an estimate of the process standard deviation ($\hat{\sigma}$) as a reflection of process variation. Let us first estimate the process standard deviation.

Standard Deviation and Range (for a Given Sample Size, the Larger the Average Range $\overline{R}$, the Larger the Standard Deviation—σ):

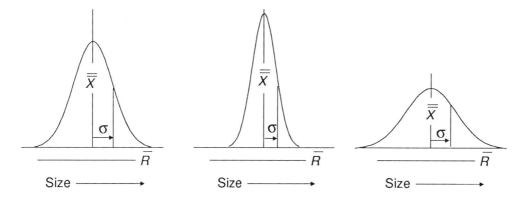

From the Example (Estimating the Process Standard Deviation from the Average Range):

$$\overline{R} = 0.169$$
$$n = 5$$
$$d_2 = 2.33$$
$$\hat{\sigma} = \overline{R} / d_2 = 0.169 / 2.33 = 0.0725$$
$$\overline{\overline{X}} = 0.738$$
$$LSL = 0.500$$
$$USL = 0.900$$

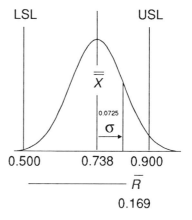

Figure 7.1 *Standard deviation and range.*

CALCULATE THE PROCESS STANDARD DEVIATION

Since the within-subgroup process variability is reflected in the subgroup ranges, the estimate of the process standard deviation, $\hat{\sigma}$ (sigma hat), can be based on the average range $(\bar{R})$. Calculate

$$\hat{\sigma} = \bar{R}/d_2$$

where $\bar{R}$ is the average of the subgroup ranges (for periods with the ranges in control) and d_2 is a constant varying by sample size, as shown in the partial table below:

n	2	3	4	5	6
d_2	1.128	1.693	2.059	2.326	2.534

n	7	8	9	10
d_2	2.704	2.847	2.970	3.078

This estimate of the process standard deviation $(\hat{\sigma})$ can be used in evaluating process capability, as long as both the ranges and averages are in statistical control and the output distribution is normal (*Figure 7.1*).

PERCENT OUT OF SPECIFICATION USING *Z* VALUES

We can estimate the percentage of output out of specification by using the area under the normal distribution curve. We can see this graphically if we:

1. Select an appropriate scale.

2. Determine the process average ($\overline{X}$) and standard deviation ($\hat{\sigma}$) from control chart data.

3. Mark off:

    a. the process average ($\overline{X}$)

    b. the $\pm 3\sigma$ process spread

    c. the distribution curve

    d. the specification limits

4. Compare the natural distribution spread ($\pm 3\sigma$) to the specification limits.

We can determine the percentage out of specification

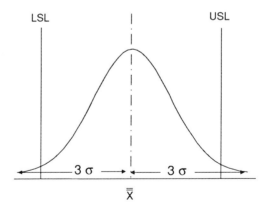

quantitatively using an index called the *Z* value and a standard normal distribution table (*Table 7.2*). The *Z* value represents the spread between the process average and the specification limits per standard deviation.

$$Z = \frac{\text{specification} - \text{average}}{\text{standard deviation}}$$

The Z value thus represents the distance of the process average from the specification in **standard deviation units**. For a bilateral tolerance:

$$Z_{USL} = \frac{USL - \overline{\overline{X}}}{\hat{\sigma}}$$

$$Z_{LSL} = \frac{\overline{\overline{X}} - LSL}{\hat{\sigma}}$$

where:

USL:	upper specification limits
LSL:	lower specification limits
$\overline{\overline{X}}$:	the process average
$\hat{\sigma}$:	the estimated standard deviation
Z_{USL}:	the Z value for the upper and lower
Z_{LSL}:	limits, respectively

The proportion of parts out of specifications can be readily estimated by calculating the area under the normal curve using the Z values and *Table 7.2* (assuming the process is in statistical control and is normally distributed).

For example, using *Table 7.2*, if $Z_{USL} = 2.21$ and $Z_{LSL} = 2.85$, we determine the proportion beyond the USL and LSL separately. In using the table, locate the value of Z along the edge of the table. The units and tenths digits are along the left edge, the hundredths digit is found along the top. The number is found where the row and column intersect (*Table 7.2*).

$P_{Z_{USL}} = 0.0136$ or 1.36%
$P_{Z_{LSL}} = 0.0022$ or 0.22%

The total beyond specification $= 0.0136 + 0.0022$
$= 0.0158$
or about
1.6%

For a unilateral tolerance, of course, only the value of Z that represents that tolerance need be calculated.

Table 7.2 *Standard normal distribution table.*

Z	X.X0	X.X1	X.X2	X.X3	X.X4	X.X5	X.X6	X.X7	X.X8	X.X9
4.0	0.00003									
3.9	0.00005	0.00005	0.00004	0.00004	0.00004	0.00004	0.00004	0.00004	0.00003	0.00003
3.8	0.00007	0.00007	0.00007	0.00006	0.00006	0.00006	0.00006	0.00005	0.00005	0.00005
3.7	0.00011	0.00010	0.00010	0.00010	0.00009	0.00009	0.00008	0.00008	0.00008	0.00008
3.6	0.00016	0.00015	0.00015	0.00014	0.00014	0.00013	0.00013	0.00012	0.00012	0.00011
3.5	0.00023	0.00022	0.00022	0.00021	0.00020	0.00019	0.00019	0.00018	0.00017	0.00017
3.4	0.00034	0.00032	0.00031	0.00030	0.00029	0.00028	0.00027	0.00026	0.00025	0.00024
3.3	0.00048	0.00047	0.00045	0.00043	0.00042	0.00040	0.00039	0.00038	0.00036	0.00035
3.2	0.00069	0.00068	0.00064	0.00062	0.00060	0.00058	0.00056	0.00054	0.00052	0.00050
3.1	0.00097	0.00094	0.00090	0.00087	0.00084	0.00082	0.00079	0.00076	0.00074	0.00071
3.0	0.00135	0.00131	0.00126	0.00122	0.00118	0.00114	0.00111	0.00107	0.00104	0.00100
2.9	0.0019	0.0018	0.0018	0.0017	0.0016	0.0016	0.0015	0.0015	0.0014	0.0014
2.8	0.0026	0.0025	0.0024	0.0023	0.0023	0.0022	0.0021	0.0021	0.0020	0.0019
2.7	0.0035	0.0034	0.0033	0.0032	0.0031	0.0030	0.0029	0.0028	0.0027	0.0026
2.6	0.0047	0.0045	0.0044	0.0043	0.0041	0.0040	0.0039	0.0038	0.0037	0.0036
2.5	0.0062	0.0060	0.0059	0.0057	0.0055	0.0054	0.0052	0.0051	0.0049	0.0048
2.4	0.0082	0.0080	0.0078	0.0075	0.0073	0.0071	0.0069	0.0068	0.0066	0.0064
2.3	0.0107	0.0104	0.0102	0.0099	0.0096	0.0094	0.0091	0.0089	0.0087	0.0084
2.2	0.0139	0.0136	0.0132	0.0129	0.0125	0.0122	0.0119	0.0116	0.0113	0.0110
2.1	0.0179	0.0174	0.0170	0.0166	0.0162	0.0158	0.0154	0.0150	0.0146	0.0143
2.0	0.0228	0.0222	0.0217	0.0212	0.0207	0.0202	0.0197	0.0192	0.0188	0.0183
1.9	0.0287	0.0281	0.0274	0.0268	0.0262	0.0256	0.0250	0.0244	0.0239	0.233
1.8	0.0359	0.0351	0.0344	0.0336	0.0329	0.0322	0.0314	0.0307	0.0301	0.0294
1.7	0.0446	0.0436	0.0427	0.0418	0.0409	0.0401	0.0392	0.0384	0.0375	0.0367
1.6	0.0548	0.0537	0.0526	0.0516	0.0505	0.0495	0.0485	0.0475	0.0465	0.0455
1.5	0.0668	0.0655	0.0643	0.0630	0.0618	0.0606	0.0594	0.0582	0.0571	0.0559
1.4	0.0808	0.0793	0.0778	0.0754	0.0749	0.0735	0.0721	0.0708	0.0694	0.0681
1.3	0.0968	0.0951	0.0934	0.0918	0.0901	0.0885	0.0869	0.0853	0.0838	0.0823
1.2	0.1151	0.1131	0.1112	0.1093	0.1075	0.1056	0.1038	0.1020	0.1003	0.0985
1.1	0.1357	0.1335	0.1314	0.1292	0.1271	0.1251	0.1230	0.1210	0.1190	0.1170
1.0	0.1587	0.1562	0.1539	0.1515	0.1492	0.1469	0.1446	0.1423	0.1401	0.1379
0.9	0.1841	0.1814	0.1788	0.1762	0.1736	0.1711	0.1685	0.1660	0.1635	0.1611
0.8	0.2119	0.2090	0.2061	0.2033	0.2005	0.1977	0.1949	0.1922	0.1894	0.1867
0.7	0.2420	0.2389	0.2358	0.2327	0.2297	0.2266	0.2236	0.2206	0.2177	0.2148
0.6	0.2743	0.2709	0.2676	0.2643	0.2611	0.2578	0.2546	0.2514	0.2483	0.2451
0.5	0.3085	0.3050	0.3015	0.2981	0.2946	0.2912	0.2877	0.2843	0.2810	0.2776
0.4	0.3446	0.3409	0.3372	0.3336	0.3300	0.3264	0.3228	0.3192	0.3156	0.3121
0.3	0.3821	0.3783	0.3745	0.3707	0.3669	0.3632	0.3594	0.3557	0.3520	0.3483
0.2	0.4207	0.4168	0.4129	0.4090	0.4052	0.4013	0.3974	0.3936	0.3897	0.3859
0.1	0.4602	0.4562	0.4522	0.4483	0.4443	0.4404	0.4364	0.4325	0.4286	0.4247
0.0	0.5000	0.4960	0.4920	0.4880	0.4840	0.4801	0.4761	0.4721	0.4681	0.4641

EXAMPLE — CALCULATING PERCENT OUT OF SPECIFICATIONS USING Z VALUES

Calculate percent out of specification using Z values.

From the example in *Figure 7.1*:

$$\bar{X} = 0.738$$
$$\hat{\sigma} = 0.0725$$
$$USL = 0.900$$
$$LSL = 0.500$$

Since this process has bilateral tolerances:

$$Z_{USL} = \frac{USL - \overline{X}}{\hat{\sigma}} = \frac{0.900 - 0.738}{0.0725} = \frac{0.162}{0.0725} = 2.23 \quad \text{No. of standard}$$

$$Z_{LSL} = \frac{\overline{X} - LSL}{\hat{\sigma}} = \frac{0.738 - 0.500}{0.0725} = \frac{0.238}{0.0725} = 3.28 \quad \text{deviations}$$

$Z_{MIN} = 2.23$

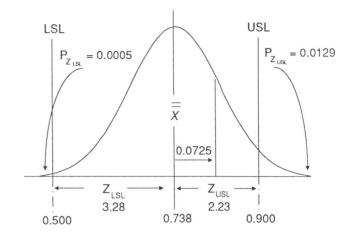

Figure 7.2 *Percentage out of specification.*
SOURCE: Ford Motor Co., <u>Continuous Process Control and Process Capability Improvement</u>, Statistical Method, Office, Operations Support, 1985.

The proportions out of specification would be:

$P_{Z_{USL}} = 0.0129$ (from the table)

$P_{Z_{LSL}} = 0.0005$ (from the table)

$P_{total} = 0.0134$ (about 1.3%)

Study the calculations for Z_{USL} and Z_{LSL} in *Figure 7.2*. Verify the percentage out of specification in the example by using the Z values and *Table 7.2* to look up $P_{Z_{USL}}$ and $P_{Z_{LSL}}$.

PROCESS CAPABILITY EXAMPLES

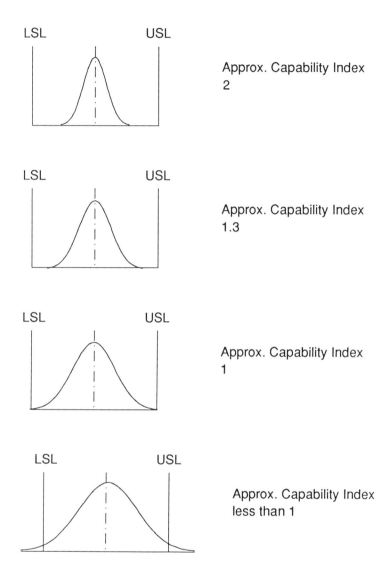

Approx. Capability Index
2

Approx. Capability Index
1.3

Approx. Capability Index
1

Approx. Capability Index
less than 1

Figure 7.3 *Process capability examples.*

CAPABILITY INDICES

The previous method (Z value and PZ) of quantifying process capability is used when an in-depth analysis is required. Large industries, such as the automobile industry, often summarize a process' ability to hold specifications with simple numbers (indices). One widely used system of capability ratios is based on two measures: C_p and C_{pk}.

Process Potential (C_p)

Process potential (C_p) can be defined as the spread where almost all of the parts or values in a distribution will fall. It is generally described as the spread including plus or minus three standard deviations ($\pm 3\sigma$) or six standard deviations (6σ). This baseline definition conveniently enables us to compare the process capability range with the process or specification tolerance. The **process capability index** (C_p) is frequently used to make this comparison and for bilateral tolerances is typically defined as:

$$C_p = \frac{\text{Specification Tolerance}}{\text{Process capability}}$$

$$= \frac{\text{USL} - \text{LSL}}{6\sigma}$$

EXAMPLE—CALCULATING C_p

From control chart data (see *Figure 5.15*) we have the following:

$\overline{X}$ = 0.143

$\overline{R}$ = 0.026

LSL = 0.100

USL = 0.180

n = 5

1. Derive the estimate of the standard deviation.

$d_2 = 2.33$

$\hat{\sigma} = \bar{R} / d_2 = 0.026/2.33 = 0.011$

and 6σ would be $0.011 \times 6 = 0.066$

2. Calculate C_p.

Since the specification tolerance is 0.180 - 0.100, the potential process capability index would be:

$$C_p = \frac{USL - LSL}{6\sigma} = \frac{0.080}{0.066} = 1.21$$

It is important to remember that the C_p number does not translate into percent out of specification. It is simply an index of capability.

If $C_p = 2.0$ The process is capable. The specs are twice as wide as the process spread.

If $C_p = 1.0$ Marginal. The specs are the same as the 6σ variability.

If $C_p = 0.8$ Not capable. The specs are only 0.8 or 80% of the 6σ variability.

Figure 7.3 shows examples of the relationship of process capability to specification tolerances. Several companies and organizational units have established minimum required C_p objectives of 1.33 or higher (the greater the better).

COMPARISON OF Cp AND Cpk

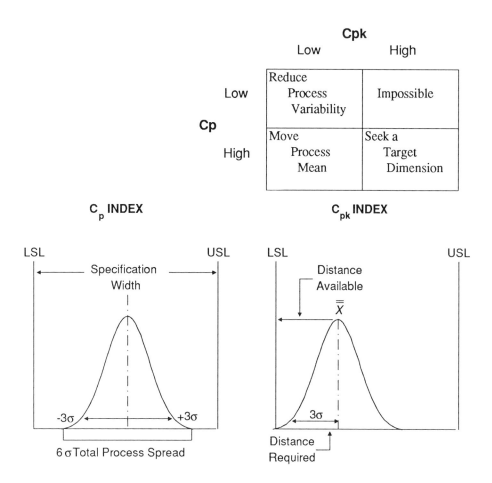

Figure 7.4 *Comparison of C_p and C_{pk}*

Process Performance (C_{pk})

We need to determine not only the potential, but the actual performance of a process. Here we must consider the effect of the actual center of the process relative to the center of the midpoint of the specification width. Any off-center or off-target condition is a reason for concern. We will see that the best performance (least out of spec) will be obtained only when the process mean, $\overline{X}$, is right on target. Any deviation from the target, especially with a marginal or poor C_p, will only increase the percentage out of specification.

The C_{pk} index was developed as a simple metric for revealing the effect of both the total underlying process variability **and** the off-target condition. The C_{pk} number is derived by calculating the ratio of the distance remaining between the process average and the closest specification divided by the amount of the distribution that must fit within this space (*Figure 7.4*). Thus,

$$C_{pk} = \frac{USL - \overline{\overline{X}}}{3\hat{\sigma}} \text{ or } \frac{\overline{\overline{X}} - LSL}{3\hat{\sigma}}$$

The **lower** of these two values is used.

If $C_{pk} = 2.0$ The process is capable. The process (6σ) is only using 50% of the specifications.

If $C_{pk} = 1.33$ The process is capable. Many companies have established a minimum critereon of $C_{pk} = 1.33$.

If $C_{pk} = 1.00$ The process is marginal.

If $C_{pk} = 0.80$ The process is not capable.

EXAMPLE — CALCULATING C_{pk}

As we have seen, the process potential capability (C_p) index would be 1.21. If the process were truly centered on the specifications, nominal (0.140), the capability index, C_{pk}, would also be 1.21. However, if it were not centered, we would be expected to determine the actual, worse-case capability index. If, for example, the process mean occurs towards the upper specification, the process is off-center toward the high side ($\overline{X} = 0.143$). The actual capability index for this case would be calculated as follows:

$$C_{pk_{USL}} = \frac{USL - \overline{\overline{X}}}{3\hat{\sigma}} = \frac{0.180 - 0.143}{3(0.011)} = \frac{0.037}{0.033} = 1.12$$

For a unilateral tolerance, the same logic prevails. We need only determine the side that is specified. In the above example (for a bilateral tolerance), the lower value (1.12) represents the true condition and is used. It is not necessary to make two separate calculations. The reported value will always be the one for the specification toward which the process average has shifted.

It should be noted that the process potential, C_p, will always be greater than or equal to the process performance, C_{pk} (*Figure 7.4*). They will be equal when the process average is exactly at the mean of the specifications. Although a C_p index can be calculated for a unilateral tolerance, it has no significant meaning—a C_{pk} number will suffice.

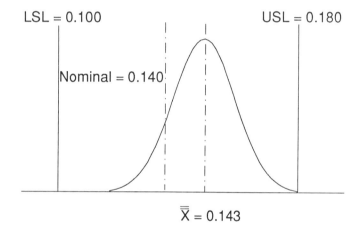

LSL = 0.100   USL = 0.180

Nominal = 0.140

$\overline{\overline{X}} = 0.143$

It is Possible to Compare C_p and C_{pk}

for Matching Processes to

Evaluate Problem Areas

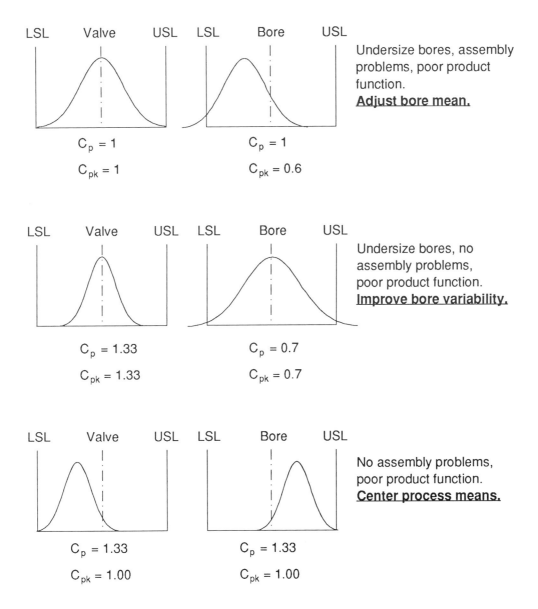

Undersize bores, assembly problems, poor product function. **Adjust bore mean.**

Undersize bores, no assembly problems, poor product function. **Improve bore variability.**

No assembly problems, poor product function. **Center process means.**

Figure 7.5 *Compare C_p and C_{pk} for matching processes to evaluate problem areas.*

7.3 EVALUATE PROCESS CAPABILITY

At this point, the process has been brought into statistical control and its capability has been described in terms of C_p and C_{pk}. The next step is to evaluate the process in terms of meeting customer requirements. The fundamental goal is never-ending improvement in process performance.

The C_p and C_{pk} of matching processes can be compared to evaluate problem areas (*Figure 7.5*).

Process Potential. C_p is a measure of process potential. It considers whether a process has the potential to meet requirements, if adjusted properly.

Process Performance. C_{pk} is a measure of process performance. It considers whether a process with a given spread and location meets specification requirements. C_{pk} is the more critical of the two indices when it comes to meeting customer requirements.

CONSIDER CAPABILITY GUIDELINES

Management often needs to establish guidelines in addition to specific capability readings to help evaluate when capability issues should be addressed. Those might include such policies as using $\pm 4\sigma$ (as a minimum criteria $C_{p_{min}} = 1.33$).

EXAMPLE — EVALUATION AND CAPABILITY GUIDELINES

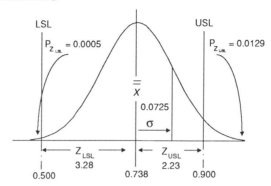

Figure 7.6a *Process not adjusted. (Not centered). SOURCE: Ford Motor Co., Continuous Process Control and Process Capability Improvement, Statistical Method, Office, Operations Support, 1985.*

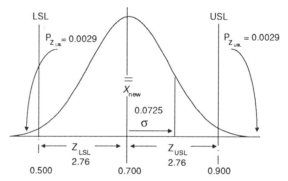

Figure 7.6b *Process Centered. SOURCE: Ford Motor Co., Continuous Process Control and Process Capability Improvement, Statistical Method, Office, Operations Support, 1985.*

From the example in *Figure 7.2*,

$$\overline{\overline{X}} = 0.738 \qquad Z_{USL} = 2.23$$
$$\hat{\sigma} = 0.0725 \qquad Z_{LSL} = 3.28$$
$$USL = 0.900 \qquad P_{Z_{USL}} = 0.0129$$
$$LSL = 0.500 \qquad P_{Z_{LSL}} = 0.0005$$
$$P_{TOTAL} = 0.0134$$
$$\text{or about } 1.3\%$$

Suppose our minimum criterreon is $C_{pk} = 1.00$. This would be equivelant to a critereon of $\overline{X} \pm 3\sigma$.

Capability Critereon of C_{pk} = 1.00 (or $\overline{\overline{X}} \pm 3\sigma$). Process Not Changed

Calculate the capability index (C_{pk}) for the process in *Figure 7.6a*.

$$C_{pk} = \frac{USL - \overline{\overline{X}}}{3\hat{\sigma}} = \frac{0.162}{0.2175} = 0.74$$

The capability index can also be derived from the Z value in the following way:

$$\text{Since } Z_{USL} = \frac{USL - \overline{\overline{X}}}{\hat{\sigma}} \text{ and } C_{pk} = \frac{USL - \overline{\overline{X}}}{3\hat{\sigma}}$$

$$\text{Therefore } C_{pk} = \frac{Z_{min}}{3}$$

$$= \frac{2.23}{3} = 0.74$$

How does this compare with our minimum critereon ($C_{pk} = 1.00$)?

Adjusting the Process Mean

If the process mean could be adjusted toward the center of the specification, the proportion of parts falling beyond either or both specification limits might be reduced, even with no change in $\hat{\sigma}$ (*Figure 7.6b*).

If control charts confirm that $\overline{X}_{new} = 0.700$ (centered), then:

$$C_{pk} = \frac{0.900 - 0.700}{0.2175} = 0.92$$

$$Z_{USL} = \frac{USL - \overline{X}_{new}}{\hat{\sigma}} = \frac{0.900 - 0.700}{0.0725} = 2.76$$

$$Z_{LSL} = \frac{\overline{\overline{X}} - LSL}{\hat{\sigma}} = \frac{0.700 - 0.500}{0.0725} = 2.76$$

We can determine the percentage out of specification from *Table 7.2*.

$$P_{\text{TOTAL}} = P_{Z_{\text{USL}}} + P_{Z_{\text{LSL}}} = 0.0029 + 0.0029 = 0.0058$$
$$\text{(or about } 0.6\%)$$

Capability Criterion of C_{pk} = 1.33 (or $\overline{\overline{X}} \pm 4\sigma$)

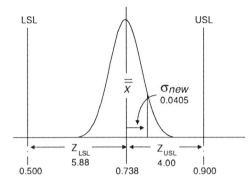

Figure 7.6c *New process spread required for $\pm 4\sigma$ capability without centered mean.*
SOURCE: Ford Motor Co., <u>Continuous Process Control and Process Capability Improvement,</u> Statistical Method, Office, Operations Support, 1985.

Suppose the capability criterion was increased to C_{pk} = 1.33 (i.e. $\overline{X} \pm 4\sigma$). Current performance of C_{pk} = 0.74 would be unacceptable, since Z_{min} = 2.23 (1.3% of output is beyond specification). Even if the process could be centered, Z_{min} = 2.76. Action must be taken.

To improve actual process performance (a long-term goal), variation from common causes must be reduced. This would result in less spread (a smaller $\hat{\sigma}$).

How much must we improve the current process performance (without centering the mean) in order for the process to meet the new C_{pk} = 1.33 criterion?

Or, what is the new spread necessary for the present process average for $\overline{X} \pm 4\sigma$ capability to existing specification limits?

The new critereon means that $\pm\, 4\sigma$ must fit within specification limits or:

$$\text{USL} - \overline{\overline{X}} \geq 4\sigma$$

The new Z_{min} value would then be:

$$Z_{min} = \frac{\text{USL} - \overline{\overline{X}}}{\sigma}$$

$$\geq \frac{4\sigma}{\sigma}$$

$$\geq 4$$

Taking $Z_{min_{new}} = 4$ we can determine the new required process spread.

$$\sigma_{new} = \frac{\text{USL} - \overline{\overline{X}}}{Z_{min_{new}}} \text{ or } \sigma_{new} = \frac{\overline{\overline{X}} - \text{LSL}}{Z_{min_{new}}}$$

Here the USL is the closest limit:

$$\sigma_{new} = \frac{0.900 - 0.738}{4} = \frac{0.162}{4} = 0.0405$$

This means that action must be taken to reduce the process standard deviation from 0.0725 to 0.0405, about a 44% improvement (*Figure 7.6c*).

Capability Criterion of C_{pk} = 1.33 (or $\overline{X} \pm 4\sigma$) with Centering the Mean

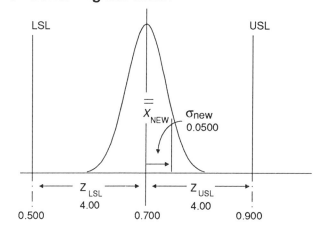

Figure 7.6d *New process spread required for $\pm 4\sigma$ capability with centered mean.*
SOURCE: Ford Motor Co., Continuous Process Control and Process Capability Improvement, Statistical Method, Office, Operations Support, 1985.

If control charts confirm that the process has been centered, and $\overline{X}_{new} = 0.700$, the process spread necessary for $\overline{X} \pm 4\sigma$ capability to existing specifications would be

$$\sigma_{new} = \frac{USL - \overline{X}_{new}}{Z_{min_{new}}}$$

$$= \frac{0.900 - 0.700}{4} = \frac{0.200}{4} = 0.0500$$

If the process can be adjusted to the center of the specification, action would need to reduce the process standard deviation from 0.0725 to 0.0500, or about 31% (*Figure 7.6d*).

A Short-Term Alternative —Increase the Specification Tolerance for $\overline{\overline{X}} \pm 4\sigma$

If all output is sorted, about 1.3% (0.6% if centered) must be scrapped or reworked. This is expensive and unreliable.

NOTE: This is a temporary measure to be used with caution. It should be used **only** as a last resort.

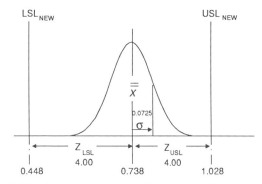

Figure 7.6e *Increasing specification tolerance for ±4σ. Process not centered. SOURCE: Ford Motor Co., Continuous Process Control and Process Capability Improvement, Statistical Method, Office, Operations Support, 1985.*

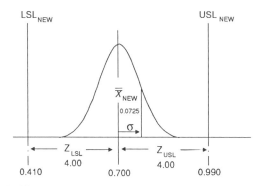

Figure 7.6f *Increasing specification tolerance for ±4σ. Process centered. SOURCE: Ford Motor Co., Continuous Process Control and Process Capability Improvement, Statistical Method, Office, Operations Support, 1985.*

Improving process performance requires management action and may take time. In some cases, if immediate action is required, a short-term alternative could be to increase the specification tolerance in order to reduce scrap and rework costs.

- If the process is not changed (not centered), new $\overline{X} \pm 4\sigma$ specifications would be (*Figure 7.6e*):

$$\overline{X} \pm 4\sigma = 0.738 \pm 4 \times 0.0725$$
$$= 0.738 \pm 0.290$$
$$= 0.448 \text{ to } 1.028 \text{ (rounded } 0.45 \text{ to } 1.03)$$

- If the process has been adjusted (confirmed by control charts that $\overline{X}_{new} = 0.700$), the new $\overline{X} \pm 4\sigma$ limits would be (*Figure 7.6f*):

$$\overline{X}_{new} \pm 4\sigma = 0.700 \pm 4 \times 0.0725$$
$$= 0.700 \pm 0.290$$
$$= 0.410 \text{ to } 0.980 \text{ (rounded } 0.40 \text{ to } 1.00)$$

This is a stop-gap measure to meet short-term needs. Sorting output for scrap and rework adds cost but altering specification limits for consistency with process performance does not improve the performance the customer sees. Both are clearly inferior to process improvement.

7.4 IMPROVE THE PROCESS CAPABILITY

The problems causing unacceptable process capability are due to common causes. Actions must be directed toward the system—the underlying process factors that account for the process variability, such as machine performance, consistency of input materials, the basic methods by which the process operates, training methods, and the working environment. As a general rule, these system-related causes of process noncapability are beyond the abilities of operators or their local supervision to correct. Instead, they require management intervention to make basic changes, allocate resources, and provide the coordination needed to improve the process performance. Attempts to correct the system with short-range local action will be unsuccessful.

Improving capability involves the following steps:

1. **Identify common causes of variation.** This is beyond the corrective abilities of line operating personnel. System-related causes include such sources as machine and tooling capability, consistency of materials, process operation, training methods, environmental conditions, etc. Management should, however, include operators in brainstorming sessions to identify common causes.

2. **Analyze common-cause variability.** Basic problem-solving tools such as Pareto diagrams and cause-and-effect diagrams can be helpful in analyzing system variability. More advanced techniques such as Taguchi design of experiments may be needed to ultimately reduce the effects of common cause variation.

7.5 CHART AND ANALYZE THE REVISED PROCESS

When systematic process actions have been taken, their efforts should be apparent in the control chart, especially in terms of reduced ranges. The charts become a way of verifying the effectiveness of the action.

As the process change is implemented, the control chart should be carefully monitored. This change period can be disruptive to operations, potentially causing new control problems that could obscure the effect of the system change.

After any instabilities of the change period have been resolved, the new process capability should be assessed and used as the basis of new control limits for future operations.

1. Monitor the control chart.

2. Look for reduced ranges.

3. Establish future control limits.

7.6 SHORT-RUN AND LONG-RUN CAPABILITY

There are two distinct approaches used to analyze process capability: short-run and long-run.

Short-run capability (sometimes referred to as machine capability) is concerned with piece-to-piece variation. Typically, 25 to 100 measurements are carried out on successive pieces of production. During this period, process conditions are maintained as constant as possible. This technique is frequently used for setup approval, evaluation of machinery condition, trouble-shooting, etc.

As the name suggests, this approach measures the variation that is present in process output over the short run. Acceptable short-run capability is required as a starting point to achieve good capability over the long run, but it does not guarantee it.

Long-run capability considers variation over a larger time period. More sources of variation are present. There are operator-to-operator differences, variation from one material batch to another, deterioration of equipment, changes in climate or measurement system, etc.

As a rule of thumb, it is not unusual to find that variation grows by up to one-third over the long run due to the different sources mentioned. Therefore, in order to have an acceptable process in the long run, tougher standards must be satisfied in the short-run capability study. Typically, $\pm 4\sigma$ must fall within specifications over the short run in order to have a reasonable chance of holding $\pm 3\sigma$ in specification in the long run.

In addition to good short-run capability, adequate control is necessary to achieve **long-run capability**. The process center and spread must be maintained at or close to their original levels. Unlike the short-run study that is concerned with measurements on successive pieces, samples for a long-run study must be taken over a period of time that is long enough so that all expected sources of variation are included.

Such a long-run capability study is usually initially performed using a control chart for variables to check whether the process is controlled (e.g., stable).

It is this long-run control and capability that is of greatest interest to the customer, since it reflects the overall quality of the product received.

PROCESS POTENTIAL STUDY

The **process potential study** may be used for preliminary estimates of process capability (e.g., evaluating a new tooling situation). A unique type of graph paper, called capability or probability paper, is used to analyze statistical data and assess capability.

Sample Size Requirements

The following sample sizes are suggested as minimums to determine acceptable short-run capability for trouble-shooting or diagnosing a process or production lot (*Table 7.3*).

Table 7.3 *Sample size guide.*

Short-Run Capability	Sample Size Minimum
± 5σ or better	25 Pieces
± 4σ to ± 5σ	50 Pieces
± 4σ or worse	100 Pieces

According to these guidelines, if short-run capability calculated on the basis of a sample of 25 pieces indicates ± 5σ within specification or better, no further measurements are required. If capability is less than ± 5σ in specification, but better than ± 4σ, a sample size of 50 is sufficient. If indicated short-run capability is less than ± 4σ, a sample size of 100 should be employed.

The accuracy of statistical methods does not depend on the lot size. It is almost entirely determined by the size of the sample.

CHECK FOR NORMALITY

All the methods of analyzing capability discussed so far are based on the normal curve model. In order for the conclusions to be valid, it is essential to always check the shape of the distribution in order to ensure that it is reasonably close to normal. If it is not, calculations based on the normal curve may contain large errors.

For practical purposes, "reasonably close to normal" means that the distribution should have one major high point with the results spread approximately symmetrically on both sides.

7.7 USING CAPABILITY ANALYSIS PAPER

Capability analysis paper can be used to check for normality and assess capability. Use of capability analysis paper involves three distinct phases:

1. Completing the data collection analysis page.

2. Completing the capability analysis sheet.

3. Evaluating the analysis sheet.

DATA COLLECTION FOR CAPABILITY ANALYSIS

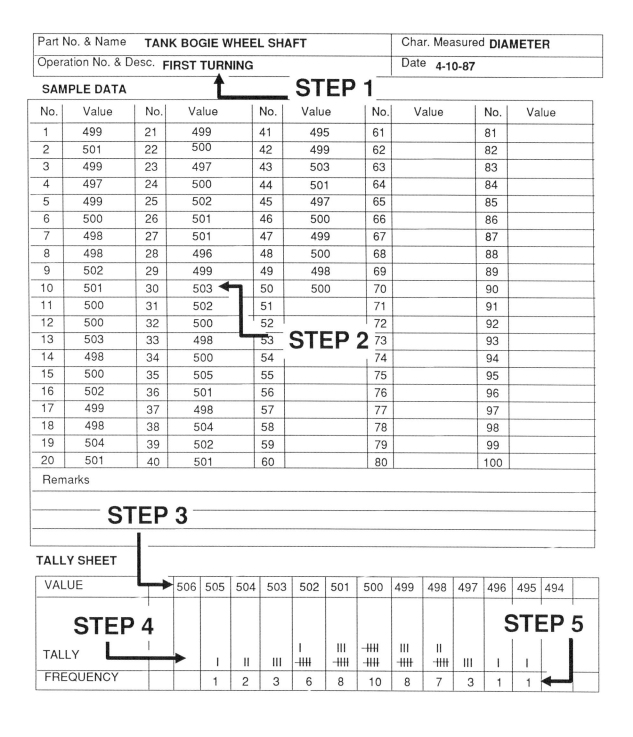

| Part No. & Name | **TANK BOGIE WHEEL SHAFT** | Char. Measured **DIAMETER** |
| Operation No. & Desc. | **FIRST TURNING** | Date **4-10-87** |

SAMPLE DATA   **STEP 1**

No.	Value	No.	Value	No.	Value	No.	Value	No.	Value
1	499	21	499	41	495	61		81	
2	501	22	500	42	499	62		82	
3	499	23	497	43	503	63		83	
4	497	24	500	44	501	64		84	
5	499	25	502	45	497	65		85	
6	500	26	501	46	500	66		86	
7	498	27	501	47	499	67		87	
8	498	28	496	48	500	68		88	
9	502	29	499	49	498	69		89	
10	501	30	503	50	500	70		90	
11	500	31	502	51		71		91	
12	500	32	500	52		72		92	
13	503	33	498	53		73		93	
14	498	34	500	54		74		94	
15	500	35	505	55		75		95	
16	502	36	501	56		76		96	
17	499	37	498	57		77		97	
18	498	38	504	58		78		98	
19	504	39	502	59		79		99	
20	501	40	501	60		80		100	

STEP 2 (points to No. 30 value 503)

Remarks

STEP 3

TALLY SHEET

VALUE		506	505	504	503	502	501	500	499	498	497	496	495	494	
TALLY			I	II	III	I -HHI	III -HHI -HHI	-HHI -HHI -HHI	III -HHI -HHI	II -HHI -HHI	III	I	I		
FREQUENCY				1	2	3	6	8	10	8	7	3	1	1	

STEP 4   **STEP 5**

Figure 7.7 *Data collection for capability analysis.*

COMPLETE THE DATA COLLECTION ANALYSIS PAGE

STEP 1: Complete the heading information.

LIST: Part number and name, operation number and description, supplier name, location and code number, date of the study, sample size, characteristics measured, tolerance.

The remaining block could contain such information as machine number, plant, shift, and type of study (long- or short-range, etc.).

Measure a minimum of 30 parts or 30 subgroups. Use the values for frequency data.

STEP 2: Record each measurement on the sample data sheet.

STEP 3: Record the range of values on the value column of the tally sheet.

STEP 4: Tally the number of measurements that fall within each value range.

STEP 5: Record the numeric frequency in each value category. Enter a zero when there is no data for a value (*Figure 7.7*).

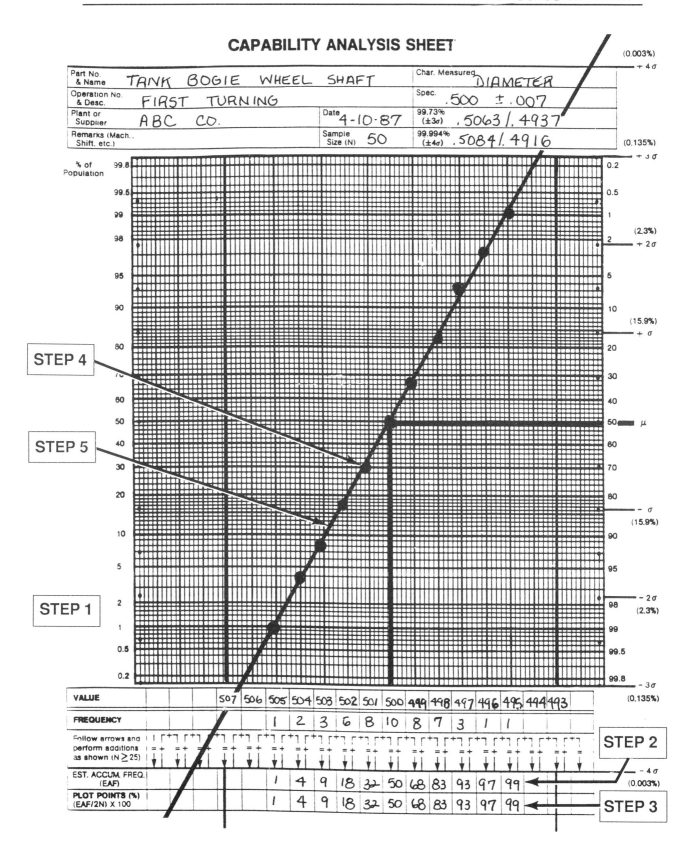

Figure 7.8 *Capability analysis sheet.*

COMPLETE THE CAPABILITY ANALYSIS SHEET

STEP 1: Transfer the data from the data collection page to the capability analysis sheet.

Place the specification midpoint in block 11, row 1.

Divide the specification range into about ten equal segments. Place half the division to the left and half to the right of the specification midpoint.

Record the frequency that each value occurs under the tolerance value (lines 1 and 2).

STEP 2: Calculate the **Estimated Accumulated Frequency (EAF)**.

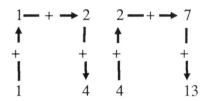

Transfer the first number in block 6 of row 2 to the corresponding column of row 3.

Add it to itself and to the value in the next column. Record the sum of the values in row 3.

The next value is derived in the same way.

STEP 3: Convert EAF values to plot-point percentages.

Take the number in row 3. Divide it by two times the sample size and multiply by 100%. This is the plot-point percentage. For example, the second plot-point percentage is:

$$\frac{\text{EAF}}{2(\text{sample size})} \times 100 = \frac{4}{2(50)} \times 100 = 4.00$$

NOTE: Because a sample of 50 was used, the plot-point percentages in the example (*Figure 7.8*) turn out to be numerically the same as in the EAF values. As we can see in *Figures 7.12* and *7.14*, in most cases this will not occur.

STEP 4: Plot each point on the graph.

Use the values in line 1 and plot-point percentages in line 4.

For example, the first point is vertically above the value 505 and at 1.0% on the left vertical scale.

Plot each point in the same way.

CAPABILITY ANALYSIS SHEET

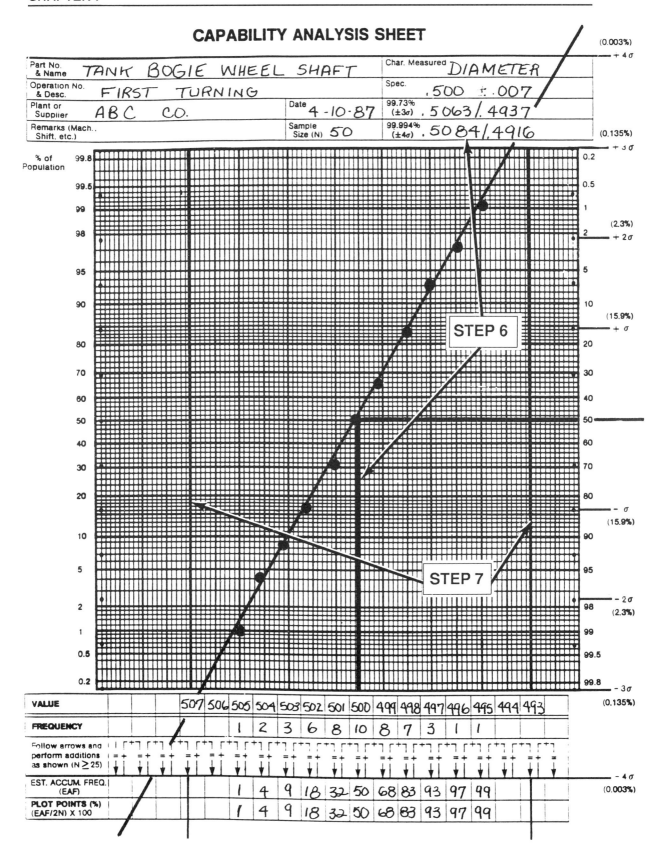

Figure 7.9 *Capability analysis sheet.*

STEP 5: Draw the **line of best fit** through the plotted points.

The best-fit line should pass through all of the indicated plot points.

Some deviation should be expected. The line should concentrate on the points that represent the largest volume of data. Make sure the line extends across the horizontal ± 4σ at the top and bottom of the sheet.

NOTE: A normal curve will plot a straight line. If there is a pattern other than a straight line, the process may not be normal (*Figure 7.8*).

STEP 6: Obtain statistical measurements.

Central Tendency: Use the right-hand scale to estimate the mean. Find the 50% point and move horizontally to the left to intersect the line of best fit. From that point, drop straight down to read the process center ($\overline{X}$) on the value scale.

Spread: Use horizontal lines at +3σ and -3σ to find the process spread. The value recorded below the intercept of the best-fit line and -3σ represents the (-3σ) lower limit (similarly for the upper limit).

Record the ± 3σ values in the 99.73 (±3σ) box on the heading.

STEP 7: Complete the capability analysis sheet.

Draw the specification limits as heavy vertical lines at the appropriate points in the value scale.

Read the percentage out of specification directly from the capability analysis sheet.

Read the percentage above the upper specification on the right-hand scale.

Read the percentage below the lower specification on the left-hand scale (*Figure 7.9*).

INTERPRETING THE RESULTS

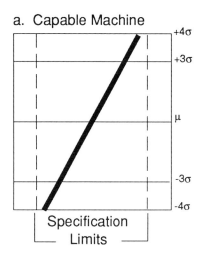

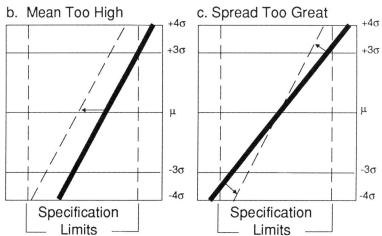

Figure 7.10 *Commonly occurring situations in analyzing the capability analysis sheet.*

EVALUATE THE ANALYSIS SHEET

A capability analysis sheet can be read like a histogram. *Figures 7.10a, 7.10b,* and *7.10c* illustrate some commonly occurring conditions. The pattern formed by the plotted points and best-fit line reveal whether:

- The process is normal

- The process is capable.

A Capable Process

When the $\pm\,4\sigma$ limits are within specifications, a process is considered capable (*Figure 7.10a*). This means that the process has sufficient short-run capability to achieve long-run goals and allow for additional sources of variability (e.g., tool wear, operator performance, etc.). The C_{pk} will be 1.33 or better.

A Process with a High Mean

When the best-fit line crosses either the high or low specification line, a process is incapable (*Figure 7.10b*). Here the mean needs to be shifted using such an activity as machine adjustment. When the adjustment is made, the sloped line on the capability analysis sheet should shift left or right while remaining parallel to the best-fit line.

A Process with Excessive Spread

When the best-fit line crosses both the upper and lower 3σ lines at a point beyond the specification lines, a process is incapable (*Figure 7.10c*). The process spread is too large.

Actions may require corrections for excessive internal machine variation. After successful action has been taken, the best-fit line should appear steeper and be within specification limits.

INTERPRETING NON-NORMAL RESULTS

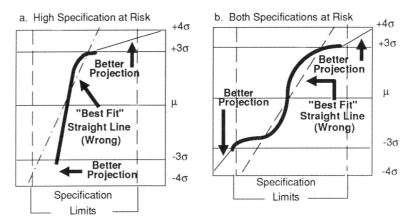

Figure 7.11 *The appearance of different non-normal distributions when plotted on normal probability paper.*

7.8 PROCESS CAPABILITY IN NON-NORMAL DISTRIBUTIONS

When the best-fit line shows a curved rather than a straight-line shape, the process has an abnormal distribution. The process distribution does not follow the rules and assumptions of the normal bell curve. This must be dealt with in assessing process capability.

Figure 7.11 shows the appearance of some different non-normal distributions when plotted on capability paper. In *Figure 7.11a*, the best-fit line bends to the right at the top. This shows the +3σ tail of the distribution to be skewed to the high side. This condition occurs with such dimensions as runout, out of control, and taper, where much of the data is clustered toward zero while some readings are fairly large.

In *Figure 7.11b,* the best-fit line slopes shallowly at both ends. The percentage of very small or very large parts coming from the combination of two normal or near-normal distributions have similar variation but different process means.

This results from the mixed output of several parallel operations, mixed lots of material causing different degrees of variability on final output, or an internal machine characteristic causing output to be divided into several distributions.

DEALING WITH NON- NORMAL DATA

Data may be non-normal because of the nature of the process or some other problem. Other more advanced analytical techniques may be required. A statistical specialist should be consulted.

For expediency, in order to continue the analysis, the data can be adjusted before process capability is assessed. One method for doing this is the mirror-image technique.

The **mirror-image technique** assumes skewness and transforms it into a symmetrical distribution. The new distribution is used to calculate the distribution average and standard deviation. This provides a better assessment of capability than calculations made on the original distribution.

This technique uses the modal value of the original distribution as a starting point. It then divides the skewed distribution into two parts and reflects either of the parts into new symmetrical distributions. (See Chapter 3 for details.)

Values for both the $\overline{\overline{X}}$ and standard deviation can be estimated and used to generate Z values, percentage out of specification, C_p, and C_{pk}.

Using the mirror-image technique gives the data symmetry, but it does not necessarily result in normality. Use of the technique should, at best, be taken as an approximation. See Chapter 3, Section 3.10, for an example of an application of the mirror-image technique.

Figures 7.12, 7.13, and *7.14* show the capability plots and corresponding histograms for various non-normal distributions.

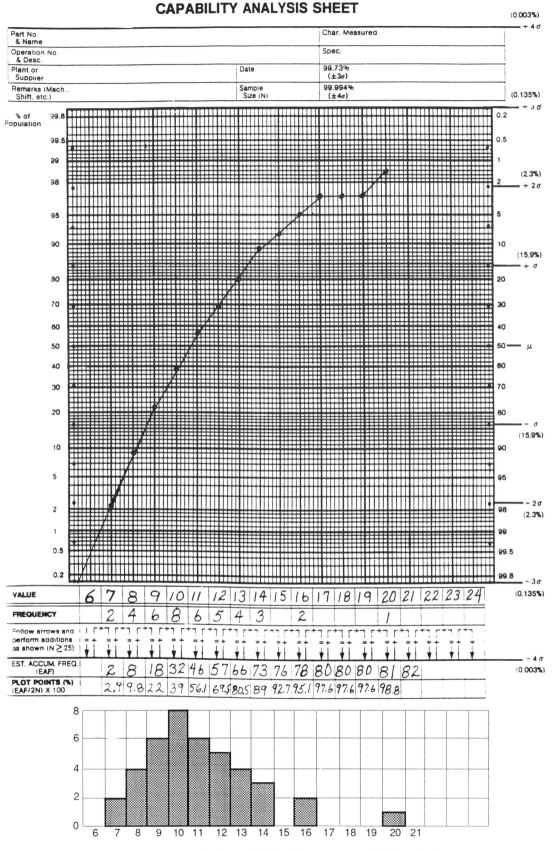

Figure 7.12 *A non-normal distribution.*

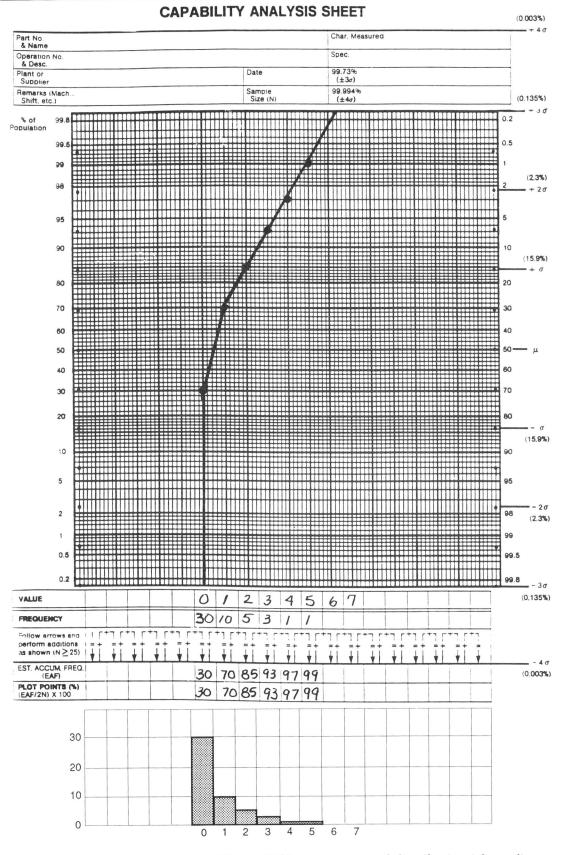

Figure 7.13 *A non-normal distribution (skewed).*

CAPABILITY ANALYSIS SHEET

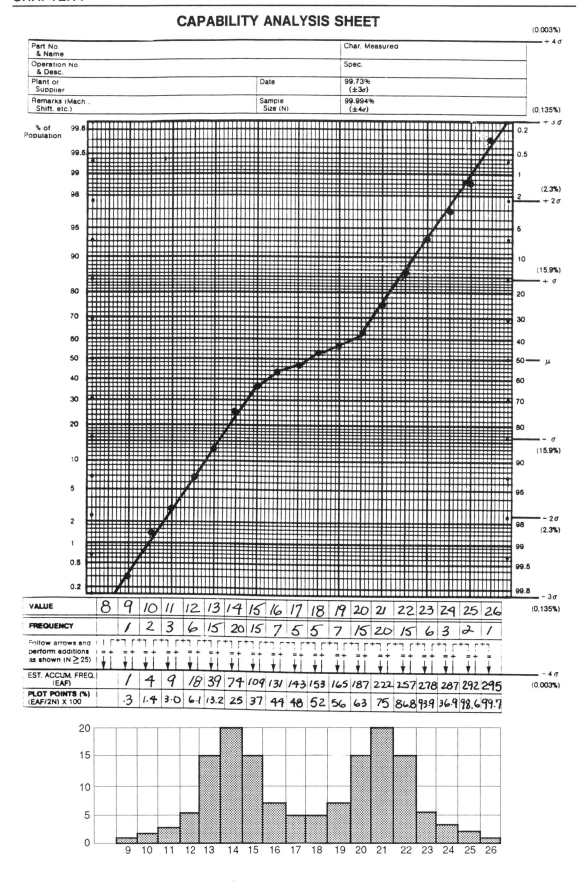

VALUE	8	9	10	11	12	13	14	15	16	17	18	19	20	21	22	23	24	25	26
FREQUENCY		1	2	3	6	15	20	15	7	5	5	7	15	20	15	6	3	2	1
EST. ACCUM. FREQ. (EAF)		1	4	9	18	39	74	109	131	143	153	165	187	222	257	278	287	292	295
PLOT POINTS (%) (EAF/2N) X 100		.3	1.4	3.0	6.1	13.2	25	37	44	48	52	56	63	75	86.8	93.9	96.9	98.6	99.7

Figure 7.14 *A non-normal distribution (bimodal).*

OTHER CONTROL CHARTS FOR VARIABLES

KEY CONCEPTS

In this chapter you will learn about the following key items and concepts:

$\overline{X}$ and s chart
Median chart
Chart for individuals
Moving range
Short runs
Constant process with too few pieces
Routine state of changeover
Short run $\overline{X}$ and R chart

OTHER CONTROL CHARTS FOR VARIABLES

8.1 $\overline{X}$ AND s CHARTS

$\overline{X}$ and s charts, like $\overline{X}$ and R charts, are developed from measured process output data and are always used as a pair. Range charts were developed as a measure of process variation because range is easy to calculate and is relatively efficient for small subgroup sample sizes. The sample standard deviation is a more efficient indicator of process variability, especially with larger sample sizes. However, it is more complex to calculate and is less sensitive in detecting special causes of variation that cause only a single value in a subgroup to be unusual. Use s charts instead of R charts when:

- The data are recorded and/or charted by computer, so a calculation routine for s is easily integrated

- Ready availability of a pocket calculator makes computation of s simple on a routine basis

- Large subgroup sample sizes are used, and the more efficient measure of variation is appropriate.

SAMPLE SIZE -10 CONSECUTIVE PIECES - ONCE/SHIFT

Part No.	Part Name		Operation No.	Machine No.	Dept No.	Shift
A-1267	MOUNTING BRACKET		470			

Characteristic checked	Sample Size	Print Limits		Date	Badge No.
THICKNESS CHECK ONCE PER SHIFT	10	Lower	Upper		

Date	1-5		1-6		1-7		1-8		1-9		1-12		1-13		1-14		1-15		1-16		1-19		1-20	
SHIFT/PIECE No.	1	2	1	2	1	2	1	2	1	2	1	2	1	2	1	2	1	2	1	2	1	2	1	2
1	.30	.01	.22	.08	.08	.12	.22	.04	.08	.20	.25	.24	.13	.08	.08	.14	.06	.14	.07	.13				
2	.10	.10	.05	.12	.30	.30	.10	.14	.02	.13	.11	.34	.16	.31	.26	.02	.12	.22	.05	.13				
3	.20	.15	.13	.11	.31	.01	.13	.18	.14	.19	.16	.40	.12	.12	.13	.14	.08	.18	.07	.12				
4	.25	.27	.08	.28	.12	.20	.02	.12	.20	.16	.04	.26	.22	.18	.14	.34	.12	.27	.05	.04				
5	.05	.25	.15	.00	.04	.11	.33	.00	.02	.03	.43	.13	.12	.13	.30	.30	.20	.17	.16	.40				
6	.35	.12	.27	.15	.10	.33	.17	.02	.04	.25	.06	.15	.07	.07	.15	.08	.02	.26	.02	.12				
7	.10	.10	.25	.15	.15	.02	.24	.05	.34	.20	.29	.08	.04	.08	.07	.24	.19	.15	.02	.15				
8	.16	.20	.11	.14	.35	.25	.28	.34	.05	.24	.42	.02	.28	.05	.02	.12	.03	.07	.14	.01				
9	.37	.04	.12	.28	.12	.05	.34	.12	.12	.10	.10	.05	.12	.00	.22	.15	.02	.02	.07	.30				
10	.25	.08	.10	.31	.26	.10	.12	.05	.06	.03	.00	.18	.10	.26	.18	.36	.09	.36	.00	.14				
X BAR	.213	.132	.148	.162	.183	.149	.195	.106	.107	.153	.186	.185	.136	.138	.155	.189	.093	.184	.065	.154				
(s) SIGMA	.110	.086	.074	.099	.111	.115	.105	.101	.100	.079	.155	.125	.070	.095	.087	.115	.065	.099	.051	.115				

Figure 8.1 *Sample size—ten consecutive pieces, once per shift.*

The details of instructions for $\overline{X}$ and s charts are very similar to those for $\overline{X}$ and R charts. Exceptions are noted below.

STEP 1: GATHER THE DATA

(See Section 5.9. Exceptions are noted below.)

If raw data are voluminous, they are often recorded on a separate data sheet, with only each subgroup's $\overline{X}$ and s appearing on the chart itself (*Figure 8.1*).

Calculate each subgroup's sample standard deviation using one of the following equivalent formulas:

$$s = \sqrt{\dfrac{\sum\limits_{i=1}^{n} (X_i - \overline{X})^2}{n-1}} \quad \text{or}$$

$$s = \sqrt{\dfrac{\sum\limits_{i=1}^{n} x_i^2 - n\overline{X}^2}{n-1}}$$

$$= \sqrt{\dfrac{X_1^2 + X_2^2 + \ldots + X_n^2 - n\overline{X}^2}{n-1}}$$

where X_i, $\overline{X}$, and n represent the subgroup's individual values, average, and sample size (*Figure 8.2*).

The scale spacing for the s chart should be the same as for its corresponding $\overline{X}$ chart.

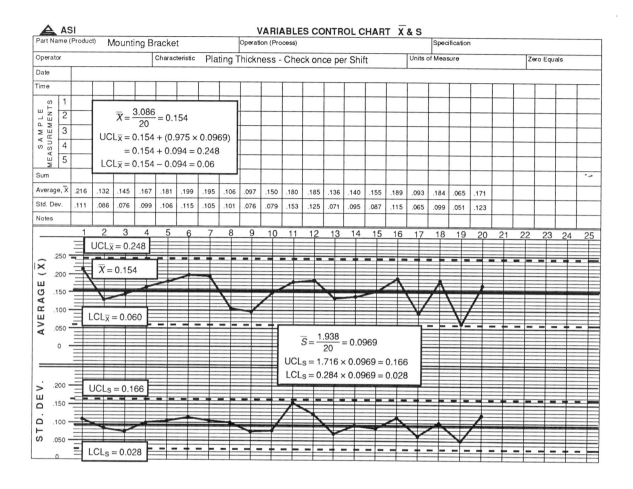

Figure 8.2 $\overline{X}$ *and s chart.*

STEP 2: CALCULATE THE CONTROL LIMITS

(See Section 5.10 . Exceptions are noted below.)

Calculate the upper and lower control limits for standard deviations and averages (UCL$_s$, LCL$_s$, UCL$_{\overline{X}}$, LCL$_{\overline{X}}$) (*Figure 8.2*).

$$UCL_s = B_4\bar{s}$$

$$LCL_s = B_3\bar{s}$$

$$UCL_{\overline{X}} = \overline{\overline{X}} + A_3\bar{s}$$

$$LCL_{\overline{X}} = \overline{\overline{X}} - A_3\bar{s}$$

where $\bar{s}$ is the average of the individual subgroup sample standard deviations, and B_4, B_3, and A_3 are constants varying by sample size, with values for sample sizes from two to ten shown in the following partial table:

n	2	3	4	5	6
B_4	3.267	2.568	2.266	2.089	1.970
B_3	*	*	*	*	0.030
A_3	2.659	1.954	1.628	1.427	1.287

n	7	8	9	10
B_4	1.882	1.815	1.761	1.716
B_3	0.118	0.185	0.239	0.284
A_3	1.182	1.099	1.032	0.975

NOTE: There is no lower control limit for standard deviations for samples sizes below six.

STEP 3: INTERPRET FOR PROCESS CONTROL

(See Section 5.11.)

STEP 4: INTERPRET FOR PROCESS CAPABILITY.

(See Section 5.11. Exceptions are noted below.)

Estimate the process standard deviation:

$$\hat{\sigma} = \bar{s} / c_4$$

where $\bar{s}$ is the average of the sample deviations (for periods with the standard deviation under control) and c_4 is a constant varying by sample size, with values for sample sizes from two to ten shown in the following partial table:

n	2	3	4	5	6
c_4	0.7979	0.8862	0 .9213	0 .9400	0.9515

n	7	8	9	10
c_4	0.9594	0.9650	0.9693	0.9727

NOTE: If the process has a normal distribution, this estimate of σ can be used directly in assessing process capability, as long as both averages and standard deviations are in statistical control.

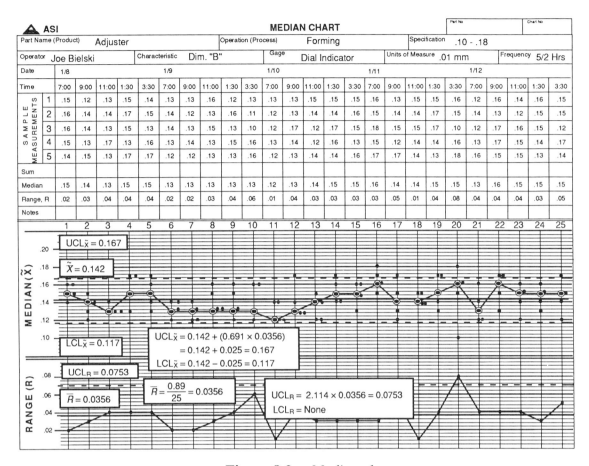

Figure 8.3 *Median chart.*

8.2 MEDIAN CHARTS

Median charts are alternatives to $\overline{X}$ and R charts for control of a process with measured data. They yield similar conclusions but have several specific advantages:

- Median charts are easy to use and do not require day-to-day calculations. This can increase shop-floor acceptance of the control chart approach.

- Since individual values as well as medians are plotted, the median chart shows the spread of process output and gives an ongoing picture of the process variation.

- Since a single chart shows both the median and spread, it can be used to compare the output of several processes or of the same process at successive stages.

Instructions for median charts are similar to $\overline{X}$ and R charts. Exceptions are noted below.

STEP 1: GATHER THE DATA

(See Section 5.9. Exceptions are noted below.)

Typically, median charts are used with subgroup sample sizes of ten or less; odd sample sizes should be used for easy determination of the median value.

Only a single graph is plotted (*Figure 8.3*). Set the scale to include the larger of (a) the product specification tolerance plus an allowance for out-of-specification readings, or (b) 1-1/2 to 2 times the difference between the highest and lowest individual measurement. The gage being used should divide the product tolerance into at least 10 increments, and the graph scales should agree with the gage.

Plot the individual measurements for each subgroup in a vertical line. Circle the median of each subgroup. To aid in interpreting trends, connect the subgroup medians by a line.

Enter each subgroup's median ($\tilde{X}$) and range (R) in the data table (*Figure 8.3*).

STEP 2: CALCULATE THE CONTROL LIMITS

(See Section 5.10. Exceptions are noted below.)

Find the average of the subgroup medians and draw this as the central line on the chart; record this as $\tilde{X}$

Find the average of the ranges; record this as $\overline{R}$.

Calculate the upper and lower control limits for ranges and medians (UCL_R, LCL_R, $UCL_{\tilde{X}}$, $LCL_{\tilde{X}}$)

$$UCL_R = D_4\overline{R}$$

$$LCL_R = D_3\overline{R}$$

$$UCL_{\tilde{X}} = \tilde{X} + \tilde{A}_2\overline{R}$$

$$LCL_{\tilde{X}} = \tilde{X} - \tilde{A}_2\overline{R}$$

where D_4, D_3, and $\tilde{A}_2$ are constants varying by sample size, with values for sample sizes two to ten shown in the following table (*Figure 8.3*):

n	2	3	4	5	6
D_4	3.267	2.574	2.282	2.114	2.004
D_3	*	*	*	*	*
$\tilde{A}_2$	1.880	1.187	0.796	0.691	0.548

n	7	8	9	10
D_4	1.924	1.864	1.816	1.777
D_3	0.076	0.136	0.184	0.223
$\tilde{A}_2$	0.508	0.433	0.412	0.362

NOTE: There is no lower control limit for ranges for sample sizes below seven.

Plot the control limits for medians on the chart.

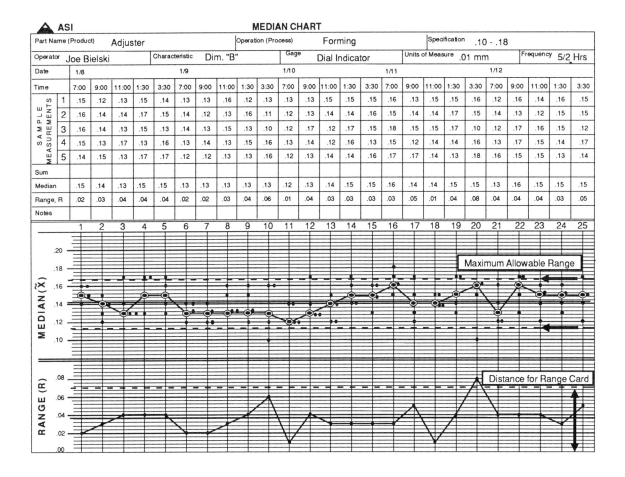

Figure 8.4 *Median chart.*

Ongoing control:

- The center line is set at the average of the subgroup medians from the previous study period.

- The control limits are based on the ranges from the previous study period.

- Medians are circled and compared to the control limits.

STEP 3: INTERPRET FOR PROCESS CONTROL

(See Section 5.11. Exceptions are noted below.)

Compare the UCL_R and LCL_R with each calculated range. Draw a narrow vertical box to enclose any subgroup with excessive range (*Figure 8.4*).

Mark any subgroup median that is beyond the median control limits, and note the spread of medians within the control limits (2/3 of points within middle third of limits) or the existence of patterns or trends.

Take appropriate process action for special causes affecting the ranges.

STEP 4: INTERPRET FOR PROCESS CAPABILITY

(See Section 5.12. Exceptions are noted below.)

Estimate the process standard deviation:

$$\hat{\sigma} = \overline{R} / d_2$$

where $\overline{R}$ is the average of the sample ranges (for periods with the range under control) and d_2 is a constant varying by sample size, with values for sample sizes from two to ten shown in the following table:

n	2	3	4	5	6
d_2	1.128	1.693	2.059	2.326	2.534
n	7	8	9	10	
d_2	2.704	2.847	2.970	3.078	

If the process has a normal distribution, this estimate of σ can be used directly in assessing process capability, as long as the medians and ranges are in statistical control.

NOTE: For ongoing process control where control limits are based on prior data, the charting process can be simplified as follows:

- A single chart may be used, with scales set at the same increments as the gage being used (at least ten increments between product specifications), and with the central line and control limits for medians already centered.

- A card (possibly plastic) is provided, marked with the control limits for ranges.

- The operator marks the chart with each individual reading, but the numerical values do not need to be recorded.

- For each subgroup, the operator compares the range card to the subgroup's highest and lowest marks; any subgroup having a range beyond the limits on the card is enclosed in a narrow vertical box.

- The operator counts to the median of each subgroup and circles it; any median beyond either control limit is marked.

- For ranges or medians beyond control limits, the operator takes appropriate actions to adjust or correct the process, or to notify supervisory or support people.

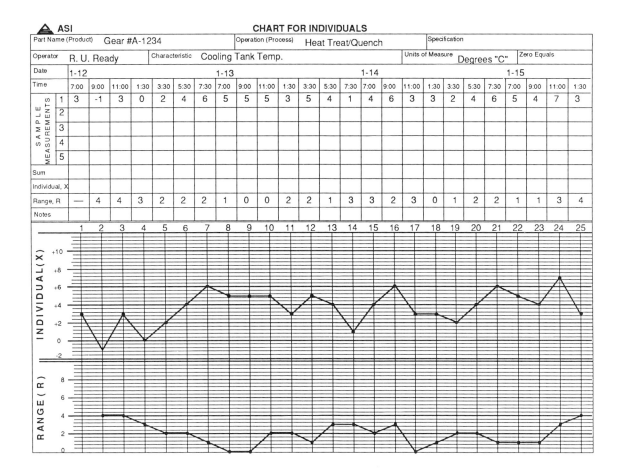

Figure 8.5 *Chart for individuals.*

8.3 CHARTS FOR INDIVIDUALS

It is sometimes necessary for process control to be based on individual readings, rather than subgroups. This typically occurs when the measurements are expensive (for example, a destructive test), or when the output at any point in time is relatively homogenous (such as the pH of a chemical solution). In these cases, control charts for individuals can be constructed as described below. Four cautions should be noted, however:

1. Charts for individuals are not as sensitive to process changes as $\overline{X}$ and R charts.

2. Care must be taken in interpretation of charts for individuals if the process distribution is not symmetrical.

3. Charts for individuals do not isolate the piece-to-piece variability of the process. In many situations, therefore, it may be better to use a conventional $\overline{X}$ and R chart with small subgroup sample sizes (from two to four even if this requires a longer period between subgroups).

4. Since there is only one individual item per subgroup, values of $\overline{X}$ and σ can have substantial variability (even if the process is stable) until the number of subgroups is 100 or more.

The detail of instructions for charts for individuals are somewhat similar to those for $\overline{X}$ and R charts. Exceptions are noted below.

STEP 1: GATHER THE DATA

(See Section 5.9. Exceptions are noted below.)

Individual readings (X) are recorded from left to right on the data chart.

Calculate the moving range (R) between individuals. It is generally best to record the difference between each successive pair of readings (such as the difference between the first and the second reading, the second and third, and so on). There will be one less such range than there are individual readings (25 readings give 24 ranges). In rare cases, the range can be based on a larger moving group (perhaps threes or fours) or on a fixed subgroup (all the readings taken on a single shift). Note that even though the measurements are individually sampled, it is the number of readings grouped to form the moving range (for example two, three, or four) that determines the nominal sample size, n (*Figure 8.5*).

Select scales for the chart for individuals (X) equal to the larger of a) the product specification tolerance plus an allowance for out-of-specification readings, or b) 1-1/2 to 2 times the difference between the highest and lowest individual readings. The scale spacing for the chart for ranges (R) should be the same as that of the X chart.

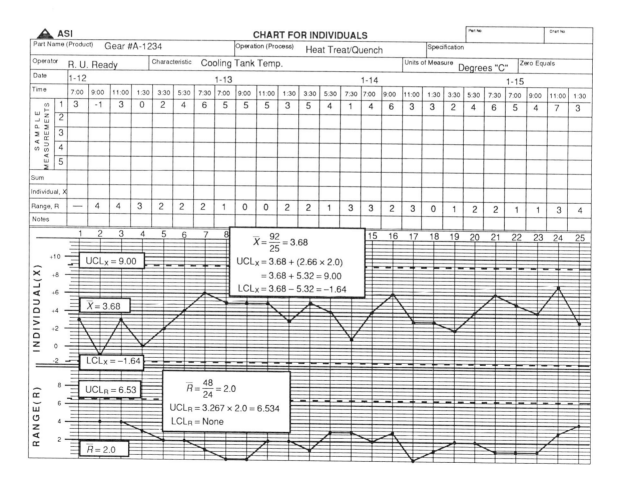

Figure 8.6 *Chart for individuals.*

STEP 2: CALCULATE THE CONTROL LIMITS.

(See Section 5.10. Exceptions are noted below.)

Calculate and plot the process average ($\overline{X}$), and calculate the average range ($\overline{R}$). Note that there is one less range value (R) than the number of individual readings (X) (*Figure 8.6*).

Calculate the control limits:

$$\text{UCL}_\text{R} = D_4 \overline{R}$$

$$\text{LCL}_\text{R} = D_3 \overline{R}$$

$$\text{UCL}_\text{X} = \overline{X} + E_2 \overline{R}$$

$$\text{LCL}_\text{X} = \overline{X} - E_2 \overline{R}$$

where $\overline{R}$ is the average moving range, $\overline{X}$ is the process average, and D_4, D_3, and E_2 are constants that vary according to the sample size used in grouping the moving ranges, as shown in the following partial table.

n	2	3	4	5	6
D_4	3.267	2.574	2.282	2.114	2.004
D_3	*	*	*	*	*
E_2	2.660	1.772	1.457	1.290	1.184

n	7	8	9	10
D_4	1.924	1.864	1.816	1.777
D_3	0.076	0.136	0.184	0.223
E_2	1.109	1.054	1.010	0.975

NOTE: There is no lower control limit for ranges for sample sizes below seven.

STEP 3: INTERPRET FOR PROCESS CONTROL

(See Section 5.11. Exceptions are noted below.)

Review the range chart for points beyond the control limits as signs of the existence of special causes. Note that successive ranges are correlated, since they have a point in common. Care must be taken when interpreting trends because of this.

The chart for individuals can be analyzed for points beyond the control limits, spread of points within the control limits, and trends or patterns. Note here, though, that if the process distribution is not symmetrical, the rules shown previously for $\overline{X}$ charts may give signals of special causes when none exist.

STEP 4: INTERPRET FOR PROCESS CAPABILITY

(See Section 5.12. Exceptions are noted below.)

As with $\overline{X}$ and R charts, the process standard deviation can be estimated by:

$$\hat{\sigma} = \overline{R} / d_2$$

where $\overline{R}$ is the average of the moving ranges and d_2 is a constant varying by the sample size, used for the moving range, as shown in the partial table below:

n	2	3	4	5	6
d_2	1.128	1.693	2.059	2.326	2.534

n	7	8	9	10
d_2	2.704	2.847	2.970	3.078

If the process has a normal distribution, this estimate of σ can be used directly in assessing process capability, as long as the process is in statistical control.

8.4 THE SPECIAL PROBLEM OF SHORT RUNS

Control charting is most often applied to processes that produce high volumes of discrete parts. Consequently, processes that produce very few pieces, or short runs, are often not easily controlled using the standard $\overline{X}$ and R chart methodology. The two situations where such difficulty arises are:

- A constant process that produces so few pieces per shift that there isn't enough time to generate control chart samples. This situation often occurs in small job shops that make minimal numbers of many different kinds of pieces.

- A constant process that is in a routine state of changing to a series of similar parts, with each having a unique level regarding a particular quality characteristic. This situation often occurs when production volumes are low, and a process is frequently shut down to set up production of similar parts with different dimensions.

CONSTANT PROCESS — TOO FEW PIECES

Often processes that produce very low production volumes, and therefore do not allow enough time for sampling, can be controlled using simple techniques. These include the following:

- **100% inspection.** If the quality characteristic of concern is easily identified, 100% inspection of the final product will establish shipping disposition.

- **Frequency distribution.** Often a simple frequency distribution that is collected and plotted to the target value of the quality characteristic in question will demonstrate the overall variability of a process. While the distinction between control and capability cannot be discerned, this technique may be valuable in problem solving.

- **Process parameters.** If the above techniques do not satisfactorily reveal the variability in a problem process, it is often necessary to analyze process parameters rather than dimensional characteristics.

The first step in conducting a process parameter study is to identify the parameters themselves. A fishbone diagram can be used in this situation to identify the sources of end-product variation and lead to the corrective action necessary to bring the process into control. Any of the previous charts may then be applied to the process characteristic.

ROUTINE STATE OF CHANGEOVER

Fortunately, many processes involved in frequent shut-down and start-up operations have a tendency to produce an overall variation that adheres to the statistical laws of performance. This situation lends itself to a particular way of producing an average and range chart for the dimension under study, which is called the **short run $\bar{X}$ and R chart**.

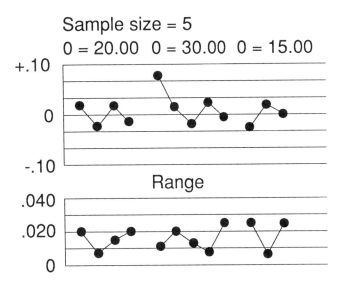

Figure 8.7 *Routine changeover control chart 1.*

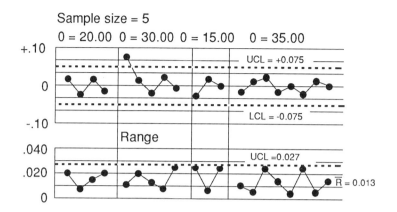

Figure 8.8 *Routine changeover control chart 2.*

SHORT RUN $\overline{X}$ AND R CHART

A short run $\overline{X}$ and R chart, also called an **aim chart**, **target chart**, and **deviation chart**, sets the zero value on the $\overline{X}$ chart as the intended target value for each part sampled from the various setups. Each sample is measured against this intended zero point.

EXAMPLE—SHORT RUN CHART

A process cuts 100 pieces to target value of 20 inches long. It next cuts 200 pieces to a target value of 30 inches long. It then cuts 50 pieces to a target value of 15 inches long. A sample of the initial control chart looks like *Figure 8.7.*

Initially, the changeover control study may only have a few samples to work with. Eventually, however, at least 20 subgroups will be obtained and a single average range can be determined. This will represent the underlying common cause variation of the process and can therefore be applied to all the parts involved. The range chart control limits are determined as in a normal $\overline{X}$ and R chart. The average chart control limits are placed plus and minus a distance of $A_2\overline{R}$ from the zero line. The finished chart will look like *Figure 8.8.*

Once the routine changeover chart is set up in the manner illustrated, it can be used as an ongoing monitor of control, even though the product nominal specifications differ from one part to another.

NOTE: Test for control ignores tolerances except for their targets. The usefulness of the changeover technique stems from the often found process or product characteristic that has the same common cause variation regardless of the intended target being run. When this is the case, the range values all seem to come from a common system over time. When this is not the case, certain points may demonstrate their own, perhaps larger, range values. If this happens, the points in question will require their own $\overline{X}$ and R chart.

CONTROL CHARTS FOR ATTRIBUTES

CONTENTS

KEY CONCEPTS

In this chapter you will learn about the following key items and concepts:

Attributes
Nonconformities
Proportion nonconforming
Number nonconforming
Number of nonconformities
Nonconformities per unit
Weighted nonconformities per unit
Demerits
p **chart**
np **chart**
c **chart**
u **chart**
d **chart**

CONTROL CHARTS
FOR ATTRIBUTES

9.1 INTRODUCTION

Control charts have also been developed for attributes. Attribute-type data have only two values (conforming/nonconforming, pass/fail, go/no-go, present/absent), but they can be counted for recording and analysis.

Examples include the presence of a required label, the continuity of an electrical circuit, and errors in a typed document. Other examples are characteristics that are measurable, where the results are recorded in a simple yes/no fashion, such as the conformance of a shaft diameter when measured on a go/no-go gage, the acceptability of door margins to a visual or gage check, or on-time delivery performance. Control charts for attributes are important for several reasons:

1. Attribute data analysis is useful in many technical and administrative processes. The most significant difficulty is to develop precise operational definitions of what is nonconforming.

2. Attribute data are already available in many situations, wherever there are existing inspections, writeups for repair, sorts of rejected material, and so on. In these cases, no additional data-collection expense is involved beyond the effort of converting the data to control data form.

3. Where new data must be collected, attribute information is generally quick and inexpensive to obtain. Simple gaging (such as a go/no-go gage) does not require specialized collection skills.

4. Much data gathered for management-type summary reporting is in attribute form and can benefit from control chart analysis. Examples include department first run OK performance, scrap rates, quality audits, and material rejections.

5. When introducing control charts into an organization, it is important to prioritize problem areas and use charts where they are most needed. Attribute control charts can be used on key overall quality measures to point the way to special process areas that need more detailed examination, including the use of control charts for variables.

The next five subsections cover the fundamentals of the four major types of attribute control charts:

- The p chart for proportion of units nonconforming (from samples not necessarily of constant size).

- The np chart for number of units nonconforming (from samples of constant size).

- The c chart for number of nonconformities (from samples of constant size).

- The u chart for number of nonconformities per unit (from samples not necessarily of constant size).

- The d chart for demerits per unit.

The discussion of the p chart is more detailed than the others because it introduces the major concepts. The other subsections concentrate on the distinguishing features of the other types of charts. The reader is referred to the appropriate page of the discussion of the p chart, when the steps are the same.

9.2 THE *p* CHART FOR PROPORTION NONCONFORMING

The *p* chart measures the proportion of nonconforming (discrepant or so-called defective) items in a group of items being inspected. This could refer to a sample of 75 pieces, taken twice a day, 100% of production grouped on an hourly or daily basis, or any other convenient sample. It may evaluate one characteristic (was a particular part installed?) or many characteristics (was anything found wrong at the electrical system check station?). It is important that:

1. Each component or vehicle checked is recorded as either conforming or nonconforming (even if an item has several specific nonconformities, it is only tallied once as a nonconforming item).

2. The results of these inspections are grouped on a meaningful basis, and the nonconforming items are expressed as a decimal fraction of the subgroup size.

Before any control chart can be used properly, preparatory steps must be taken. These steps are essentially the same as those described for variable control charts in Chapter 5, Section 5.8.

- Establish an environment suitable for action.

- Define the project

- Determine the characteristic to be charted. Consider:

  — Customer needs

  — Current and potential problem areas

  — Correlation between characteristics

- Define the categories

- Minimize unnecessary variation.

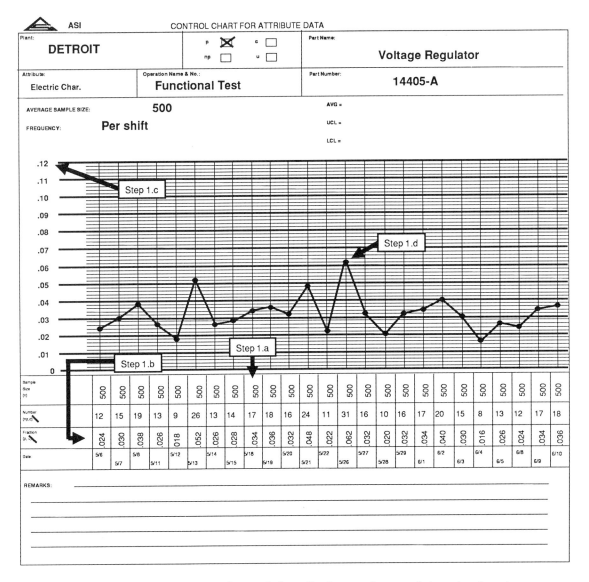

Figure 9.1 *Gather and record data (p chart).*

9.2.1 STEP 1: GATHER DATA

1.A SELECT THE SIZE, FREQUENCY, AND NUMBER OF SUBGROUPS

Subgroup size. Proportion nonconforming (p) charts for attributes generally require large subgroup sizes (such as 50 to 200 or more) to be able to detect moderate shifts in performance. For the chart to show analyzable patterns, the subgroup size should be large enough to expect to have several nonconforming items per subgroup (for example, as a guideline, sample size n should be about equal to $5/P_o$, where P_o is the average of the fraction defective).

Note that large subgroup sizes can be a disadvantage if each subgroup represents a long period of process operation. It is most convenient if subgroup sizes are constant or if they vary by no more than $\pm 25\%$ of the mean sample average, but this need not be the case (*Figure 9.1*).

Subgroup frequency. The subgroup frequency should make sense in terms of production periods to aid in analysis and correction of problems found. Short time intervals allow faster feedback but may conflict with requirements for larger subgroup sizes.

Number of subgroups.: The data collection period should be long enough to capture all the likely sources of variation affecting the process. It should also include 25 or more subgroups to give a good test for stability and, if stable, a reliable estimate of process performance.

1.B CALCULATE EACH SUBGROUP'S PROPORTION NONCONFORMING (p)

The following data should be recorded for each subgroup:

*   The number of items inspected, n

*   The number of nonconforming items found, d.

From these, calculate the proportion nonconforming:

$$p = \frac{d}{n}$$

These data should be recorded on a data form as the basis of initial analysis. When the most recent historical data are available, they may be used to accelerate this phase of the study.

1.C SELECT SCALES FOR THE CONTROL CHART

The chart where the data are plotted should be laid out with the proportion (or percent) nonconforming as the vertical scale and the subgroup identification (hour, day, etc.) as the horizontal scale. The highest vertical scale should extend from zero to about 1-1/2 times the highest proportion nonconforming noted in the initial data readings.

1.D PLOT THE PROPORTION NONCONFORMING ON THE CONTROL CHART

Plot the values of p for each group. It is usually helpful to connect the points with lines to help visualize patterns and trends.

As the points are plotted, briefly scan them to see if they are reasonable. If any points are substantially higher or lower than the others, confirm that the calculations are correct.

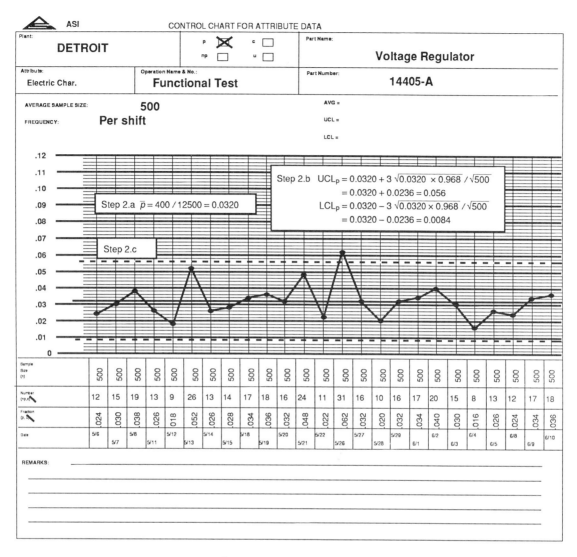

Figure 9.2 *Calculate process average and control limits (p chart).*

9.2.2 STEP 2: CALCULATE CONTROL LIMITS

2.A CALCULATE THE PROCESS AVERAGE PROPORTION NONCONFORMING ($\bar{p}$)

For the study period of k subgroups, calculate the average proportion nonconforming:

$$\bar{p} = \frac{d_1 + d_2 + \ldots + d_k}{n_1 + n_2 + \ldots + n_k}$$

where $d_1, d_2, \ldots$ and $n_1, n_2, \ldots$ are the number of nonforming items and number of items inspected in each subgroup (*Figure 9.2*).

2.B CALCULATE THE UPPER AND LOWER CONTROL LIMITS (UCL, LCL)

The control limits are the process average plus or minus an allowance for the variation that could be expected if the process was in statistical control, given the typical subgroup sample size. For the study period of k subgroups, calculate the upper and lower control limits (UCL and LCL):

$$\text{UCL}_p = \bar{p} + 3 \sqrt{\bar{p} \, (1 - \bar{p}) \, / \, n}$$

$$\text{LCL}_p = \bar{p} - 3 \sqrt{\bar{p} \, (1 - \bar{p}) \, / \, n}$$

where n is the sample size (*Figure 9.2*).

NOTE: When $\bar{p}$ is low and/or n is small, the LCL can sometimes be calculated as a negative number. In this case there is no lower control limit, since even a value of $p = 0$ for a particular period is within the limits of random variation.

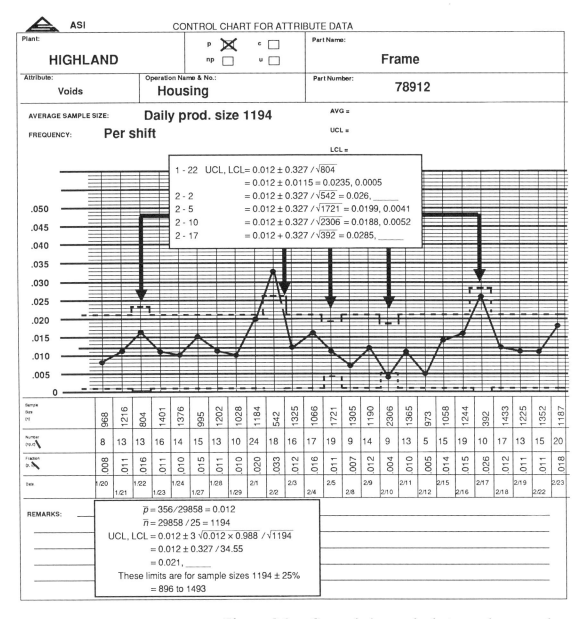

Figure 9.3 *Control chart calculations when sample size changes (p chart).*

2.C DRAW AND LABEL LINES

- Process average ($\bar{p}$)—solid horizontal line

- Control limits (UCL, LCL)—dashed horizontal lines.

During the initial study phase, these are considered trial control limits.

CONTROL CHART CALCULATIONS WHEN SAMPLE SIZE CHANGES

The control limits calculations given above are appropriate when the subgroup sizes are all equal (as they would be in a controlled sampling situation). Theoretically, whenever the sample size changes (even for a single subgroup), the control limits change, and unique limits would be calculated for each subgroup having a unique sample size. However, for practical purposes, control limits calculated with an average sample size ($\bar{n}$) are acceptable when the individual subgroup sizes vary from the average by no more than $\pm 25\%$ (typical of actual production volumes under relatively stable conditions). When subgroup sizes vary by more than this amount, separate control limits are required for the periods with particularly small or large samples. A reasonable procedure, which should be documented in the "remarks" section of the form, is:

- Determine the range of sample sizes that would vary from the average by $\pm 25\%$; identify all subgroups with sample sizes that lie outside this range.

- Recalculate the precise limits for those points as follows:

$$\text{UCL}_p, \text{LCL}_p = \bar{p} \pm 3 \sqrt{\bar{p}\,(1 - \bar{p})\,/\,n}$$

where n is the sample size of the particular subgroup. Only the $\sqrt{n}$ term changes from point to point (*Figure 9.3*).

- Plot the new UCL and LCL on the chart for the affected subgroups and use as the basis for identifying special causes.

Note that any procedure for handling variable control limits is going to be cumbersome. Variable control limits may lead to potential confusion among people trying to interpret the charts. It is much better, wherever possible, to **structure** the **data-collection plan so that constant sample sizes can be used**.

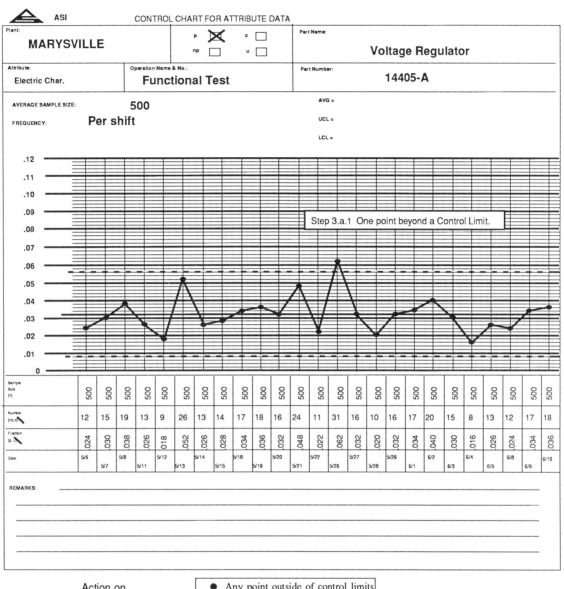

Figure 9.4 *Interpret for process control: points outside of control limits (p chart).*

9.2.3 STEP 3: INTERPRET FOR PROCESS CONTROL

3.A ANALYZE THE DATA PLOT FOR EVIDENCE OF NONCONTROL

Objective: Identify any evidence that the process is no longer operating at the same level—that it is out of control—and take appropriate action. Points beyond control limits, or obvious trends or patterns in the data beyond what would likely occur due to chance, suggest the presence of special causes of variation.

3.A.1 Points Beyond the Control Limits

The presence of one or more points beyond either control limit is evidence of instability at that point. Since points beyond the control limits would be very rare if the process was stable and only common cause variation was present, we presume that special causes have accounted for the extreme value. The special cause may be either favorable or unfavorable. Either warrants immediate investigation. This is the primary decision rule for action on any control chart. Any point beyond the control limits should be marked (*Figure 9.4*).

A point above the UCL (higher proportion nonconforming) is generally a sign that:

- The control limit or plot point is in error.

- The process performance has worsened, either at that point in time or as part of a trend.

- The measurement system has changed (for example, inspector, quality standard, etc.).

A point below the LCL (lower proportion nonconforming) is generally a sign that:

- The control limit or plot point is in error.

- The process performance has improved (this should be studied for improvements that might be incorporated on a permanent basis).

- The measurement system has changed.

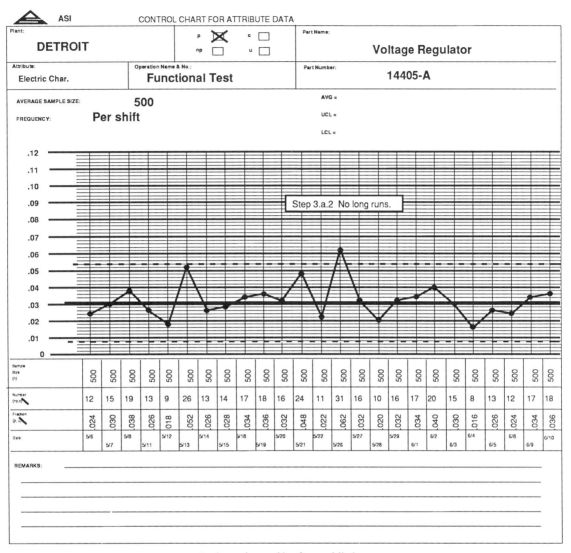

● Any point outside of control limits

● A run of 7 points—all above or below the center line
● A run of 7 intervals up or down

● Any other obviously non-random pattern

Figure 9.5 *Interpret for process control: runs or trends within control limits (p chart).*

3.A.2. Runs or Trends within Control Limits

The presence of unusual patterns or trends, even when all points are within the control limits, can be evidence of noncontrol or a change in the level of performance during the period of the pattern or trend. This can give advance warning of conditions that, if left uncovered, could cause variation beyond the control limits.

NOTE: When the average number of nonconforming items per subgroup, $n\bar{p}$, is moderately large (nine or more), the distribution of the subgroup, p's, is nearly normal, and trend analysis similar to that used for $\bar{X}$ charts can be used. When $n\bar{p}$ becomes small (five or fewer), the following rules are not directly applicable.

In a process under control, with np moderately large, approximately equal numbers of points should fall on either side of the average. Either of the following could be a sign that a process shift or trend has begun:

- Seven points in a row show on one side of the average

- Seven intervals in a row are consistently increasing (equal or greater than the preceding points) or consistently decreasing (*Figure 9.5*).

In these cases, the point that prompts the decision should be marked (for example, the eighth point above the average); it may be helpful to extend a reference line back to the beginning of the run. The analysis should consider the approximate time that the trend or shift first began.

Runs above the process average, or runs up, generally signify that:

- The process performance has worsened, and may still be worsening.

- The measurement system has changed.

Runs below the process average, or runs down, generally signify that:

- The process performance has improved (the causes should be studied for permanent incorporation).

- The measurement system has changed.

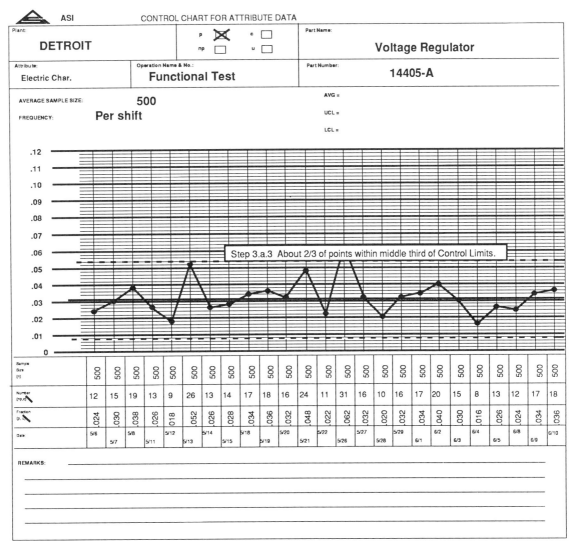

- ● Any point outside of control limits
- ● A run of 7 points—all above or below the center line
- ● A run of 7 intervals up or down
- ● Any other obviously non-random pattern

Figure 9.6 *Interpret for process control: any other obvious non-random pattern (p chart).*

NOTE: When *np* is small (below five), the likelihood of runs below $\bar{p}$ increases, so a run length of eight or more could be necessary to signal a decrease in the proportion nonconforming.

3.A.3 Obvious Nonrandom Patterns

Other distinct patterns may indicate the presence of special causes of variation, although care must be taken not to misinterpret the data. Among these patterns are trends, cycles, unusual spread of points within the control limits, and relationships among values within subgroups (for example, if all nonconforming items occur within the first few readings taken for the subgroup). One test for unusual spread is given below.

Distance of points from the process average: In a process under statistical control, with only common cause variation present and np moderately large, about 2/3 of the data points will be within the middle third of the region between the control limits; about 1/3 of the points will be in the outer two-thirds of the region; and about 1/20 will lie relatively close the control limits (in the outer third of the region) (*Figure 9.6*).

If substantially more than 2/3 of the points lie close to the process average, this could mean that:

- The control limits or plot points have been miscalculated or misplotted.

- The process or the sampling method is stratified; each subgroup systematically contains measurements from two or more process streams that have very different average performance (for example, the mixed output of two parallel production lines).

- The data have been edited (values that would have deviated much from the average have been altered or removed).

If substantially fewer than 2/3 of the points lie close to the process average (for 25 subgroups if 40% or fewer are in the middle third), this could mean that:

- Calculation or plotting errors have been made.

- The process or the sampling method causes successive subgroups to contain measurements from two or more process streams that have very different average performance (such as performance differences between shifts).

- The process is unstable.

If several process streams are present, they should be identified and tracked separately.

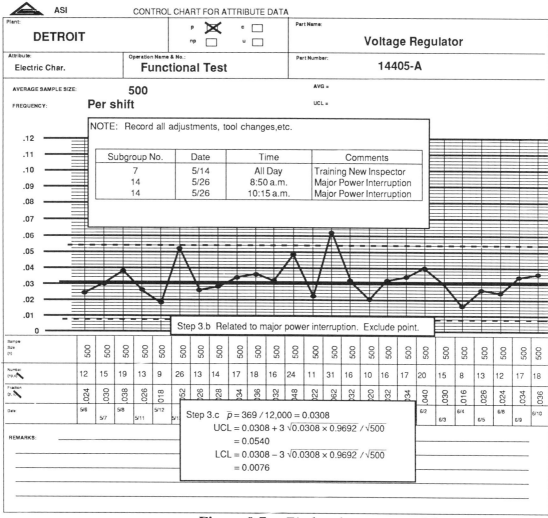

Figure 9.7 *Find and correct special causes. Recalculate control limits, if necessary (p chart).*

3.B FIND AND CORRECT SPECIAL CAUSES

When an out-of-control condition has been identified in the data, the operation of the process must be studied to determine the cause. This cause must then be corrected and, to the extent possible, prevented from recurring. Since a special cause was indicated by the control chart, analysis of the operation is called for. One would expect to find causes of variation within the ability of the operator or local supervision to correct. Problem-solving techniques such as Pareto analysis and cause-and-effect analysis can be helpful.

NOTE: For information, see Chapter 11 of this book and Ishikawa in the Background References section.

For ongoing studies with real-time data, analysis of out-of-control conditions involves timely investigation of a process. Emphasis should be on finding what, if any, changes occurred that might explain the abnormal performance. When this analysis results in corrective action, it should be apparent in the control chart (*Figure 9.7*).

The passage of time may make analysis of process operating changes more difficult, especially for symptoms that come and go. The analysis must be made as complete as possible in order to identify the condition and to prevent its recurrence.

3.C RECALCULATE CONTROL LIMITS

When conducting an initial process study or a reassessment of process capability, the trial control limits may need to be recalculated to exclude the effects of periods whose state of control was affected by special causes that have been corrected. The control limits should be recalculated excluding the points associated with the special causes and plotted on the chart (*Figure 9.7* step 3.c). The historical data should again be checked against the revised limits to confirm that no further points suggest the presence of assignable causes.

Once the historical data show consistent performance within trial control limits, the limits can be extended forward to cover future control periods. Future data will be evaluated against them.

The limits for ongoing control may be altered from those developed during the analysis period by changing the sample size. In such a case, the basic formulas from subsections 2.a and 2.b are used with the new sample size.

NOTE: For more extensive discussions of interpretation and problem solving, see Grant and Leavenworth or Duncan in the Background References section.

Calculate the Process Capability

From the example:

$$\bar{p} = 0.0308$$

Process capability currently is 3.08% failures of the functional check (96.92% OK).

Evaluate the Process Capability

If the functional check is performed 100% and nonconforming products are set aside, outgoing product is being protected, but the 3% average failure rate (requiring rework or scrap) is wasteful. Actions to improve the performance level should be developed.

Figure 9.8 *Calculation and evaluation of process capability (p chart).*

9.2.4 STEP 4: INTERPRET FOR PROCESS CAPABILITY

When control issues have been resolved (special causes identified, analyzed, and corrected/prevented from recurring), the control chart reflects the underlying process capability.

4.A CALCULATE THE PROCESS CAPABILITY

For a p chart, the process capability (in the same sense as the capability developed from variable data) is reflected by the process average nonconforming $\bar{p}$ calculated when all points are in control. If desired, this can be expressed as the proportion conforming to specification $(1 - \bar{p})$ (*Figure 9.8*).

For a preliminary estimate of process capability, use historical data but exclude data points associated with special causes.

For a formal process capability study, new data should be run, preferably for 25 or more periods, with the points all reflecting statistical control. The $\bar{p}$ for these consecutive in-control periods is a better estimate of the current capability of the process.

4.B EVALUATE THE PROCESS CAPABILITY

The process capability as just calculated reflects the ongoing level of performance that the process is generating and can be expected to generate, as long as the process remains in control and does not experience any basic change in performance. On a period-to-period basis, the measured proportion nonconforming will vary between the control limits. Barring any changes in the process, or periods where the process goes out of control, the average proportion nonconforming will tend to be stable.

This average capability, not the fluctuating individual values, must be evaluated against the philosophy of continuous improvement. Analysis of the nature and cause of the underlying defective level (Pareto analysis, cause-and-effect analysis) becomes the more important effort. The power of the control chart lies in its ability to avoid chasing special cause situations in the process capability improvement effort.

IMPROVE THE PROCESS CAPABILITY

To improve the performance of the process, concentrate on the common causes that affect all periods. These will usually require management action.

CHART AND ANALYZE THE REVISED PROCESS

Confirm the effectiveness of system changes by continued monitoring of the control chart.

4.C IMPROVE THE PROCESS CAPABILITY

Once the process is demonstrating statistical control, the remaining average level of nonconformities will reflect the systematic causes of variation in the underlying process—the process capability. The types of analysis performed in diagnosing the special cause (control) issues, which focused on operations, will no longer be appropriate in diagnosing common causes affecting the system. Unless management action is directed toward the system itself, no improvement in the process capability can be expected. Long-term solutions are necessary to correct the sources of chronic nonconformities.

Problem-solving techniques such as Pareto analysis and cause-and-effect analysis can be helpful (see Ishikawa in the Background References section). However, understanding the problems can be difficult when only attribute data is used. In general, problem solving is aided by going upstream in the process as far as possible toward the source of suspected causes of variation and by using variable data for analysis (such as in $\bar{X}$ and R charts).

4.D CHART AND ANALYZE THE REVISED PROCESS

When systematic process actions have been taken, their effects should be apparent in the control chart. The chart becomes a way of verifying the effectiveness of the action.

As the process change is implemented, the control chart should be monitored carefully. This change period can be disruptive to operations and may cause new control problems that could obscure the true effect of the system change.

After any special causes of variation that appear during the change period have been identified and corrected, the process will be in statistical control at a new process average. This new average reflects in-control performance. It can be used as the basis of ongoing process control. However, investigation and improvement of the system should continue.

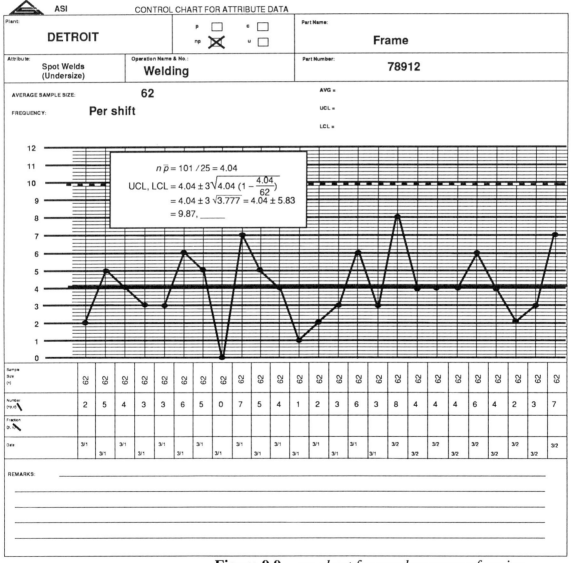

Figure 9.9 *np chart for number nonconforming.*

9.3 THE *np* CHART FOR NUMBER NONCONFORMING

The *np* chart measures the number of nonconforming (discrepant or so-called defective) items in an inspection lot. It is identical to the *p* chart except that the actual number of nonconforming items, rather than their proportion of the sample, is recorded. Both *p* and *np* charts are appropriate for the same basic situations, with the choice being the *np* chart if a) the actual number of nonconformities is more meaningful or simpler to report than the proportion, and b) the sample size remains constant from period to period. The details of instructions for the *np* chart are virtually identical to those of the *p* chart; exceptions are noted below.

STEP 1: GATHER THE DATA

(See Section 9.2.1. Exceptions are noted below.)

The inspection sample sizes must be equal. The period of subgrouping should make sense in terms of production intervals and feedback systems, and samples should be large enough to expect several nonconforming items to appears in each subgroup. Record the sample size on the form.

Record and plot the number nonconforming in each subgroup (*np*).

STEP 2: CALCULATE THE CONTROL LIMITS

(See Section 9.2.2. Exceptions are noted below.)

Calculate the process average number nonconforming ($n\bar{p}$):

$$n\bar{p} = \frac{d_1 + d_2 + \ldots + d_k}{k}$$

where d_1, d_2, ... are the number nonconforming in each of the *k* subgroups (*Figure 9.9*).

Calculate the UCL, LCL:

$$\text{UCL}_{np} = n\overline{p} + 3\sqrt{n\overline{p}\,(1 - \overline{p})}$$

$$\text{LCL}_{np} = n\overline{p} - 3\sqrt{n\overline{p}\,(1 - \overline{p})}$$

where n = the subgroup sample size, and $\overline{p} = \dfrac{\sum np}{\sum n}$.

STEP 3: INTERPRET FOR PROCESS CONTROL

(See Section 9.2.3.)

STEP 4: INTERPRET FOR PROCESS CAPABILITY

(See Section 9.2.4. Exceptions are noted below.)

The process capability is $n\overline{p}$, the average number nonconforming in a fixed sample size n.

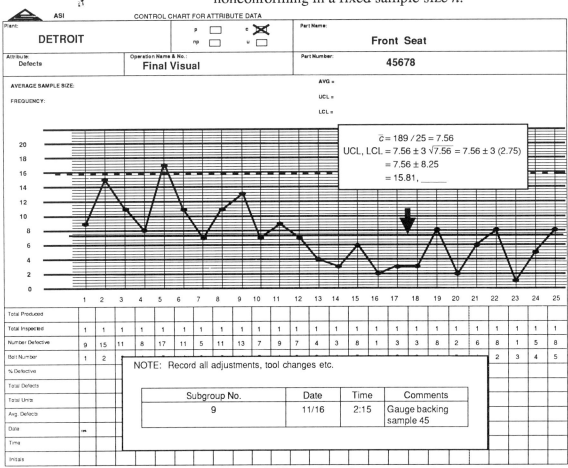

Figure 9.10 *c chart for number of nonconformities.*

9.4 THE *c* CHART FOR NUMBER OF NONCONFORMITIES

The *c* chart measures the number of nonconformities (discrepancies or so-called defects) in a sample lot (as opposed to the number of units found nonconforming, as plotted on an *np* chart). **The *c* chart requires a constant sample size or amount of material inspected.** It is applied in two major types of inspection situations:

1. Where the nonconformities occur through a more or less continuous flow of product (such as flaws in a bolt of vinyl, bubbles in glass, or spots of thin insulation on wire), and where the average rate of nonconformities can be expressed as nonconformities per unit (for example, in flaws per 100 square meters of vinyl).

2. Where there are nonconformities from many different potential units, such as the writeups at a departmental repair station, or where each individual vehicle or component could have one or more of a wide variety of potential nonconformities.

SAMPLING DIFFERENCES: THE *p* CHART AND THE *c* CHART

A major difference between the *p* chart and the *c* chart lies in the sample size. Whereas the *p* chart requires very large sample sizes to determine control, the *c* chart needs only a sample size large enough to be a source of finding at least one nonconformity each time the process is sampled. With a very complex product, a sample of one may suffice.

The following are the steps in construction and application of a *c* chart, which are similar to the basic approach described previously for *p* charts; exceptions are noted below.

STEP 1: GATHER THE DATA

(See Section 9.2.1. Exceptions are noted below.)

The inspection sample sizes (for example, number of units, area of fabric, or length of wire) need to be equal so that the plotted values of c will reflect changes in quality performance (likelihood of a nonconformity occurring) rather than changes in exposure (the sample size: n). Record the sample size on the form.

Record and plot the number of nonconformities in each subgroup (c).

STEP 2: CALCULATE THE CONTROL LIMITS

(See Section 9.2.2. Exceptions are noted below.)

Calculate the process average number of nonconformities ($\bar{c}$):

$$\bar{c} = \frac{c_1 + c_2 + \ldots + c_k}{k}$$

where c_1, c_2...are the number of nonconformities in each of the k subgroups.

Calculate the control limits (UCL$_c$ and LCL$_c$)

$$\mathrm{UCL_c} = \bar{c} + 3\sqrt{\bar{c}}$$

$$\mathrm{LCL_c} = \bar{c} - 3\sqrt{\bar{c}}$$

(See *Figure 9.10.*)

STEP 3: INTERPRET FOR PROCESS CONTROL

(See Section 9.2.3.)

STEP 4: INTERPRET FOR PROCESS CAPABILITY

(See Section 9.2.4. Exceptions are noted below.)

The process capability is $\bar{c}$, the average number of nonconformities in a sample of fixed size n.

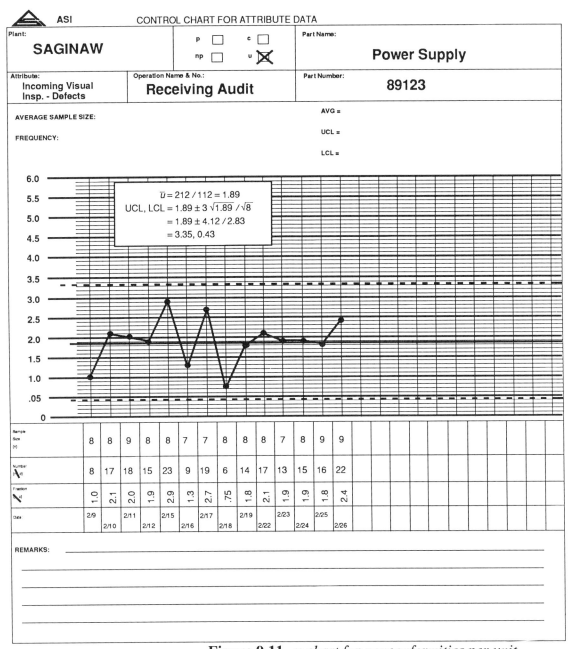

Figure 9.11 *u chart for nonconformities per unit.*

9.5 THE *u* CHART FOR NONCONFORMITIES PER UNIT

The *u* chart measures the number of nonconformities (discrepancies or so-called defects) per inspection reporting unit in subgroups **that can have varying sizes (or amounts of material inspected)**. It is similar to the *c* chart except that the number of nonconformities is expressed on a per-unit basis. Both *u* and *c* charts are appropriate for the same basic data situations. However, the *u* chart may be used if the sample includes more than one unit (to make the reporting more meaningful), and it must be used if the sample size can vary from period to period. The details of instructions for the *u* chart are similar to those for the *p* chart; exceptions are noted below.

STEP 1: GATHER THE DATA

(See Section 9.2.1. Exceptions are noted below.)

Samples do not need to be constant from subgroup to subgroup, although maintaining them within 25% above or below the average simplifies the calculation of common control limits.

Record and plot the nonconformities per unit in each subgroup (*u*):

$$u = \frac{c}{n}$$

where *c* is the number of nonconformities found, and *n* is the sample size (number of inspection reporting units) of the subgroup; *c* and *n* should also be recorded on the form (*Figure 9.11*).

NOTE: The sample size for each subgroup, *n*, is expressed in terms of inspection reporting units. Sometimes the reporting unit is a single production unit, such as an engine. Often, however, the inspection reporting unit is other than one production unit. For instance, in reports showing nonconformities per 100 units, the reporting unit is 100 production units, and *n* shows how many hundreds were inspected.

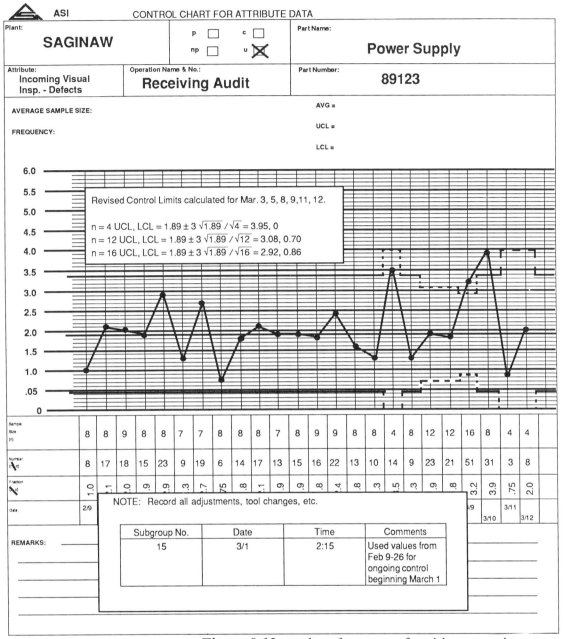

Figure 9.12 *u chart for nonconformities per unit.*

STEP 2: CALCULATE THE CONTROL LIMITS

(See Section 9.2.2. Exceptions are noted below.)

Calculate the process average nonconformities per unit $(\bar{u})$:

$$\bar{u} = \frac{c_1 + c_2 + \ldots + c_k}{n_1 + n_2 + \ldots + n_k}$$

where c_1, c_2, ...and n_1, n_2, ...are the number of nonconformities and sample size of each of the k subgroups.

Calculate the control limits (UCL_u and LCL_u)

$$UCL_u = \bar{u} + 3\sqrt{\bar{u}/\bar{n}}$$

$$LCL_u = \bar{u} - 3\sqrt{\bar{u}/\bar{n}}$$

where $\bar{n}$ is the average sample size.

NOTE: If any individual subgroup sample size is more than 25% above or below the average sample size, recalculate the precise control limits as follows:

$$UCL_u, LCL_u = \bar{u} \pm 3\sqrt{\bar{u}/n}$$

where $\bar{u}$ is the process average and n is the sample size (number of inspection reporting units) of a particular subgroup. Change the limits on the chart and use the basis for identifying special causes (*Figure 9.12*).

Note that any use of variable control limits is cumbersome and potentially confusing. It is **much better wherever possible to avoid this situation using constant subgroup sample sizes.**

STEP 3: INTERPRET FOR PROCESS CONTROL

(See Section 9.2.3.)

STEP 4: INTERPRET FOR PROCESS CAPABILITY

(See Section 9.2.4. Exceptions are noted below.)

The process capability is $\bar{u}$, the average number of nonconformities per reporting unit.

9.6 THE *d* CHART FOR DEMERITS PER UNIT

The *d* chart assigns weights or demerits per unit. The chart is useful because other attributes charts consider all defect types equally important, while the real world views things differently. For instance, uniform car audits see brake problems as a more critical factor than paint defects. Consequently, inspection plans have been assigning demerits per unit for years. Some of the classifications used to assign relative importance to various characteristics have included critical, major, and minor. Other more detailed classifications have been cited in the *Bell System Technical Journal*. They include:

Class A defects. These defects are very serious. They are weighted with 100 demerits and will render a unit totally unfit for service, or will cause operating failure in service that cannot be readily corrected on the job.

Class B defects. These defects are serious and are weighted with 50 demerits. Class B defects will probably cause Class A operating failure in service, will most likely cause trouble of a nature less serious than Class A operating failure, and will surely cause increased maintenance or decreased life.

Class C defects. These defects are moderately serious and are weighted with ten demerits. They will possibly cause operating failure in service or may cause trouble less serious than an operating failure, are likely to cause increased maintenance or decreased life, and may cause major defects of appearance, finish, or workmanship.

Class D defects. These defects are not serious and are weighted with one demerit. They will not cause operating failure in service, and may cause minor defects of appearance, finish, or workmanship.

NOTE: A series of weights may be assigned by consensus for any given product. Weights may be applied separately by defect and by area of occurrence on the product.

STEP 1: $D_1 = (5)\,(3) + (1)\,(7) + (2)\,(5) + (10)\,(6)$
$= 15 + 7 + 10 + 60 = 92$

STEP 2: $\overline{D} = \dfrac{92 + 94 + 51 + \ldots + 99}{20} = 94.9$

STEP 3:

$$UCL_D = 94.9 + 3\sqrt{(5)^2\,(4.85) + (1)^2\,(7.45) + (2)^2\,(7.1) + (10)^2\,(4.9)} = 171.2$$

$$LCL_D = 94.9 - 3\sqrt{(5)^2\,(4.85) + (1)^2\,(7.45) + (2)^2\,(7.1) + (10)^2\,(4.9)} = 18.6$$

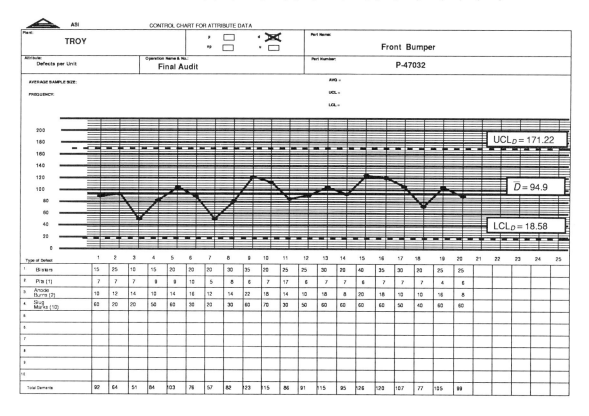

Figure 9.13 *d chart for weighted number of defects per unit (front bumper defects).*
SOURCE: Charbonneau, Harvy C., and Webster, Gordon L., Industrial Quality Control, Prentice-Hall, Inc., Englewood Cliffs, N.J., 1978.

CONSTRUCTING THE *d* CHART

The *d* chart is a precise way of determining control when weighted demerits are used. As an example, it may base the weights on rework costs while providing a control chart that is easy to interpret. Fluctuation on the chart should be stable or show a downward trend. An upward trend indicates increasing product cost while downward trends may reflect an uneconomic situation. For example, a reduction in cost at final inspection could be attributed to excessive rework cost at some point earlier in the system.

When constructing the *d* chart, use the steps listed below.

NOTE: D, the plotted statistic, is the total demerits per inspection unit. The center line $(\overline{D})$ is the average number of demerits per unit.

Step 1: Calculate D

To calculate D multiply the individual defect quantity, c_1, by its respective weight, w_1, and take the sum for each inspection unit. Use the following formula:

$$D = w_1 c_1 + w_2 c_2 + \ldots + w_d c_d$$

where c_1 is the number of Type I defects, c_2 is the number of Type II defects, etc., w_1 is the weight for Type I defects, w_2 is the weight for Type II defects, etc.

Step 2: Calculate $\overline{D}$

When calculating $\overline{D}$, use the following formula:

$$\overline{D} = \frac{\sum D}{k}$$

where k is the number of inspection units.

Step 3: Calculate The Control Limits

When calculating the control limits, use the following formula:

$$UCL_D = \overline{D} + 3\sigma_D$$

$$LCL_D = \overline{D} - 3\sigma_D$$

Where:

$$\sigma_D = \sqrt{w_1^2 \overline{c_1} + w_1^2 \overline{c_2} + \ldots + w_d^2 \overline{c_d}}$$

and $\overline{c_1}$ is the sum of Type I defects divided by the number of inspection units, $\overline{c_2}$ the sum of the Type II defects divided by the number of inspection units, etc. So:

$$\overline{c_i} = \frac{\sum c_i}{k} \quad \text{or}$$

$$\overline{c_1} = \frac{\sum c_1}{k}, \overline{c_2} = \frac{\sum c_2}{k}, \text{etc.}$$

Interpretation for process control and assessment of process capability are similar to procedures for the *u* chart.

MEASUREMENT SYSTEM VARIATION

CONTENTS

KEY CONCEPTS

In this chapter you will learn about the following key items and concepts:

Measurement system
Measurement error
Gage accuracy
Gage repeatability
Gage reproducibility
Gage stability
Gage linearity
Variable gage study (short method)
Variable gage study (long method)

MEASUREMENT SYSTEM VARIATION

10.1 MEASUREMENT SYSTEM VARIATION

It is frequently assumed that measurements taken in studies and experiments are exact. However, there is variation in all measurement systems, and this affects the individual measurements and the decisions based on that data.

A measurement system is not simply a measuring device. It includes the following elements:

• The instrument or measuring device

• The human operator

• The product itself.

These factors all contribute to measurement variation and measurement error. Measuring equipment is subject to variation. Bias exists when equipment is not calibrated (accuracy) or when different persons use the equipment (reproducibility). Variation is caused by wear, deterioration, or environmental conditions (stability). Random variation can be introduced by friction in meters or gages (repeatability).

Companies try to make sure that measurements are dependable by implementing instrument calibration programs. Regular calibration of instruments is necessary, but it only addresses one source of measurement error—accuracy. **The objective of a measurement system study is to determine the type and amount of measurement error**. It is often more practical to recognize repeatability and calibration bias and establish limits for them, than to provide extremely accurate gages with very high repeatability.

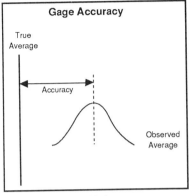

Figure 10.1a

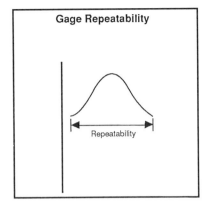

Figure 10.1b

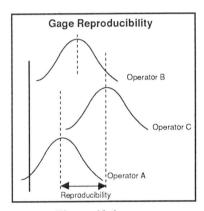

Figure 10.1c

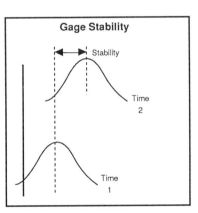

Figure 10.1d

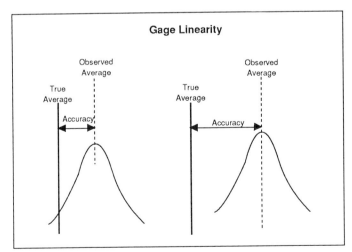

Figure 10.1e

10.2 DEFINITIONS

The following definitions and diagrams help illustrate the types of error associated with a measurement system:

- **Gage accuracy (a).** Gage accuracy is the difference between the observed average of measurements and the true average. Establishing the true average is best determined by measuring with the most accurate measuring equipment available.

- **Gage repeatability(b).** Gage repeatability is the variation in measurements obtained when one operator uses the same gage for measuring the identical characteristics of the same parts.

- **Gage reproducibility (c).** Gage reproducibility is the variation in the average of measurements made by different operators using the same gage and parts.

- **Gage stability (d).** Gage stability refers to the difference in the average of at least two sets of measurements obtained with the same gage on the same parts taken at different times.

- **Gage linearity (e).** Gage linearity is the difference in the accuracy values through the expected operating range.

10.3 PREPARING FOR A MEASUREMENT SYSTEM STUDY

The first step in preparing for a measurement system study is establishing the purpose of the study and determining the type of information needed to satisfy the purpose. The following questions should be answered:

- What approach should be used?

- How many operators are to be involved?

- How many sample parts are to be tested?

- What number of repeat readings will be needed?

Once that information is outlined, the next step is to choose the operators and select the sample parts to be used for the study, etc.

NOTE: Measurements for the study should be taken in random order to prevent bias.

Parts	Operator A	Operator B	Range (A, B)
1	4	2	2
2	3	4	1
3	6	7	1
4	5	7	2
5	9	8	1
6	8	7	1
7	4	6	2
8	5	6	1
9	3	4	1
10	4	2	2
		Sum of Ranges	14

Figure 10.2 *Variable Gage Study (short method).*

$$\text{Average Range } (\bar{R}) = \frac{\sum R}{10} = \frac{14}{10} = 1.4$$

$$\text{Gage Error (GRR)} = 4.44\,(\bar{R}) = 4.44\,(1.4) = 6.2$$

Table 10.1 *Variable gage study (short method)—table of $d_2 *$ values.*

Number of Parts	Number of Operators			
	2	**3**	**4**	**5**
1	1.41	1.91	2.24	2.48
2	1.28	1.81	2.15	2.40
3	1.23	1.77	2.12	2.38
4	1.21	1.75	2.11	2.37
5	1.19	1.74	2.10	2.36
6	1.18	1.73	2.09	2.35
7	1.17	1.73	2.09	2.35
8	1.17	1.72	2.08	2.35
9	1.16	1.72	2.08	2.34
10	1.16	1.72	2.08	2.34

10.4 VARIABLE GAGE STUDY (SHORT METHOD)

The short-method variable gage study of gage repeatability and reproducibility (GRR) provides a quick and meaningful way of determining the acceptability of gage variation.

Only two operators are needed, and each operator measures the same set of ten parts. Each part is measured only once by each person.

In the short method, gage repeatability and reproducibility cannot be isolated. The results reflect a combination of both types of gage error.

CONDUCTING THE STUDY

As mentioned, only two operators and ten parts are used in the study. Parts are selected at random and should have different values. Each operator gages the ten parts just once. The results should be recorded on a form similar to the one shown in *Figure 10.2*.

The difference between measurements of operator A and B is calculated for each part tested and the result is entered in the column labeled RANGE (A, B). Notice that only positive numbers are entered in this column as it is the absolute difference that matters, not the sign. The **average range** (indicated by the symbol $\bar{R}$) is calculated next. It is merely the total of all ranges divided by the number of parts. In this case the sum of the ranges is 14 and there are ten parts being measured. As one can see by the formula in *Figure 10.1*, the result is $\bar{R} = 1.4$.

Gage error is calculated by multiplying the average range (1.4 in this example) by a constant, 4.44. The value is derived from the ratio $5.15/d_2^*$ where the value 5.15 is a given constant and d_2^* is determined from *Table 10.1*. As can be seen from the example, $d_2^* = 1.16$, which is the intersection of the row representing ten parts and the column representing two operators: as calculated in *Table 10.1*.

$$GRR = \frac{5.15\,(\bar{R})}{1.16} = 4.44\,(\bar{R})$$

The result is GRR = 6.2, which represents the combined gage error. To convert this number to a percentage of tolerance, divide by the tolerance and multiply by 100.

Example:

If the tolerance is 20 for the study above, then:

$$GRR \text{ as a \% of tolerance} = \frac{6.2 \times 100}{20} = 31.0\%$$

Once the process performance is known, one may wish to compare the GRR to performance, rather than the tolerance.

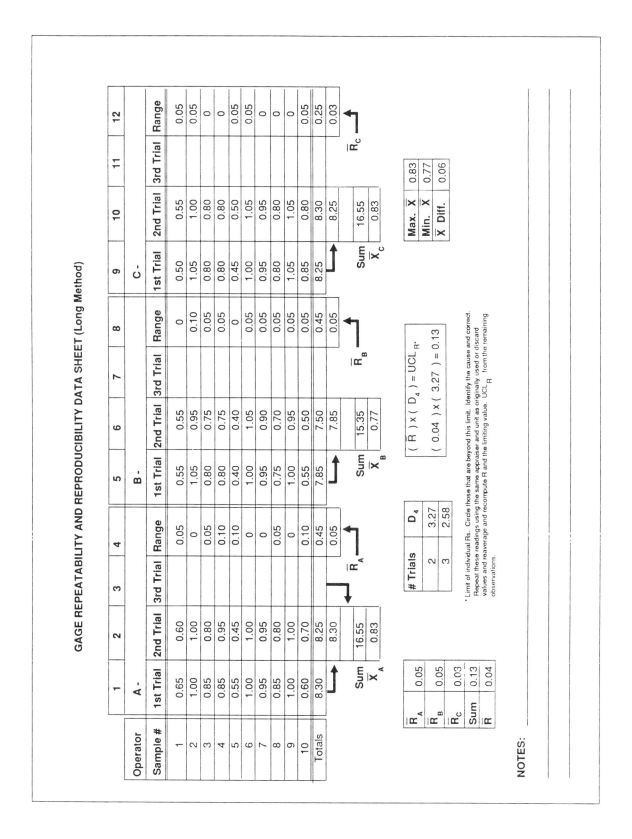

Figure 10.3 *Gage repeatability and reproducibility data sheet (long method).*

10.5 VARIABLE GAGE STUDY (LONG METHOD)

The long-method variable gage study can determine errors of repeatability and reproducibility separately. Study results can also provide information concerning the causes of gage error.

For example, if lack of reproducibility is large compared to repeatability, then possible causes could be:

- The operator is not properly trained in how to use and read the gage instrument.

- Calibrations on the gage dial are not clear.

If lack of repeatability is large compared to reproducibility, the reasons may be:

- The gage instrument needs maintenance.

- The gage should be redesigned to be more rigid.

- The clamping or location gaging needs to be improved.

CONDUCTING THE STUDY

Even though the number of operators, the number of trials, and the number of parts may vary, one should conduct the study according to the following steps:

1. Select operators A, B, and C, and number the parts one through ten so that the numbers are not visible to the operators.

2. Calibrate the gage.

3. Let operator A measure ten parts in a random order and enter the results in Column 1.

4. Repeat step 3 with operators B and C.

5. Repeat the cycle, with the ten parts measured in another random order, for the number of trials required.

6. Steps 3 through 5 may be modified for large parts, unavailability of parts, or when operators are on different shifts.

7. Using the form shown in *Figures 10.3* and *10.4* enter the observations on one side and calculate GRR using the formulas shown on the reverse side.

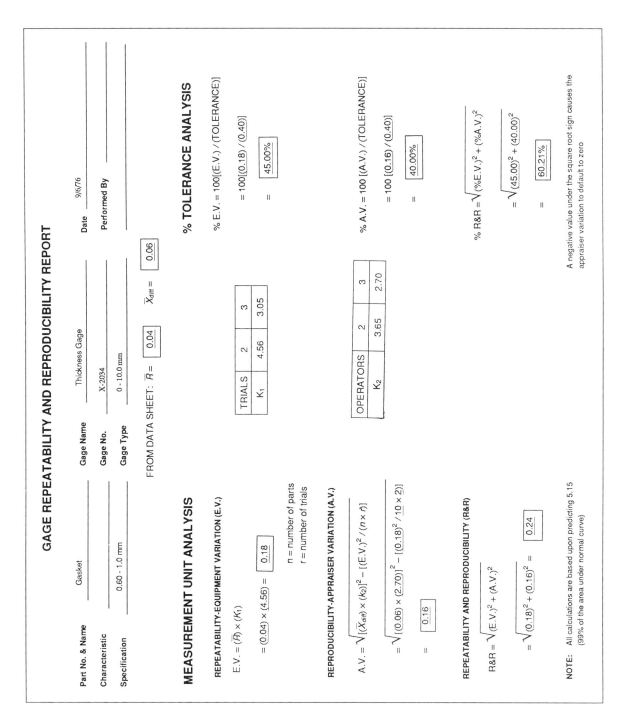

Figure 10.4 *Gage repeatability and reproducibility report.*

10.6 GAGE ACCURACY

Lack of gage accuracy generally is not as predominant a gage error as repeatability and reproducibility. Nevertheless, it should be identified. To determine gage accuracy, it is necessary to obtain the true measurement of the sample parts. This can be done with tool room or layout inspection equipment. A true average is derived from these readings to be compared later with the operators' observed averages (identified as $\bar{X}_A$, $\bar{X}_B$, $\bar{X}_C$) from the GRR study.

If it is not possible to measure all of the sample parts in this manner, the following alternative method can be used.

Measure one of the sample parts precisely on tool room or layout inspection equipment. Have one operator measure the same part a minimum of ten times, using the gage being evaluated and average the results.

The difference between the true measurement and the observed averages represents gage accuracy. To convert accuracy to a percentage of tolerance, multiply by 100 and divide by the tolerance.

If gage accuracy is relatively large, look for these possible causes:

- Error in the master

- Worn gage

- Gage made to the wrong dimension

- Gage is measuring the wrong characteristic

- Gage not calibrated properly

- Gage being used improperly by operator.

10.7 GAGE STABILITY

Gage stability should be computed, although it typically is not as large a problem as repeatability and reproducibility. How gage stability is determined depends upon how often the gage is used between normal calibrations. The need for calibration results from factors such as these:

- Time—long idle periods

- Number of measurements taken

- Air pressure change

- Warm-up.

Given that any of these factors are known, the need to calibrate the equipment can be established to help minimize gage error due to lack of stability.

If a gage is used intermittently, then its stability may be determined at the same time as the GRR study is made. The gage must be calibrated before and after each trial to determine the amount of calibration change.

This difference is the gage stability **for that trial only**. To calibrate overall gage stability, the calibration change for each trial must be added up and divided by the number of trials:

$$\text{gage stability} = \frac{\text{sum of calibration changes}}{\text{number of trials}}$$

If a gage is normally used for relatively long periods of time without calibration (such as start of a shift or after lunch), the stability can be determined without recalibrating for each trial. One would simply conduct another GRR study just prior to the time calibration is due. Gage stability would be the positive difference between the grand averages calculated using all of the measurements in the first and second studies.

gage stability = range of (grand average study one - grand average study two)

To convert gage stability to a percentage of tolerance, multiply by 100 and divide by the tolerance. If gage stability error is relatively large, look for these possible causes:

- Gage not being calibrated as frequently as needed.

- Air pressure regulator or filter may be needed for air gaging.

- Warm-up may be required for electronic gages.

10.8 GAGE LINEARITY

Gage linearity can be determined by conducting gage accuracy studies through the expected operating range. A minimum of two accuracy studies should be conducted, one at each end of the operating range.

Gage linearity can be computed by subtracting the smaller accuracy value from the larger.

gage linearity = larger accuracy value - smallest accuracy value

If gage linearity error is relatively large, look for these possible causes:

- The gage may not be calibrated properly at both lower and upper end of the operating range.

- There may be an error in the minimum or maximum master.

- The gage may be worn.

- The internal gage design characteristics may require reviewing 1.

10.9 GENERAL GUIDELINES

Results of gage studies should be carefully evaluated to determine if the gage is acceptable for its intended application. Whether or not a measurement system is satisfactory depends largely upon the percentage of parts tolerance that is reflected by gage system error—a combination of gage accuracy, repeatability, reproducibility, stability, and linearity. Generally, the criteria for acceptance of gage repeatability and reproducibility are:

- Under 10% error—acceptable

- 10 to 30% error—may be acceptable based upon importance of the application, gage cost, cost of repairs, etc.

- Over 30%—generally not acceptable. Make every effort to identify the problem and get it corrected.

When dealing with gages having more than 30% error, consult the applicable customer for resolution.

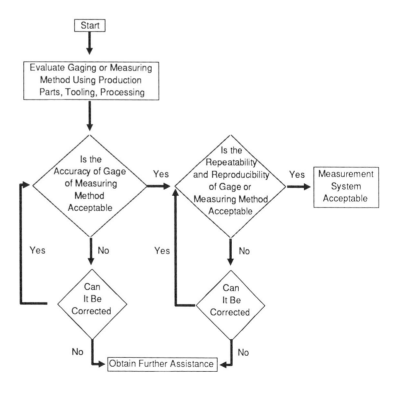

Figure 10.5 *Measurement system evaluation flow chart.*

TOOLS FOR PROBLEM SOLVING

CONTENTS

KEY CONCEPTS

In this chapter you will learn about the following key items and concepts:

PDCA cycle
Pareto analysis
Process flowchart
Cost of quality report
Cause-and-effect diagram (fishbone)
Scatter diagram
Design of experiments
Taguchi Methods
Regression analysis

TOOLS FOR PROBLEM SOLVING

11.1 INTRODUCTION

Control charts are useful and powerful tools that enable us to determine if and when a problem exists. But we must first decide where to apply control charts—where to begin and where to concentrate our improvement efforts. The technical solution to a problem, which has been discovered using the control chart, is also accomplished by using other problem-solving tools (*Figure 11.1*).

In examining our processes we should ask the following questions:

- Where do I begin to improve quality?

- Can I collect accurate, reliable, timely data?

- Are there problems in the process?

- What are those problems and how do I eliminate them?

This section reviews some of the tools that can be applied to the identification, definition, and prioritization of problems in production processes, as well as to the identification and elimination of causes.

The tools for collecting data (check lists and techniques for measurement-system evaluation) are discussed in Chapters 4 and 10. The use of histograms is covered in Chapter 3 and control charts are discussed in Chapters 5 through 9.

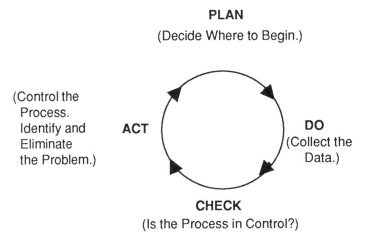

PLAN
(Decide Where to Begin.)

(Control the
Process.
Identify and   ACT   DO
Eliminate   (Collect the
the Problem.)   Data.)

CHECK
(Is the Process in Control?)

ACTIVITY	TOOLS
Deciding where to begin	- Pareto analysis - Flow diagrams - Cost of quality report
Collecting the data	- Check lists - Measurement system evaluation
Deciding whether a process is in control (Are there problems? Is the process capable?)	- Histograms - Control charts
Identifying and defining problems	- Cause-and-effect diagram - Scatter diagrams

Figure 11.1 *The PDCA Cycle*

11.2 TOOLS FOR DECIDING WHERE TO BEGIN

Where should we begin to apply control charts? It is neither wise nor practical to apply them to every process in a plant. We need to know where to concentrate our process-improvement program in order to have the greatest impact. There are three tools that can help us prioritize and direct our efforts and to decide where and how to begin. These are Pareto analysis, flow diagrams, and the cost of quality report.

PARETO ANALYSIS

Each problem usually consists of so many smaller problems that it is difficult to know where to begin solving them. The severity of a series of problems should be quantified and placed in the relative order of importance. When this is done and presented graphically in the form of a Pareto diagram, we can begin to prioritize our problem-solving effort. This will help to decide where to begin.

The Pareto principle states that a relatively few number of causes usually account for a disproportionately large amount of the total effect. It has been called the "80/20 rule" because often 20% of the causes account for 80% of the problem. For example, employers may observe that 80% of their absenteeism is caused by fewer than 20% of their employees. These small numbers of causes are called the "vital few", and the large number of items that account for a small part of the problem are called the "trivial many". Our quality improvement efforts are best spent concentrating on the vital few.

Data on defectives from a process is shown in *Table 11.1a*. The defectives have been divided into five categories: caulking, fitting, connection, improper torque, and gapping. Data from the table is then made into a bar graph (*Figure 11.2*). The left vertical axis shows the number of defectives for each defective item, and the right vertical axis shows the percent contribution for each defective item. The horizontal axis lists the defective items, starting with the most frequent item on the left to the least frequent item on the extreme right. The cumulative total of the number of defectives is shown by the line graph.

According to this graph, we should concentrate on caulking first, connecting second, etc. Bar graphs allow us to see which defects are more important more easily than a table of numbers does, and are thus extremely useful in factory quality control. In the above example, a secondary Pareto diagram could be made to identify and prioritize the major sources of the caulking problem, which may need to be further subdivided.

Table 11.1a *Process defective data.*

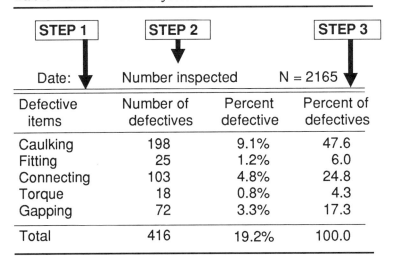

Defective items	Number of defectives	Percent defective	Percent of defectives
Caulking	198	9.1%	47.6
Fitting	25	1.2%	6.0
Connecting	103	4.8%	24.8
Torque	18	0.8%	4.3
Gapping	72	3.3%	17.3
Total	416	19.2%	100.0

Table 11.1b *Items ranked in descending order.*

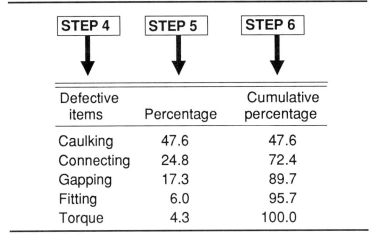

Defective items	Percentage	Cumulative percentage
Caulking	47.6	47.6
Connecting	24.8	72.4
Gapping	17.3	89.7
Fitting	6.0	95.7
Torque	4.3	100.0

CONSTRUCTING A PARETO DIAGRAM

STEP 1: Define the category to be analyzed. The category might be number of defects by machine, scrap by part number, rework by department, customer complaints, etc.

STEP 2: Select the measurement unit. This can include number of defects, weight of scrap, etc. The most useful unit is usually dollars and the unit used should be proportional to dollars.

STEP 3: List the items to be investigated and determine the value assigned to each.

STEP 4: Rank the items in descending order.

STEP 5: Find the total effect (e.g., total number of defectives) and calculate the percentage of each item.

STEP 6: Calculate the cumulative percentage.

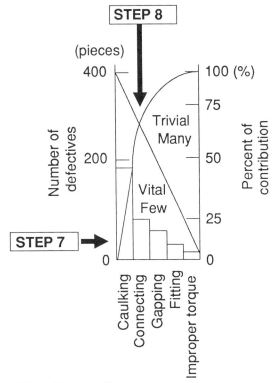

Figure 11.2 *Pareto diagram.*

STEP 7: Construct a bar graph of the percentages and a line graph for the cumulative percentages.

STEP 8: Draw a diagonal line from the 100% point on the left vertical axis to the last point on the horizontal axis. The rough dividing line between the vital few and the trivial many will be the point where this line crosses the cumulative percentage curve. The higher the percentage at the intersection, **the greater the benefits of concentrating on the vital few (the Pareto effect).**

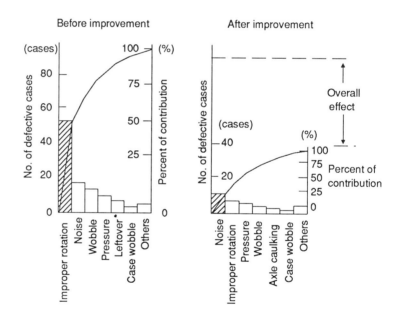

Figure 11.3 *Pareto diagrams for process defects —before and after improvement.*

USING A PARETO DIAGRAM

A Pareto diagram is useful for obtaining the cooperation of all concerned with a problem because one look tells everyone what the major problem is. Experience has shown that it is easier to reduce the problem reflected by a tall bar by half than to reduce a short bar to zero. Pareto diagrams can be applied to a wide range of problems: efficiency, conservation of materials, energy saving costs, safety, and so on. They can also be used to confirm the impact of improvement: If effective measures have been taken, the order of items on the horizontal axis will usually shift (*Figure 11.3*).

As with any tool, care must be taken in applying Pareto analysis and pitfalls must be avoided. Data for a Pareto chart can be classified by problem type (e.g., defects) or by cause (materials, operators, etc.). Problems can be detected through a problem Pareto and corrective action implemented via a cause Pareto.

1. If an initial Pareto analysis fails to give useful insight, break the data into different cause categories and repeat the analysis.

    For example, Pareto charts analyzing "downtime by machine" in a shop may show all the potential causes (presses) to be equal in downtime (i.e., no visible Pareto effect). However, a Pareto chart analyzing "downtime by reason" (e.g., maintenance, die repair, die change, tool repair, operator adjustment, etc.) may well show a clear Pareto effect, and a basis for focusing efforts in reducing downtime.

2. With data gathered over a short period of time, there is danger of drawing unwarranted conclusions.

    With a poorly controlled process the cause system may be unstable. The vital few problems may change from week to week. Short time periods may not be representative.

3. With data gathered over long periods, examine the data for stratification or changes in the vital few over time.

Long time periods may include changes. Problems may differ during different periods in a process (e.g., start up, the first two weeks, full-scale production). Rather than relying on one Pareto analysis, separate Pareto charts may reveal that defect types important during the start up period may be resolved by the second week of production.

4. With multiple Pareto charts comparing different suppliers, time periods, processes, etc., use a common basis for comparison.

Comparison between charts is made easier using a common scale against a production baseline such as defects per 1000 units, scrap cost per hundred parts, etc. Number of items inspected and quantity defective should always be included on the chart.

**PHOTO-RECEPTOR MANUFACTURING
FLOW DIAGRAM**

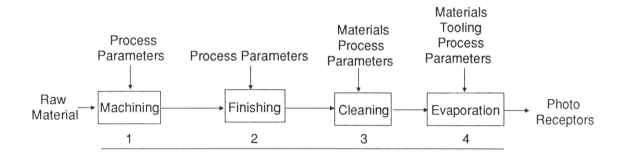

FLOW CHART

Single Line

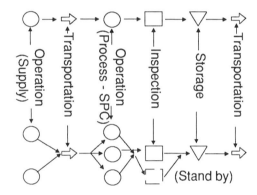

Multiple source/Multiple process

Figure 11.4 *Flowchart examples.*

PROCESS FLOWCHART

A process flowchart is a sketch or schematic drawing that depicts the steps or activities in a manufacturing process, in the order they occur (*Figure 11.4*). In developing a process flowchart:

*   Important operations and parameters should be included.

*   The process should be identified as either a single or multiple operation.

*   Material sources should be indicated.

The flowchart can be used to help identify points where control activity needs to be initiated. One should be developed at the start of every process control effort.

COST OF QUALITY REPORT

The cost of quality report is an effective tool for assessing real-time costs of actual and potential deviations from quality standards. It can be used to:

- Quantify the cost of nonconformities

- Identify and prioritize areas in need of improvement

- Justify expenditure for improvement (in terms of return on investment)

- Identify and measure the results of improvement efforts.

To be effective, quality costs must include both off-line activities, such as product and process engineering, and on-line activities, such as production. The report should be used to estimate progress resulting from many areas. Attention should be given to upstream activity. Dollars spent on prevention and continuous improvement tend to minimize quality costs in the long run.

```
┌─────────────────────────────────────────────────────┐
│                  COSTS OF CONTROL                     │
│                                                       │
│  PREVENTION                    APPRAISAL              │
│                                                       │
│  Quality planning              Inspection             │
│                                                       │
│  Process control               Testing                │
│                                                       │
│  Quality training              Quality audits          │
│                                                       │
│  Product design                Purchased part          │
│  verification                   inspections            │
│                                                       │
│           COSTS OF FAILURE TO CONTROL                 │
│                                                       │
│  INTERNAL FAILURE              EXTERNAL FAILURE        │
│                                                       │
│  Scrap                         Warranty claims         │
│                                                       │
│  Rework                        Post-warranty complaints│
│                                                       │
│  Repair                        Product recall          │
│                                                       │
│  Factory contact engineering   Product liability       │
│                                                       │
└─────────────────────────────────────────────────────┘
```

Figure 11.5 *Cost of control.*

How To Construct a Cost of Quality Report

1. Choose activity accounts appropriate for a given operation. Examples could include inspection and customer relations for a quality control department report, and rework and setup for a processor's report.

2. Establish cost of quality accounts for the four quality/cost categories: appraisal, prevention, internal and external failure.

3. Establish rules regarding the use and meaning of each account.

4. Divide the report into two sections. Put actions or assets (e.g., prevention) on the left. Put results or liabilities (i.e., failures) on the right.

5. Place the costs of each activity into the different cost of quality accounts according to the reason for the activity.

6. Evaluate the various costs in order to define the activities needed for a more efficient and effective quality improvement program.

11.3 TOOLS FOR IDENTIFYING AND DEFINING PROBLEMS

Solving a problem typically involves four steps:

1. Problem identification and definition

2. Identification of causes

3. Correcting the problem (eliminating the causes)

4. Sustaining the correction (controlling the process).

Tools that can be applied to the identification and definition of problems include cause-and-effect diagrams and scatter diagrams.

CAUSE-AND-EFFECT DIAGRAMS

When a problem has been defined, the next step is to determine the possible causes. Typical causes will include the following process elements:

- Material

- Machine

- Method

- People

- Measurement

- Environment.

One of the most effective ways to study the relationship between a visible problem and its underlying causes is through the use of a cause-and-effect diagram. The cause-and-effect diagram (also referred to as a fishbone diagram or Ishikawa diagram) shows the relationship between a quality characteristic, the effect, and the causes of variation. It can assist us in understanding complex situations so that causes can be isolated and corrective action taken (*Figure 11.6*).

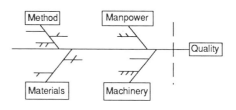

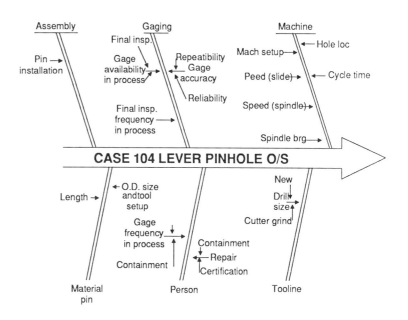

Figure 11.6 *Cause-and-effect diagram example.*

Brainstorming is an open, team discussion technique for listing potential causes. It stimulates and encourages the free and open exchange of ideas among team members.

In brainstorming, initially no idea is considered too outrageous. The more ideas presented, the better. Ideas presented can then be evaluated in terms of quality control objectives. Cause-and-effect diagrams enable the team to sort factors visually. Principal causes are listed and reduced to subcauses. This process continues until all conceivable contributing factors are listed. Causes are then analyzed in terms of their relationship to the effect to provide a direction for action.

Constructing a Cause-and-Effect Diagram

1. **Decide** on the quality characteristic to be analyzed.

2. **Represent** the process to be analyzed by a horizontal arrow pointing to a box with the characteristic or effect to be analyzed.

3. **Write major causes** in boxes, parallel to and of some distance from the main arrow. Each individual group will form a branch slanting toward the main arrow.

4. **Write minor causes** around the major causes. Minor causes are further subdivided until most of the causes are listed.

5. By consensus, select those causes that are identified as important sources of the effect.

Using a Completed Cause-and-Effect Diagram

1. **Compare** all the causes listed with the standards and methods of operation.

2. **Identify** the degree of influence of the various causes. This can be done using techniques of correlation analysis, design of experiments and analysis of variance.

3. **Implement** the solution and monitor the results.

4. Refer to the diagram as new problems arise.

5. Revise the diagram as improvements occur.

SCATTER DIAGRAMS

The scatter diagram is another useful diagnostic tool. It can be used to determine if a relationship between two variables exists and the nature of such a relationship. Numerous factors can influence the quality of a product. Preparing scatter diagrams is a first step in understanding the relationship between factors. In manufacturing, the ability to meet specifications can sometimes depend on controlling one of a pair of dependent variables to control the effect the variable has on a quality characteristic. Using scatter diagrams, one can determine the optimal level of one variable that will result in the desired effect.

When plotting paired data on a scatter diagram, the horizontal axis usually denotes the measurement values and the vertical axis, the process element values, such as temperature, pressure, current, or voltage (*Figure 11.7*). Data is obtained from the process (*Table 11.2*) and points are tabulated and plotted on a graph, which is then interpreted for levels of correlation (e.g., positive, negative, no correlation, or nonlinear correlation).

Table 11.2 *Process data for scatter diagram —severed length vs. conveyor speed.*

Severed length y	1	4	3	10	8	9	12	2	1	50
1050									I	1
1045							I			1
1040					I	I	II			4
1035				I		III	III			7
1030					III	III	III	II		11
1025		I	II	IIII	II	I	I			11
1020		I		III	II	I				7
1015		II		I			II			5
1010	I		I	I						3
1005										
	5.0	5.5	6.0	6.5	7.0	7.5	8.0	8.5	9.0	

Conveyor speed x

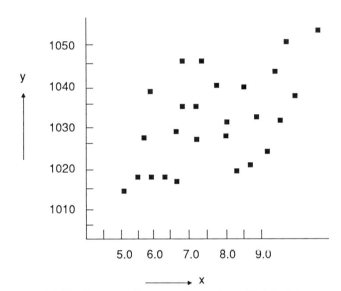

Figure 11.7 *Scatter diagram based on Table 11.2*

Some examples of scatter diagrams are shown in *Figure 11.8*. The relationships between factors are:

- **Positive correlation (a).** If an increase in *y* follows an increase in *x*, then if *x* is controlled, *y* will naturally be controlled. The correlation is strong.

- **Positive correlation may be present (b).** If *x* is increased, *y* will increase, but the relationship is not as strong as that in 1 (*Figure 11.8a*). The *y* variable may be dependent on some other variable as well.

- **No correlation (c).** There is no correlation between x and y.

- **Negative correlation may be present (d).** An increase in x will cause a tendency for a decrease in y.

- **Negative correlation (e).** An increase in x will cause a decrease in y. Therefore, x may be controlled instead of y.

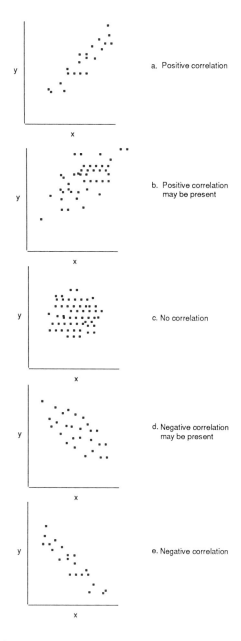

Figure 11.8 *Scatter diagrams—relationships between factors.*

11.4 OTHER TOOLS

Control charts aid in problem solution by relating the existence of special causes of variation to the time of manufacture. Pareto diagrams are useful in deciding which problem to study first in process improvement. Fishbone diagrams allow us to study cause-and-effect relationships in an orderly manner, and scatter diagrams allow us to determine whether any kind of relationship exists between two variables. Other more advanced statistical tools allow us to solve more involved problems and to optimize manufacturing processes. These methods include:

- Methods for hypotheses testing

- Statistical sampling techniques

- Regression analysis and multivariate analysis

- Design of experiments (classical methods and Taguchi Methods).

The fundamental purpose of a designed experiment is to determine a course of action based on firm information. The primary reason for using designed experiments is to obtain maximum information for a minimum expenditure. Methods for designing experiments allow information to be gathered on all factors simultaneously, leading to economies of cost, efficiency, and output over single-factor experiments. Design of experiments is a powerful methodology for optimizing processes and improving quality.

In the past, such experimentation has been expensive. Dr. Genichi Taguchi has developed an approach to product and process design that has renewed interest in industrial experimentation. He has solved many of the problems of applying classical experimentation to industrial situations by redefining assumptions about quality, cost, factors, effects, and objectives of design. Called Quality Engineering, Taguchi Methods emphasize engineering knowledge rather than advanced statistical techniques. They significantly reduce the time and cost of experimentation while maintaining the reliability of experimental results. Their objective is to develop designs that are "robust" (e.g., insensitive to the many causes of variation that a product encounters in production and in the hands of the customer).

The details of these tools are beyond the scope of this manual. If use of one or more of these methods is indicated, you should consult with a specialist in these techniques.

11.5 SPECIAL CONSIDERATIONS

There are a number of other special items that should be considered if we are to apply the techniques of process control effectively. They affect and can enhance our ability to interpret, manage, and take action on statistical data. Time prohibits discussing all of them; some are peculiar to specific application situations and some involve more advanced techniques. This section discusses three common and important considerations:

- The effect of small sample size

- The effect of tweaking

- Recording effective and useful information

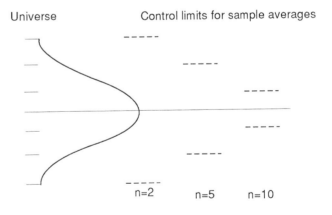

Figure 11.9 *Sample size and control limits.*

THE EFFECT OF SMALL SAMPLE SIZES

A Type I error suggests that a process has gone out of control when it has not. It sends the operator looking for trouble when none exists. Using a $\pm 3\sigma$ range to plot control limits, 3/10 of a percent of all data will be outside the limits (3 out of every 1000 plotted points) and indicate trouble when none exists. Practically, the possibility of a Type I error affecting a control chart is so small that these errors are usually ignored.

Type II errors are another matter. If a process goes out of control or shifts from its target, will the operator know this has happened the next time he samples the process? This is equivalent to asking: How good is the control chart in sensing lack of control?

Type II errors do not have a fixed percentage of occurrence. They are due to many factors, including the degree of change in the process, the amount of underlying common cause variation, and sample size. Selection of sample size is one of the most important factors affecting Type II errors.

Manufacturers tend to select the smallest possible sample size for economic reasons. However, small samples create problems while larger sample sizes minimize Type II errors.

Figure 11.9 illustrates the relationship between sample size and control limits. Consider the control limit position for a sample of five ($n=5$). If this distribution should drift off target to a point where the process average coincides with the upper control limit (a distance of little more than one standard deviation), the next time the operator samples the process there will be a 50-50 chance that the new sample average ($n=5$) will fall on either side of its process average. If it falls on the lower side, the plotted statistic will be within control limits. Otherwise it will be outside control limits and call for corrective action.

The operator has a 50-50 chance of knowing that the process has shifted a bit more than one σ at the next sampling. For some critical characteristics, this may permit the process to wander by more than a desirable amount. Here we will want to decrease the possibility of Type II errors. This can be done by increasing the sample size.

If we had elected to take samples of ten rather than five, we would have significantly lowered the probability of the process shifting without the operator's knowledge (*Figure 11.9*).

Experience has shown that a sample size of five usually proves to be a fairly good starting point for most Statistical Process Control applications for variable data. A sample of five represents a reasonably even balance between the need to economize with small samples and the need to minimize Type II error.

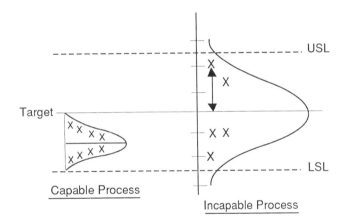

Figure 11.10 *The effect of tweaking in a capable and noncapable process.*

THE EFFECT OF TWEAKING

Tweaking is a term that describes the tendency of an operator to make adjustments to a process without using a statistical discipline, such as a control chart, often on the basis of a sample of one. The tendency is to overadjust a process—operators often continue adjustments or even adjust the process for no reason whatsoever. It is the author's opinion that tweaking is a practice that prevails throughout manufacturing.

Taking single-sample readings is dangerous, especially with marginal or incapable processes. When a single sample is taken without a statistical sorting mechanism, such as an $\overline{X}$ and R chart, the operator does not know where it lies within the distribution. With a normal distribution, the single sample will be within ± one standard deviation two-thirds of the time. Without a statistical signalling mechanism better than this, he will probably tweak the process unnecessarily.

Figure 11.10 compares a process that is highly capable but off target, with a process that is not capable (the ± 3σ boundaries exceed specification limits), but on target. If the operator takes a single sample from either process, he does not know from where within the distribution it has come.

With the highly capable process, it doesn't matter what piece the operator picks. Each piece is so close to the others in measurement value that making an adjustment on this basis won't harm the situation. With a well-optimized, highly capable process, alternative means of control (even with samples of one) can be used satisfactorily (*Figure 11.10*).

When there is a high degree of variability due to common causes in a process, this is not the case. If the operator takes a piece from position X in the distribution in the incapable process (*Figure 11.10*) and measures it, he may mistakenly adjust the process based on deviation from the target value. Here he will move the whole distribution to a new, lower level, causing a process that was on target to go off target. He will continue to do this if he makes adjustments based on samples of one—the process will continually go up and down, causing even more inconsistency. Tweaking makes things worse.

One of the most significant, short-term improvements that can be made in a system is to teach operators the effect of tweaking and provide them with a basis for making adjustments on a sounder, more scientific basis.

The best solution would be to provide control chart discipline, fix on a certain sample size, and teach operators to make adjustments when the chart shows lack of control; otherwise, to leave the process alone. If the situation is not critical enough for a full-fledged control chart, the operator may be given some control limit guidelines, and taught how to take a sample, calculate the average, determine if it is within predetermined boundaries, and make adjustments accordingly. This could be simplified even further, for set-up people as well as operators, by using the median of the sample and median control limits.

Processes often include equipment that automatically adjusts the process. If such equipment operates on the basis of a sample of one, it becomes the "tweaker." With highly capable processes, no harm is done. With incapable processes, it can make matters worse. The equipment might be reprogrammed to work with sample averages or a moving average.

If measurement error is large, it also affects tweaking —a substantial amount of measurement error can be the principal source of tweaking. Good product control is impossible for an operator if measurement error is a major source of variability.

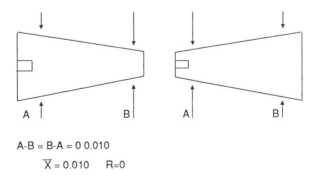

A-B = B-A = 0 0.010

$\overline{X}$ = 0.010   R=0

Figure 11.11a *Taper measurements recorded in absolute units.*

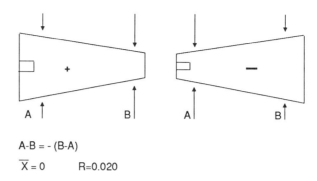

A-B = - (B-A)

$\overline{X} = 0$ R=0.020

Figure 11.11b *Taper measurements recorded considering direction.*

RECORDING EFFECTIVE DATA FOR CONTROL

A control chart should reflect information of immediate use to the operator. The sampling scheme, the way measurements are recorded, and the way data is displayed on this chart should allow the operator to easily use and react to information. The chart should be designed with the adjustments and changes available to the operator in mind.

For example, the way measurements are recorded can make a difference in their interpretation. An operator may be concerned with measuring taper in a shaft that is supposed to be perfectly cylindrical. He measures two shafts for taper (*Figure 11.11a*). If he records only the absolute difference between readings A and B (e.g., differences of 0.010 inch) the operator sees the differences as an average of 0.010 and a range of zero. If he considers direction, by assigning + and - values as in *Figure 11.11b*, he is given a different signal—an average of zero and range of 0.020. The target is zero, and deviations from the target are recorded. The control chart should be set up so that the operator's ability to achieve the quality objective is enhanced.

Every effort should be made to acknowledge the operator's needs in relation to the process and improvement objectives.

11.6 SUMMARY

PROCESS CONTROL AND CAPABILITY IMPROVEMENT

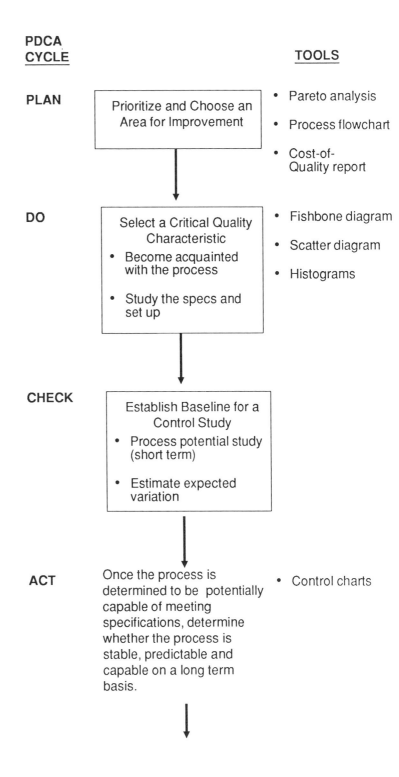

PDCA CYCLE | | **TOOLS**

PLAN — Prioritize and Choose an Area for Improvement
- Pareto analysis
- Process flowchart
- Cost-of-Quality report

DO — Select a Critical Quality Characteristic
- Become acquainted with the process
- Study the specs and set up

- Fishbone diagram
- Scatter diagram
- Histograms

CHECK — Establish Baseline for a Control Study
- Process potential study (short term)
- Estimate expected variation

ACT — Once the process is determined to be potentially capable of meeting specifications, determine whether the process is stable, predictable and capable on a long term basis.
- Control charts

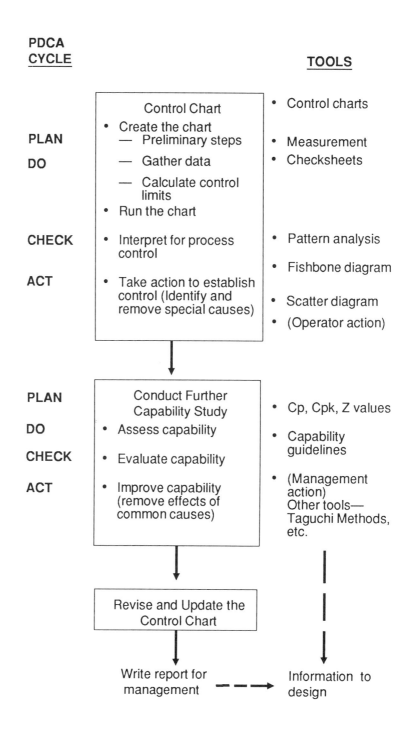

IMPLEMENTING THE SPC PROGRAM

CONTENTS

KEY CONCEPTS

In this chapter you will learn about the following key items and concepts:

Implementation
Management support
Employee involvement
In-house coordination
Quality assurance
Supplier involvement
Pilot program
Continuous improvement
Periodic review
Cross-functional teams
Single-source policy

IMPLEMENTING THE SPC PROGRAM

12.1 INTRODUCTION

There is no one best way to implement a Statistical Process Control (SPC) program. The approach taken will differ with the nature of the company and the product involved. It is possible to identify certain key issues that most companies confront. The following guidelines provide a suggested method for implementing the use of statistical techniques in a plant. Implementation involves the following steps:

- Management support

- Employee involvement

- In-house coordination
  (Leadership and teamwork)

- Training for the entire company, from top to bottom

- Supplier involvement

- A pilot program

- Regular review by management and employees.

12.2 MANAGEMENT SUPPORT

COMMITMENT AND INVOLVEMENT

The commitment and active involvement of top management is vital to the success of any implementation program. Management support means more than passive delegation for change. Management must learn and practice the principles of continuous improvement and SPC. If they do not understand the methods, management will not be able to plan effectively for introducing SPC, or be prepared to support the changes and resources required for its success.

Middle managers tend to keep the problems of employees from upsetting top managers. Top management must be visible in its support and listen to its work force. Otherwise, it can find itself planning directions that are out of phase with the vision and desires of employees.

"Management by walking around" can be a highly visible and very supportive form of participatory management. It allows a manager to be visible and get to know employee needs.

COMMON VISION AND PHILOSOPHY

Management must develop a common vision and philosophy and communicate it to all employees. Continuous improvement provides such a vision. It is the view that every process has an endless potential for improvement. Each person is responsible for finding such opportunities and utilizing them. Policies and procedures as well as the nature and requirements of jobs should be redesigned to fit the concept of continuous improvement. Common standards and tools should be established. The job of quality control is easier when everyone uses similar standards and tools.

EMPHASIS ON TEAMWORK

In the past, management viewed quality control and SPC as tools for specialists. With continuous improvement comes a decentralization of authority. Each employee is responsible for his own contribution to quality.

Teamwork must be emphasized. Work teams should be established. Work teams are small groups of workers (five to nine people) in a common area of study. Such groups should be cross-functional teams of workers from different departments involved in a common quality objective.

Management support, in terms of time, resources, and rewards, is essential for the success of such teams. Such teams need time to meet, proper equipment, and channels of communication with other departments.

Effective training and coordination is absolutely essential. Managers must be active participants and promoters of teams and their efforts.

Teams promote the sharing of ideas, techniques, and decisions. If teams are not emphasized, individuals fall back on the more familiar ways of following supervisors' dictates.

PLANT MANAGERS

It is essential that plant managers be visibly committed to the statistical approach to quality and the philosophy of continuous improvement. The plant manager must understand the various statistical techniques and their analysis in order to enhance implementation. This cannot be delegated. Statistical awareness must continue down the chain of management to every employee responsible for quality. All company activities should be exposed to such awareness to some degree.

12.3 EMPLOYEE INVOLVEMENT

It is essential that the initial implementation of an SPC program be well-planned, well-coordinated, and involve all pertinent employees, management, supervisory, and hourly. When using SPC, production employees become the "eyes and ears" of the quality system. Employees will not only keep up charts, but their supervisor's observations and input on process conditions are critical for diagnosis of problems. Above all, a climate must be established that encourages free flow of information on a timely basis.

SPC will enable production personnel to identify the occurrence of many problems affecting quality. Production will be able to resolve some of these problems itself. However, others will require help from management, maintenance, engineering, the toolroom, or purchasing to solve. Problems that require cooperation often cause bottlenecks unless the affected departments are included in the implementation plan.

12.4 IN-HOUSE COORDINATION

One individual in the plant should be selected to coordinate the program details. That person should assist in developing the pilot program plans, participate in the management phase, and conduct or coordinate elementary statistical training. It is advisable to have at least one other person as a backup.

If the individuals selected have not had previous training in basic statistics or SPC techniques, formal training must be provided. Sufficient time should be allocated for these persons to get their feet on the ground, before they start to apply what was learned. Remember, this has to be a full-time occupation to be successful. It is not something added on to other duties and responsibilities.

The in-house coordinator should not be seen as a problem solver. His primary mission is administration and training. Problem solving should be clearly assigned to line management and staff.

12.5 TRAINING

Effective implementation of any new program requires training for the entire organization, from top management to line operators. The nature and content of the training will vary according to the needs of the group concerned.

Training should begin with top management. This is essential for management to develop the understanding required to support the program. For operating employees, intensive training should be planned so that they have the opportunity to immediately put their new skills to use on the job.

Both salaried and hourly people should be given appropriate basic statistical training, depending on their respective roles in the statistical effort. This may be done with data from their production areas, if available. Salaried personnel (process engineers, production supervisor, and quality control engineers, for example) should be provided the most extensive training. Training for hourly people is usually less extensive, depending on their roles, interests, and capabilities. Understanding and acceptance on their part is the most important aspect.

Employee training is the vital element of successful strategy. Unless it is carried out in a framework that includes management support, sound planning, and adequate resources, training will produce limited long-run results.

12.6 THE ROLE OF QUALITY ASSURANCE

With the implementation of an SPC program, the concept of inspection is replaced by a company-wide effort that strives for continuous improvement. This means that the quality control department must change.

The quality assurance department must now become the key interdepartmental support group for the quality effort. This means new roles for quality assurance personnel. Quality assurance personnel become facilitators and coordinators for the quality effort, and auditors and support staff for the company-wide quality control system. They will serve as instructors, internal consultants, and resource people in the training and support of staff. They will function interdepartmentally in the coordination of cross-functional teams. Continuous improvement means that production and quality assurance must work much more closely with product development and design.

Quality assurance will serve as auditors of the quality system:

- With production operators to see if continuous improvement is being supported

- With marketing, sales, and service to audit final product performance.

- Management, production, and marketing will all use this information. Quality assurance personnel will work closely with purchasing to audit supplier materials, facilities, programs, etc. Such information should be shared with suppliers to develop a dialogue for improvement. Quality personnel may even provide technical support for suppliers for implementation.

12.7 SUPPLIER INVOLVEMENT

Company suppliers are a part of the SPC system. All company activities should be conducted under one operating philosophy and one quality control system. This includes all purchased materials, parts, components, etc. Lines of communication with suppliers should be established. Clear standards, including the use of SPC, process capability requirements, specifications, etc., should be established. These should be based on hard numbers.

At some companies, multiple sourcing has been eliminated. Companies have gone to a single-source policy, with one supplier for each component or part purchased. The goal of such policies is to obtain the highest quality at minimal cost.

Suppliers must also take an active role in getting their subsuppliers to utilize SPC methodology. The total product is the result of all elements in the total process. All processes, including subsupplier performance, must be involved in a continuous improvement program. Subsupplier management must know about SPC and be aware of its responsibility to improve operations and reduce variation. Quality improvement will only be achieved when buyers and suppliers form a cooperative effort.

12.8 DEVELOPING A PILOT PROGRAM

A key step in implementation is the development of a successful pilot program. Select one or two plant areas to implement a pilot program to demonstrate these effective statistical techniques. To set the stage for true quality accountability, responsibility for the pilot program should be assigned to line management personnel, with support from various staff personnel, including quality assurance. A specific operation or series of operations should be identified for study and control. Factors that determine the pilot area(s) can be both quantitative and qualitative. They include:

Improvement is needed. This may be evidenced by plant scrap and/or rework records. Customer returns, complaints, or warranty costs are prime information sources that reveal a need for improvement.

People involved exhibit a cooperative attitude. Both salaried and hourly personnel should be willing to learn the new methodology.

Improvement can be measured. Plant scrap and rework records, customer returns, complaints, and warranties are accounts that should show the effect of an improved quality product. If $\overline{X}$ and R charts are the immediate control device, evidence of statistical control would illustrate improvement. This would also be revealed on a proportion nonconforming chart.

Significant disruptions are not present. Avoid short-run production jobs for an initial study, since the job could be completed before the study. The initial study should also preclude operations that have never run satisfactorily. Concentrate on process areas where the first applications have a good chance to succeed.

Statistical techniques can be easily applied. The problem identification tools are: control charts, histograms, check sheets for data collection, Pareto diagrams, graphs, cause-and-effect (fishbone) diagrams, and scatter plots. Any one or all of these tools can be effectively integrated in the pilot program and should be utilized to demonstrate statistical problem solving. Participation should focus on production personnel in applying statistical techniques.

Visual presentation of defects to production workers should not be made until the manufacturing process is statistically and technically in control. A production worker can be held responsible for the rejects he himself has caused. He can report irregularities caused by machinery or materials, but these are beyond his control; other sources must be enlisted to remedy these. A visual presentation of quality at this stage brings the worker nothing but uncertainty and disturbance.

Once the decisive factors for quality are determined and controlled, mistakes of a human origin, which the worker can now address, become self-evident. A visual presentation can now be made. In applying statistical techniques in the plant, the visual presentation of quality is frequently one of the last measures to be taken.

BASIC STATISTICAL TRAINING FOR PEOPLE IN THE PILOT AREA(S)

Both salaried and hourly people should be given appropriate basic statistical training, depending on their respective roles in the statistical effort. This may be done with locally developed material, if available. Salaried personnel (process engineers, production supervisors, quality control engineers, for example) should be provided the most extensive training. Training for hourly people is usually less extensive, depending on their roles, interests, and capabilities. Understanding and acceptance on their part is the most important aspect.

REVIEWING MACHINES OR PROCESSES TO BE STUDIED

Before beginning the pilot program, the process(es), machine(s), and/or related equipment must be in proper operating condition. Sources of special cause variation should be eliminated or minimized to the greatest extent possible, so that only common causes remain. Variation depicted on whatever charts are employed has to be operator controllable.

DESIGNING THE STUDY

This involves the control plan to collect statistical data relative to either the product or process. Remember that a separate chart is required for each variable data characteristic.

COLLECTING AND EVALUATING

Data collection and recording begins when the preceding steps have been completed.

Evaluating the statistical data to control the process should be performed at specified intervals by the individuals assigned that responsibility. With control charts, for example, the initial data (perhaps one or two weeks) would be used to calculate control limits. Analyzing the results would determine whether revisions to the process are required. Whenever significant process changes are made, the control limits would probably have to be recalculated. When satisfactory results have been obtained, the control plan would be finalized.

OPERATING THE PROCESS USING STATISTICAL TECHNIQUES

This will only involve using the appropriate statistical techniques, referred to earlier, to monitor and control the process. Research has shown that quality is made visible most frequently by means of average and range charts and check sheets. People interviewed maintained that these charts offered maximum readability and comprehensiveness.

PERIODIC REVIEW AND EXPANSION

Based on the results obtained from the pilot studies, the approach may be modified or expanded to include other areas in the plant. The best advice is to proceed slowly and carefully. Many programs have failed in the past because success was thought to be correlated with the quantity of charts displayed. Use only those techniques that will accomplish the desired objective of improved quality, increased production, and reduced cost.

12.9 THE NEXT STEP

The information gained through SPC on process capabilities, causes of variation, and quality problems must be communicated to design engineers. Engineers are the main designers of higher quality and more cost effective processes. SPC supplies the first feedback on the manufacturability of a product. It supplies information on reliability, maintenance, and manufacturability.

SPC allows production to work more closely with design engineering to help maintain and improve a manufacturing process—to monitor and maintain manufacturability and reduce manufacturing costs. By reading the information in control charts and process logs, an engineer is better able to create specifications for manufacturing capability, rate of production, and levels of quality.

Finally, regular reports and presentations on implementation must be made to management. The results of SPC implementation should be reviewed by management on a regular basis in order to 1) evaluate and maintain gains already achieved, and 2) provide a basis for directing resources to new areas of improvement.

The skills of SPC are relatively easy to learn. It is always more difficult to change attitudes and habits. Training alone does not make for change, but a visible change in expectations and rewards from management does. The vision, drive, and support for improvement in quality and productivity must continually come from top management.

American society is rapidly moving from a production based manufacturing economy to an information based service economy. In his book *The Third Wave*, Alan Toffler predicted that information would become the nation's number one product. The need for statistical thinking in manufacturing is a part of that wave.

Today every product must be accompanied by information. This has an impact on every employee. Each employee needs the training and ability to deal with statistical data at an appropriate level. A company must provide the support and training to continuously upgrade employee skills. Each person must be given a chance to participate in the system.

OTHER METHODS OF CONTROL CHARTING: CUSUM AND EWMA

INTRODUCTION

Control charts provide a signal that alerts the operator to the fact that immediate action is required. The basic signal is a single point outside of the control limits. But the meaning of a single point being outside the limits is related to the history of the process (to previous data points). These previous data points, or patterns, are important for control chart interpretation. Pattern analysis is one way of incorporating process history into the signal.

SHEWHART CONTROL CHARTING

There are several methods of control charting for incorporating process history into the statistical signal. By far the most commonly used is the method developed by Dr. Walter A. Shewhart and described in Chapters 5 through 9 of this book. This method is often referred to as **classical Shewhart control charting**.

With the classical Shewhart control chart, a single point falling beyond the $\pm 3\sigma$ limits signals that the process is out of control. By itself, this single point tells us nothing about the immediate history of the process. The analysis of patterns within control limits (runs, trends, cycles, etc.) is a supplement that allows us to use immediate process history to interpret the chart for control. It provides an informal use of recent process history that is very effective in assessing process control, especially when used by an experienced analyst.

OTHER METHODS OF CONTROL CHARTING

There are other methods of control charting that directly incorporate data on process history into a single point signal. **These include cumulative sum (CUSUM) control charting and exponentially weighted moving average (EWMA) control charting**. Both are more advanced techniques requiring statistical training beyond the scope of this book.

This section merely describes CUSUM and EWMA control charts in general terms. The construction and use of these charts are advanced topics. References are provided for those who wish to read about these techniques in detail.

Cusum Charting

The CUSUM method takes sequential observations of a process characteristic and plots the cumulative sum of their deviations from a target value. Thus, if:

y_t = observation of a characteristic
T = target value
d_t = deviation from the target value

Then $d_t = y_t - T$

The CUSUM is the cumulative sum of the deviations of sample averages from the target. The CUSUM is plotted against time (*Table A.1*).

$$\text{CUSUM} = \sum_{t=1}^{n} (Y_t - T)$$

$$= \sum_{t=1}^{n} d_t$$

Table A.1 *CUSUM example data.*

CUSUM EXAMPLE DATA

Sample Number	Data	CUSUM
1	-1.0	-1.0
2	+4.3	3.3
3	-1.4	1.9
4	-.3	1.6
5	-.2	1.4
6	-6.0	-4.6
7	2.3	-2.3
8	-4.4	-6.7
9	5.4	-1.3
10	-7.4	-8.7
11	10.7	2.0
12	10.0	12.0
13	-2.5	9.5
14	1.1	10.6
15	-1.6	9.0
16	5.4	14.4
17	3.9	18.3
18	-3.9	14.4
19	5.9	20.3
20	7.1	27.4
21	9.8	37.2

The CUSUM chart plots the cumulative sum of deviations of the mean from the target value. If the mean equals the target value, then the CUSUM will wander randomly around zero. If the mean is off target by a slight amount, δ, then the plotted CUSUM will add δ with each observation. The plot of the CUSUM will increase or decrease, depending on the sign of δ (*Figure A.1*). The analyst watches for a change in the slope of the CUSUM plot as an indication of a shift in the mean away from the target.

A CUSUM CHART

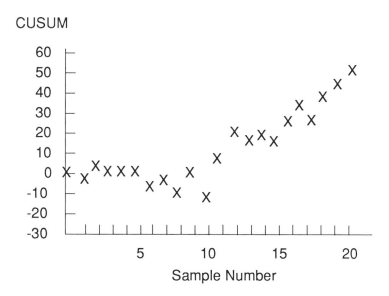

Figure A.1 *A CUSUM chart (based on example data from Table A.1).*

For statistical control purposes the CUSUM chart uses a sideways V (>), called the **V mask**. The V mask can be drawn on a clear transparency and moved with each observation. The vertex of the V mask is placed a fixed distance from the last plotted CUSUM point (*Figure A.2*). As long as all previous points lie within the arms of the V, no signal is provided. If any previous point lies outside the arms of the mask, an out-of-control situation is indicated. The lead distance and interior angle of the V mask take into account both the α and the β risks and the shift, δ, that is felt to be economically significant for action on the process.

CUSUM CHART
WITH "V" MASK

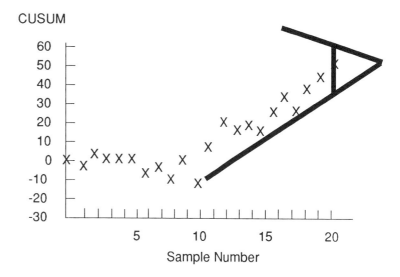

Figure A.2 *A CUSUM chart with the V mask placed at the 21st observation.*

The ordinary CUSUM chart incorporates all of the process history into the single-point signal. It accumulates process data to give a quick signal if the process mean shifts. The CUSUM chart is faster than the Shewhart chart in detecting small or moderate shifts in the mean. It usually provides tighter process control and is used when there is more emphasis on process aim (the mean being on target) than on allowing the process to drift between limits.

There are several varieties of CUSUM charts, including CUSUM charts with parallel control limits; combined Shewhart-CUSUM charts, which combine control features of both methods and Fast Initial Response (FIR) CUSUM charts which are often used for quickly detecting an out-of-control situation at start-up.

The construction and use of CUSUM charts are described in Johnson and Leone (1962), Ewan (1963), Woodward and Goldsmith (1964), Lucas (1976, 1982, 1985), and Lucas and Crosier (1982).

EWMA Charting

Even though more recent process data is more important than very old data, the CUSUM method gives equal weight to all process data. The **exponentially weighted moving average (EWMA)** is a statistic that gives less weight to process data as they get older. The EWMA chart plots a weighted moving average—a point based on an average of observations that ignores previous information. The plotted points incorporate process history and can be given a "long memory," similar to the ordinary CUSUM chart, or a "short memory," similar to a Shewhart chart.

The EWMA point is plotted one time-position ahead of the most recent observation. It is weighted to favor more recent data. Weighting is based on a constant (λ) that determines the memory of the EWMA statistic (the amount of historical information secured). The value of λ is left to the judgment of the control analyst.

$$EWMA = \hat{Y}_t + \lambda (Y_t - \hat{Y}_t)$$

Where Y_t = observation at time t
Y_t = previous EWMA value at time t

$Y_t - \hat{Y}_t$ = observed and predicted difference at time t
λ = constant determining depth of memory

The EWMA plot point is computed at time t, but plotted at time position $t+1$.

The current EWMA point, at time $t + 1$, contains all required process history information. As with CUSUM charts, there is no need to keep records of previous observations or patterns. The new EWMA point is updated by taking a measurement and adding $\lambda (Y_t - \hat{Y}_t)$ to the old EWMA value (see *Figure A.3*).

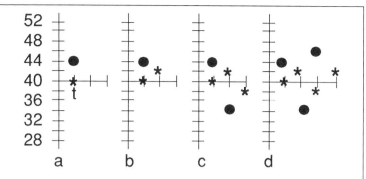

a. The target ($T = 40$) is the first EWMA point. The first observation is made at time t.

b. The next EWMA point is plotted, on the basis of the observation and previous EWMA plot point, at time position $t +1$.

c. The next EWMA point is plotted at time position $t + 2$, based on the observation and previous EWMA point at time $t + 1$.

d. The next EWMA point is plotted at time $t + 3$, etc.

Figure A.3   *Plotting EWMA points.*

Shewhart and EWMA control charts can be constructed and plotted simultaneously. The standard deviation and control limits for EWMA control charts can be derived from information used in establishing $\pm 3\sigma$ Shewhart control limits. With an EWMA control chart, a signal is produced wherever the last plotted point falls beyond the appropriate control limits (*Figure A.4*).

The construction and use of EWMA control charts are described in Cox (1961), Pandit and Wu (1983), Box and Jenkins (1976) and Hunter (1986).

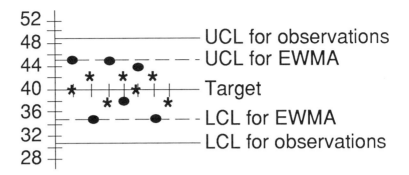

Figure A.4 *Observations (.) and EWMA points (*) can be plotted with their respective upper and lower control limits.*

COMPARING SHEWHART, CUSUM AND EWMA CHARTING

Shewhart control charts have the advantage of being simple to use and will detect large shifts in a process faster than other control techniques. CUSUM and EWMA charts respond more quickly to small shifts in the mean and provide tighter control than the standard Shewhart chart. A CUSUM chart is able to detect a persistent small change (about one standard deviation) from the target. In the hands of an experienced analyst, the use of pattern analysis makes the Shewhart chart take on aspects of the CUSUM or EWMA chart.

EWMA and CUSUM control charts provide a forecast of where the process will be in the next instant of time. They thus provide a method of real-time dynamic process control: If the forecast is too large, the process operator, or some electromechanical device, can take action to adjust the process mean to the target. The operator must know what corrective action to perform and care must be taken to avoid making changes too often (tweaking). CUSUM or EWMA control limits can be developed to inform the operator when adjustment is necessary.

CONSTANTS AND FORMULAS FOR CONTROL CHARTS

	$\overline{X}$ AND R CHARTS				$\overline{X}$ AND s CHARTS			
	Chart for Averages $(\overline{X})$	Chart for Ranges (R)			Chart for Averages $(\overline{X})$	Chart for Standard Deviations (s)		
Subgroup Size	Factors for Control Limits	Divisors for Estimate of Standard Deviation	Factors for Control Limits		Factors for Control Limits	Divisors for Estimate of Standard Deviation	Factors for Control Limits	
n	A_2	d_2	D_3	D_4	A_3	c_4	B_3	B_4
2	1.880	1.128	-	3.267	2.659	0.7979	-	3.267
3	1.023	1.693	-	2.574	1.954	0.8862	-	2.568
4	0.729	2.059	-	2.282	1.628	0.9213	-	2.266
5	0.577	2.326	-	2.114	1.427	0.9400	-	2.089
6	0.483	2.534	-	2.004	1.287	0.9515	0.030	1.970
7	0.419	2.704	0.076	1.924	1.182	0.9594	0.118	1.882
8	0.373	2.847	0.136	1.864	1.099	0.9650	0.185	1.815
9	0.337	2.970	0.184	1.816	1.032	0.9693	0.239	1.761
10	0.308	3.078	0.223	1.777	0.975	0.9727	0.284	1.716
11	0.285	3.173	0.256	1.744	0.927	0.9754	0.321	1.679
12	0.266	3.258	0.283	1.717	0.886	0.9776	0.354	1.646
13	0.249	3.336	0.307	1.693	0.850	0.9794	0.382	1.618
14	0.235	3.407	0.328	1.672	0.817	0.9810	0.406	1.594
15	0.223	3.472	0.347	1.653	0.789	0.9823	0.428	1.572
16	0.212	3.532	0.363	1.637	0.763	0.9835	0.448	1.552
17	0.203	3.588	0.378	1.622	0.739	0.9845	0.466	1.534
18	0.194	3.640	0.391	1.608	0.718	0.9854	0.482	1.518
19	0.187	3.689	0.403	1.597	0.698	0.9862	0.497	1.503
20	0.180	3.735	0.415	1.585	0.680	0.9869	0.510	1.490
21	0.173	3.778	0.425	1.575	0.663	0.9876	0.523	1.477
22	0.167	3.819	0.434	1.566	0.647	0.9882	0.534	1.466
23	0.162	3.858	0.443	1.557	0.633	0.9887	0.545	1.455
24	0.157	3.895	0.451	1.548	0.619	0.9892	0.555	1.445
25	0.153	3.931	0.459	1.541	0.606	0.9896	0.565	1.435

$$\text{UCL}\overline{X}, \text{LCL}\overline{X} = \overline{\overline{X}} \pm A_2\overline{R}$$
$$\text{UCL}_R = D_4\overline{R}$$
$$\text{LCL}_R = D_3\overline{R}$$
$$\hat{\sigma} = \overline{R} / d_2$$

$$\text{UCL}\overline{X}, \text{LCL}\overline{X} = \overline{\overline{X}} \pm A_3\overline{s}$$
$$\text{UCL}_s = B_4\overline{s}$$
$$\text{LCL}_s = B_3\overline{s}$$
$$\hat{\sigma} = \overline{s} / c_4$$

MEDIAN CHARTS

CHARTS FOR INDIVIDUALS

	Charts for Medians ($\tilde{X}$)		Chart for Ranges (R)			Charts for Individuals (X)		Chart for Ranges (R)	
	Factors for Control Limits	Divisors for Estimate of Standard Deviation	Factors for Control Limits		Factors for Control Limits	Divisors for Estimate of Standard Deviation	Factors for Control Limits	
Subgroup Size	$\tilde{A}_2$	d_2	D_3	D_4	E_2	d_2	D_3	D_4
2	1.880	1.128	-	3.267	2.660	1.128	-	3.267
3	1.187	1.693	-	2.574	1.772	1.693	-	2.574
4	0.796	2.059	-	2.282	1.457	2.059	-	2.282
5	0.691	2.326	-	2.114	1.290	2.326	-	2.114
6	0.548	2.534	-	2.004	1.184	2.534	-	2.004
7	0.508	2.704	0.076	1.924	1.109	2.704	0.076	1.924
8	0.433	2.847	0.136	1.864	1.054	2.847	0.136	1.864
9	0.412	2.970	0.184	1.816	1.010	2.970	0.184	1.816
10	0.362	3.078	0.223	1.777	0.975	3.078	0.223	1.777

$$\text{UCL}\tilde{x}, \text{LCL}\tilde{x} = \overline{\overline{X}} \pm \tilde{A}_2 \overline{R}$$
$$\text{UCL}_R = D_4 \overline{R}$$
$$\text{LCL}_R = D_3 \overline{R}$$
$$\hat{\sigma} = \overline{R} / d_2$$

$$\text{UCL}_X, \text{LCL}_X = \overline{X} \pm E_2 \overline{R}$$
$$\text{UCL}_R = D_4 \overline{R}$$
$$\text{LCL}_R = D_3 \overline{R}$$
$$\hat{\sigma} = \overline{R} / d_2$$

CONTROL CHARTS FOR VARIABLES

Calculate the Average ($\overline{X}$) and Range (R) of Each Subgroup

$$\overline{X} = \frac{X_1 + X_2 + \ldots + X_n}{n}$$

$$R = X_{max} - X_{min}$$

Calculate the Average Range ($\overline{R}$) and the Process Average ($\overline{\overline{X}}$)

$$\overline{\overline{X}} = \frac{\overline{X}_1 + \overline{X}_2 + \ldots + \overline{X}_k}{k}$$

$$\overline{R} = \frac{R_1 + R_2 + \ldots + R_k}{k}$$

Calculate the Control Limits

$$UCL_R = D_4\overline{R} \qquad\qquad LCL_R = D_3\overline{R}$$

$$UCL_X = \overline{\overline{X}} + A_2\overline{R}$$

$$LCL_X = \overline{\overline{X}} - A_2\overline{R}$$

Factors

n	D_4	D_3	A_2	d_2
3	2.57	*	1.02	1.69
4	2.28	*	0.73	2.06
5	2.11	*	0.58	2.33

CONTROL CHARTS FOR ATTRIBUTES

The p Chart

$$p = \frac{\text{number of rejects in subgroup}}{\text{number inspected in subgroup}}$$

$$\overline{p} = \frac{\text{total number of rejects}}{\text{total number inspected}}$$

$$UCL_p = \overline{p} + \frac{3\sqrt{\overline{p}(1-\overline{p})}}{\sqrt{n}}$$

$$LCL_p = \overline{p} - \frac{3\sqrt{\overline{p}(1-\overline{p})}}{\sqrt{n}}$$

The np Chart

$$UCL_{np} = n\overline{p} + 3\sqrt{n\overline{p}(1-\overline{p})}$$

$$LCL_{np} = n\overline{p} - 3\sqrt{n\overline{p}(1-\overline{p})}$$

The c Chart

$$UCL_c = \overline{c} + 3\sqrt{\overline{c}}$$

$$LCL_c = \overline{c} - 3\sqrt{\overline{c}}$$

The u Chart

$$\overline{u} = \frac{\text{total nonconformities}}{\text{total units inspected}}$$

$$UCL_u = \overline{u} + \frac{3\sqrt{\overline{u}}}{\sqrt{n}}$$

$$LCL_u = \overline{u} - \frac{3\sqrt{\overline{u}}}{\sqrt{n}}$$

NORMAL CURVE

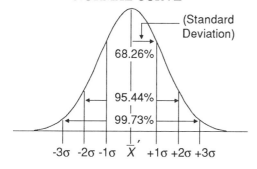

(Standard Deviation)

68.26%

95.44%

99.73%

-3σ -2σ -1σ $\overline{X}$ +1σ +2σ +3σ

PROCESS CAPABILITY

C_p Index

$$C_p = \frac{\text{spec. width}}{\text{natural tolerance}}$$

$$C_p = \frac{\text{upper spec.} - \text{lower spec.}}{6\hat{\sigma}}$$

C_{pk} Index

$$\hat{\sigma} = \overline{R} / d_2$$

$$Z_U = \frac{USL - \overline{\overline{X}}}{\hat{\sigma}} \qquad Z_L = \frac{\overline{\overline{X}} - LSL}{\hat{\sigma}}$$

$$Z_{min} = \text{Minimum}\{Z_U, Z_L\}$$

$$C_{pk} = \frac{Z_{min}}{3} = \text{Minimum}\left\{\frac{USL - \overline{\overline{X}}}{\sigma}, \frac{\overline{\overline{X}} - LSL}{\sigma}\right\}$$

Proportions Out of Specification

$$P_{Z_U}, P_{Z_L} = \text{Value from standard normal distribution table}$$

$$P_{TOTAL} = P_{Z_U} + P_{Z_L}$$

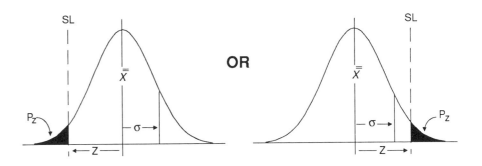

|z|	x.x0	x.x1	x.x2	x.x3	x.x4	x.x5	x.x6	x.x7	x.x8	x.x9
4.0	0.00003									
3.9	0.00005	0.00005	0.00004	0.00004	0.00004	0.00004	0.00004	0.00004	0.00003	0.00003
3.8	0.00007	0.00007	0.00007	0.00006	0.00006	0.00006	0.00006	0.00005	0.00005	0.00005
3.7	0.00011	0.00010	0.00010	0.00010	0.00009	0.00009	0.00008	0.00008	0.00008	0.00008
3.6	0.00016	0.00015	0.00015	0.00014	0.00014	0.00013	0.00013	0.00012	0.00012	0.00011
3.5	0.00023	0.00022	0.00022	0.00021	0.00020	0.00019	0.00019	0.00018	0.00017	0.00017
3.4	0.00034	0.00032	0.00031	0.00030	0.00029	0.00028	0.00027	0.00026	0.00025	0.00024
3.3	0.00048	0.00047	0.00045	0.00043	0.00042	0.00040	0.00039	0.00038	0.00036	0.00035
3.2	0.00069	0.00066	0.00064	0.00062	0.00060	0.00058	0.00056	0.00054	0.00052	0.00050
3.1	0.00097	0.00094	0.00090	0.00087	0.00084	0.00082	0.00079	0.00076	0.00074	0.00071
3.0	0.00135	0.00131	0.00126	0.00122	0.00118	0.00114	0.00111	0.00107	0.00104	0.00100
2.9	0.0019	0.0018	0.0018	0.0017	0.0016	0.0016	0.0015	0.0015	0.0014	0.0014
2.8	0.0026	0.0025	0.0024	0.0023	0.0023	0.0022	0.0021	0.0021	0.0020	0.0019
2.7	0.0035	0.0034	0.0033	0.0032	0.0031	0.0030	0.0029	0.0028	0.0027	0.0026
2.6	0.0047	0.0045	0.0044	0.0043	0.0041	0.0040	0.0039	0.0038	0.0037	0.0036
2.5	0.0062	0.0060	0.0059	0.0057	0.0055	0.0054	0.0052	0.0051	0.0049	0.0048
2.4	0.0082	0.0080	0.0078	0.0075	0.0073	0.0071	0.0069	0.0068	0.0066	0.0064
2.3	0.0107	0.0104	0.0102	0.0099	0.0096	0.0094	0.0091	0.0089	0.0087	0.0084
2.2	0.0139	0.0136	0.0132	0.0129	0.0125	0.0122	0.0119	0.0116	0.0113	0.0110
2.1	0.0179	0.0174	0.0170	0.0166	0.0162	0.0158	0.0154	0.0150	0.0146	0.0143
2.0	0.0228	0.0222	0.0217	0.0212	0.0207	0.0202	0.0197	0.0192	0.0188	0.0183
1.9	0.0287	0.0281	0.0274	0.0268	0.0262	0.0256	0.0250	0.0244	0.0239	0.0233
1.8	0.0359	0.0351	0.0344	0.0336	0.0329	0.0322	0.0314	0.0307	0.0301	0.0294
1.7	0.0446	0.0436	0.0427	0.0418	0.0409	0.0401	0.0392	0.0384	0.0375	0.0367
1.6	0.0548	0.0537	0.0526	0.0516	0.0505	0.0495	0.0485	0.0475	0.0465	0.0455
1.5	0.0668	0.0665	0.0643	0.0630	0.0618	0.0606	0.0594	0.0582	0.0571	0.0559
1.4	0.0808	0.0793	0.0778	0.0764	0.0749	0.0735	0.0721	0.0708	0.0694	0.0681
1.3	0.0968	0.0951	0.0934	0.0918	0.0901	0.0885	0.0869	0.0853	0.0838	0.0823
1.2	0.1151	0.1131	0.1112	0.1093	0.1075	0.1056	0.1038	0.1020	0.1003	0.0985
1.1	0.1357	0.1335	0.1314	0.1292	0.1271	0.1251	0.1230	0.1210	0.1190	0.1170
1.0	0.1587	0.1562	0.1539	0.1515	0.1492	0.1469	0.1446	0.1423	0.1401	0.1379
0.9	0.1841	0.1814	0.1788	0.1762	0.1736	0.1711	0.1685	0.1660	0.1635	0.1611
0.8	0.2119	0.2090	0.2061	0.2033	0.2005	0.1977	0.1949	0.1922	0.1894	0.1867
0.7	0.2420	0.2389	0.2358	0.2327	0.2297	0.2266	0.2236	0.2206	0.2177	0.2148
0.6	0.2743	0.2709	0.2676	0.2643	0.2611	0.2578	0.2546	0.2514	0.2483	0.2451
0.5	0.3085	0.3050	0.3015	0.2981	0.2946	0.2912	0.2877	0.2843	0.2810	0.2776
0.4	0.3446	0.3409	0.3372	0.3336	0.3300	0.3264	0.3228	0.3192	0.3156	0.3121
0.3	0.3821	0.3783	0.3745	0.3707	0.3669	0.3632	0.3594	0.3557	0.3520	0.3483
0.2	0.4207	0.4168	0.4129	0.4090	0.4052	0.4013	0.3974	0.3936	0.3897	0.3859
0.1	0.4602	0.4562	0.4522	0.4483	0.4443	0.4404	0.4364	0.4325	0.4286	0.4247
0.0	0.5000	0.4960	0.4920	0.4880	0.4840	0.4801	0.4761	0.4721	0.4681	0.4641

TERMS AND SYMBOLS

Accuracy (of measurement vs. precision)	Difference between the average result of a measurement with a particular instrument and the true value of the quantity being measured.
Advanced Statistical Methods	More sophisticated and less widely applicable techniques of statistical process analysis and control than included in basic statistical methods. This can include more advanced control chart techniques, regression analysis, design of experiments, advanced problem-solving techniques, etc.
Assignable Cause	A factor contributing to variation that is feasible to detect and identify.
Attribute Data	Qualitative data that can be counted for recording and analysis. Examples include such characteristics as the presence of a required label, the installation of all required fasteners, and the absence of errors on an expense report. Other examples are characteristics that are inherently measurable (i.e., could be treated as variable data), but where the results are recorded in a simple yes/no fashion, such as acceptability of a shaft diameter when checked on a go/no-go gage or the presence of any engineering changes on a drawing. Attribute data are usually gathered in the form of nonconforming units or of nonconformities; they are analyzed by p, np, c, and u control charts. (See also Variable Data.)
Average	The sum of values divided by the number (sample size) of values; designated by a bar over the symbol for the values being averaged: e.g., $\bar{X}$ (X bar) is the average of the X values within a subgroup: $\bar{\bar{X}}$ (X double bar) is the average of subgroup averages; $\bar{\tilde{X}}$ (X tilde-bar) is the

.

	average of subgroup medians: $\bar{p}$ (p bar) is the average of ps from all the subgroups. (See also Mean.)
Awareness	Personal understanding of the interrelationship of quality and productivity, directing attention to the requirement for management commitment and statistical thinking to achieve never-ending improvement.
Basic Statistical Methods	Applies the theory of variation through use of basic problem-solving techniques and Statistical Process Control; includes control chart construction and interpretation (for both variable and attribute data) and capability analysis.
Bell-Shaped Curve	A curve or distribution showing a central peak and tapering off smoothly and symmetrically to "tails" on either side. A normal curve is an example.
Bias (in measurement)	Difference between the average result of repeated measurements with a particular instrument and the true value of the quantity being measured.
Bimodal Distribution	A frequency distribution that has two peaks.
Binomial Distribution	A discrete probability distribution for attribute data that applies to conforming and nonconforming units and underlies the p and np charts.
Calibration (of instrument)	Adjusting an instrument to reduce the difference between the average reading of the instrument and the "true" value of some standard being measured, i.e., to reduce measurement bias.
Capability (Can be determined only after the process is in statistical control)	When the process average plus and minus the 3σ spread of the distribution of individuals ($\bar{X} \pm 3\sigma$) is contained within the specification tolerance (variable data), or when at least 99.73% of individuals are within specification (attribute data), a process is said to be capable. Efforts to improve capability must continue, however, consistent with the operational philosophy of never-ending improvement in quality and productivity.

Cause-and-Effect Diagram A simple tool for individual or group problem solving that uses a graphic description of the various process elements to analyze potential sources of process variation. Also called the fishbone diagram (after its appearance) or Ishikawa diagram (after its developer).

Cell See Class.

Central Line The line of a control chart that represents the overall average value of the items being plotted.

Central Limit Theorem If samples of a population with size n are drawn, and the values of $\bar{X}$ are calculated, and the distribution of $\bar{X}$ is found, the distribution's shape is found to approach a normal distribution for sufficiently large n. This theorem allows one to use the assumption of a normal distribution when dealing with $\bar{X}$. "Sufficiently large" depends on the population's distribution and on what range of $\bar{X}$ is being considered; for practical purposes, the easiest approach may be to take a number of samples of a desired size and see if their means are normally distributed. If not, the sample size should be increased.

Central Tendency A measure of the point about which a group of values is clustered; some measures of central tendency are mean, mode, and median.

Chance Causes (Random Causes) Factors, generally numerous and individually of relatively small importance, which contribute to variation, but which are not feasible to detect or identify.

Chance Variation (Random Variation) Variation due to chance causes.

Characteristic A distinguishing feature of a process or its output on which variable or attribute data can be collected.

Class (of frequency distribution and/or histogram)

A class is an interval of the variable for which all the elements falling in that interval will be summed together. Usually the full range of the variable is divided into classes of equal size, and only the total number of elements falling into each class is used in working with the frequency distribution and/or histogram. This greatly reduces the amount of information that must be dealt with, as opposed to treating each element individually. Also called a cell or group.

Cluster

A group with similar properties. For control charts and scatter plots: A group of points falling in the same area of the chart.

Common Cause

A source of variation that affects all the individual values of the process output being studied: in control chart analysis it appears as part of the random process variation.

Conformance (of product)

Adherence to some standard of the product's properties. The term is used often in attribute studies of product quality, i.e., a given unit of the product is either in conformance to the standard or it is not.

Consecutive

Units of output produced in succession; a basis for selecting subgroup samples.

Continuous Variable

A variable that can assume any of a range of values; an example would be the measured size of a part.

Control

See Statistical Control.

Control Chart

A graphic representation of a characteristic of a process, showing plotted values of some statistic gathered from that characteristic, a central line, and one or two control limits. It minimizes the net economic loss from Type I and Type II errors. It has two basic uses: As a judgment to determine if a process has been operating in statistical control and as an operation to aid in maintaining statistical control.

Control Limit

A line (or lines) on a control chart used as a basis for judging the significance of the variation from subgroup to subgroup. Variation beyond a control limit is evidence that special causes are affecting the process. Control limits are calculated from process data and are not to be confused with engineering specifications. (See also Lower Control Limit and Upper Control Limit.)

C_p Index

For process capability studies. C_p is a capability index used to measure the theoretical capability that would be obtained if the process was centered at mid-spec. Cp may range in value from 0 to infinity, with a larger value indicating a more capable process. A value of 1.33 or above is normally considered acceptable.

$$C_p = \frac{(USL - LSL)}{6\sigma}$$

C_{pk} Index

For process capability studies. An index that indicates whether the process will produce units within the tolerance limits. C_{pk} has a value equal to C_p if the process is centered on the mid-spec; if C_{pk} is negative, the process mean is outside the specification limits; if C_{pk} is between 0 and 1 then some of the 6σ spread falls outside the tolerance limits. If C_{pk} is larger than 1, the 6σ spread is completely within the tolerance limits. A value about 1.33 is generally considered acceptable, with higher values indicating a more capable process.

C_{pk} = The lesser of:

$$\frac{(USL - MEAN)}{3\sigma} \text{ or } \frac{(MEAN - LSL)}{3\sigma}$$

CR (Capability Ratio)	For process capability studies. The *CR* is a ratio that measures the theoretical capability that would be obtained if the process is centered at mid-specification. *CR* can range from 0 to infinity in value, with a smaller value indicating a more capable process. A value of 0.75 or less is normally considered acceptable.

$$CR = \frac{6\sigma}{(USL - LSL)}$$

Detection	A past-oriented strategy that attempts to identify unacceptable output after it has been produced and then separate it from the good output. (See also Prevention.)
Distribution	A way of describing the output of a common cause system of variation, in which individual values are not predictable but in which the outcomes as a group form a pattern that can be described in terms of its location, spread, and shape. Location is commonly expressed in terms of the mean or median and spread is commonly expressed in terms of the standard deviation or the range of a sample. Shape involves many characteristics such as symmetry and peakedness. These are often summarized by using the name of a common distribution such as the normal, binomial, or Poisson.
Flow Chart (for programs, decision making, process development)	A pictorial representation of a process indicating the main steps, branches, and eventual outcomes of the process.
Frequency Distribution	For a sample drawn from a statistical population, the number of times each outcome was observed.
Group	See Class.
Goodness of Fit	Any measure of how well a set of data matches a proposed form. Simple visual inspection of histogram is a valid way to determine goodness of fit.

Histogram	A graphic representation of a frequency distribution. The range of the variable is divided into a number of intervals of equal size (called classes) and an accumulation is made of the number of observations falling into each class. The histogram is essentially a bar graph of the results of this accumulation.
Individual	A single unit or a single measurement of a characteristic.
Instability (of a process)	A process is said to show instability if it exhibits variations larger than its control limits, or shows a systematic pattern of variation.
Linearity	The extent to which a measuring instrument's response is proportional to the measured quantity.
Location	A general concept for the typical values or central tendency of a distribution.
LCL (Lower Control Limit)	For control charts, the lower limit above which a process remains, if it is in control.
Mean (of a statistical sample)	The average value of some variable. The mean is given by the formula, where X is the value of the variable for the nth element, and n is the number of elements in the sample.

$$\overline{X} = \frac{x_1 + x_2 + \ldots + x_n}{n}$$

Measurement Accuracy	See Accuracy.
Measurement Error	The difference between the actual and measured value of measured quantity.
Measurement Precision	The extent to which a repeated measurement gives the same result. Variations may arise from the inherent capabilities of the instrument, from changes in operating condition, etc. (See also Repeatability and Reproducibility.)

Median	The middle value in a group of measurements, when arranged from lowest to highest; if the number of values is even, by convention the average of the middle two values is used as the median. Subgroup medians form the basis for a simple control chart for process location. Medians are designated by a tilde (~) over the symbol for the individual values. $\tilde{X}$ is the median of a subgroup.
Never-Ending Improvement in Quality and Productivity	The operational philosophy that makes best use of the talents within a company to produce products of increasing quality for customers in an increasingly efficient way that protects the return on investment to stockholders. This is a dynamic strategy designed to enhance the strength of the company in the face of present and future market conditions. It contrasts with any static strategy that accepts (explicitly or implicitly) some particular level of outgoing defects as inevitable.
Nominal Dimension	For a product whose size is of concern: The desired mean value for the particular dimension.
Nonconforming Units	Units that do not conform to a specification or other inspection standard; sometimes called discrepant or defective units. p and np control charts are used to analyze systems producing nonconforming units.
Nonconformities	Specific occurrences of a condition that does not conform to specifications or other inspection standards; sometimes called discrepancies or defects. An individual nonconforming unit can have the potential for more than one nonconformity (e.g., a door could have several dents and dings; a functional check of a carburetor could reveal any of a number of potential discrepancies). c and u control charts are used to analyze systems producing nonconformities.

Normal Distribution

A continuous, symmetrical, bell-shape frequency distribution for variable data that underlies the control charts for variables. When measurements have a normal distribution, about 68.26% of all individuals lie within plus or minus one standard deviation unit of the mean, about 95.44% lie within plus and minus two standard deviation units of the mean, and about 99.73% lie within plus and minus three standard deviation units of the mean. These percentages are the basis for control limit and control chart analysis (since subgroup averages tend to be normally distributed even if the output as a whole is not) and for many capability decisions (since the output of many industrial processes follows the normal distribution).

Operational Definition

A means of clearly communicating quality expectations and performance; it consists of 1) a criterion to be applied to an object or to a group, 2) a test of the object or of the group, 3) a decision: yes or no—the object or the group did or did not meet the criterion.

Out of Control

A process that exhibits variation larger than the control limits is said to be out of control.

p Chart (percent defective)

A control chart for the percentage of defective units. Used for attribute quality control.

Pareto Chart

A simple tool for problem solving that involves ranking all potential problem areas or sources of variation according to their contribution to cost or to total variation. Typically, a few causes account for most of the cost (or variation), so problem-solving efforts are best prioritized to concentrate on the "vital few" causes temporarily ignoring the "trivial many."

Poisson Distribution

A discrete probability distribution for attribute data that applies to nonconformities and underlies the c and u control charts.

Precision (of measurement)

The extent to which repeated measurement of a standard with a given instrument yields the same result.

Prevention	A future-oriented strategy that improves quality and productivity by directing analysis and action toward correcting the process itself. Prevention is consistent with a philosophy of never-ending improvement. (See also Detection.)
Primary Reference Standard	For measurements: A standard maintained by the National Bureau of Standards for a particular measuring unit. The primary reference standard duplicates as nearly as possible the international standard and is used to calibrate other (transfer) standards, which in turn are used to calibrate measuring instruments for industrial use.
Problem-Solving	The process of moving from symptoms to causes (special or common) to actions that improve performance. Among the techniques that can be used are Pareto charts, cause-and-effect diagrams, and Statistical Process Control techniques.
Process	The combination of people, equipment, materials, methods, and environment that produce output of a given product or service. A process can involve any aspect of our business. A key tool for managing processes is Statistical Process Control.
Process Average	The location of the distribution of measured values of a particular process characteristic, usually designated as an overall average, $\overline{X}$.
Process Capability	The level of uniformity of a product that a process is capable of yielding. Process capability may be expressed by the percent of defective products, the range or standard deviation of some product dimension, etc. Process capability is usually determined by performing measurements on some (or all) of the product units produced by the process.
Process Control	Maintaining the performance of a process at its capability level. Process control involves a range of activities, such as sampling the process product, charting its performance, determining causes of any problems, and taking corrective actions.

Process Spread
The extent to which the distribution of individual values of the process characteristic vary; often shown as the process average plus or minus some number of standard deviations (e.g., $\overline{X} \pm 3\sigma$).

Randomness
A condition in which individual values are not predictable, although they may come from a definable distribution.

Range
The difference between the highest and lowest values in a subgroup. The expected range increases both with sample size and with the standard deviation.

Rational Subgrouping
For control charting: a subgroup of units selected to minimize the differences due to assignable causes. Usually samples taken consecutively from a process operating under the same conditions will meet this requirement.

Repeatability (of a measurement)
The variation in repeated measurements of a particular object with a particular instrument by a single operator.

Reproducibility (of measurements)
Reproducibility is the variation in the average of measurements made by different operators using the same instrument when measuring identical characteristics of the same parts.

Resolution (of a measuring instrument)
The smallest unit of measure that an instrument is capable of indicating.

Run
A consecutive number of points consistently increasing or decreasing, or above or below the central line. Can be evidence of the existence of special causes of variation.

Run Chart
A simple graphic representation of a characteristic of a process, showing plotted values of some statistic gathered from the process (often individual values) and central line (often the median of the values), which can be analyzed for runs. (See also Control Charts.)

Sample	In process control applications, this term is synonymous with subgroup. This use is totally different from the purpose of providing an estimate of larger groups of people, items, etc.
Sample Size	The number of elements, or units, in a sample.
Sampling	The process of selecting a sample of a population and determining the properties of the sample. The sample is chosen in such a way that its properties are representative of the population.
Sampling Variation	The variation of a sample's properties from the properties of the population from which it was drawn.
Sensitivity (of a measuring instrument)	The smallest change in the measured quantity that the instrument is capable of detecting.
Skewed	A nonsymmetric distribution is said to be skewed.
Shape	A general concept for the overall pattern formed by a distribution of values.
Sigma (σ)	The Greek letter used to designate a standard deviation.
Special Cause	A source of variation that is intermittent, unpredictable, and unstable; sometimes called an assignable cause. It is signalled by a point beyond the control limits or a run or other nonrandom pattern of points within the control limits.
Specification	The engineering requirement for judging acceptability of a particular characteristic. A specification is never to be confused with a control limit.
Spread	A general concept for the extent by which values in a distribution differ from one another; dispersion. (See also Process Spread.)
Stability	The absence of special causes of variation; the property of being in statistical control.
Stable Process	A process that is in statistical control.

Standard Deviation   A measure of the spread of the process output or the spread of a sampling statistic from the process (e.g., of subgroup averages); denoted by the Greek letter σ (sigma).

Statistic   A value calculated from or based upon sample data (e.g., a subgroup average or range), used to make inferences about the process that produced the output from which the sample came.

Statistical Control   The condition describing a process from which all special causes of variation have been eliminated and only common causes remain; evidenced on a control chart by the absence of points beyond the control limits and by the absence of nonrandom patterns or trends within the control limits.

Statistical Process Control   The use of statistical techniques, such as control charts, to analyze a process or its output so as to take appropriate actions to achieve and maintain a state of statistical control and to improve process capability.

Subgroup   One or more events or measurements used to analyze the performance of a process. Rational subgroups are usually chosen so that the variation represented within each subgroup is as small as feasible for the process (representing the variation from common causes), and so that any changes in the process performance (i.e., special causes) will appear as differences between subgroups. Rational subgroups are typically made up of consecutive pieces, although random samples are sometimes used.

Trend   A gradual, systematic change with time or other variables.

Type I Error   Rejecting an assumption that is true; e.g., taking action appropriate for a special cause when in fact the process has not changed; over control. Also called the α error or "producer's risk."

Type II Error

Failing to reject an assumption that is false; e.g., not taking appropriate action when in fact the process is affected by special causes; under control. Also called β error or "consumer's risk."

***u* Chart**

Attribute data: A control chart for the number of defects per unit or sample. May use varying sample sizes (or amounts of material inspected).

**UCL
(Upper Control Limit)**

For control charts, the upper limit below which a process remains if it is in control.

**USL
(Upper Specification Limit)**

The highest value of a product dimension or measurement that is acceptable.

Variability

The property of exhibiting variation, i.e., changes or differences in particular in the product or a process.

Variable Data

Quantitative data, where measurements are used for analysis. Examples include the diameter of a bearing journal in millimeters, the closing effort of a door in kilograms, the concentration of an electrolyte in percent, or the torque of a fastener in newton-meters. $\overline{X}$ and R, $\overline{X}$ and s, median, and individuals control charts are used for variable data. (See also Attribute Data).

Variation

The inevitable differences among individual outputs of a process; the sources of variation can be grouped into two major classes: common causes and special causes.

SYMBOLS USED IN THIS MANUAL

A_2 A multiplier of $\bar{R}$ used to calculate the control limits for averages.

$\tilde{A}_2$ A multiplier of $\bar{R}$ used to calculate the control limits for medians.

A_3 A multiplier of $\bar{s}$ used to calculate the control limits for averages.

c The number of nonconformities in a sample.

$\bar{c}$ The average number of nonconformities in samples constant size n.

c_4 A divisor of $\bar{s}$ used to estimate the process standard deviation.

C_p A capability index.

C_{pk} A capability index.

CR Capability ratio.

d_2 A divisor of $\bar{R}$ used to estimate the process standard deviation.

D_3, D_4 A multiplier of $\bar{R}$ used to calculate the lower and upper control limits, respectively, for ranges.

E_2 A multiplier of $\bar{R}$ used to calculate control limits for individuals.

k In this manual: The number of subgroups used to calculate control limits.

LCL The lower control limit; LCL_X, LCL_R, LCL_P, etc., are, respectively, the lower control limits for averages, ranges, proportion nonconforming, etc.

LSL	The lower engineering specification limit.
n	The number of individuals in a subgroup; the subgroup sample size.
$\bar{n}$	The average subgroup sample size.
np	The number of nonconforming items in a sample of size.
$n\bar{p}$	The average number of nonconforming items in samples of constant size n.
p	The proportion of units nonconforming in a sample.
$\bar{p}$	The average proportion of units nonconforming in a series of samples (weighted by sample size).
p_z	In this manual: The proportion of output beyond a point of interest, such as a particular specification limit which is z standard deviations away from the process average.
R	The subgroup range (highest minus lowest value).
$\bar{R}$	The average range of a series of subgroups of constant size.
s	The sample standard deviation.
$\bar{s}$	The average sample standard deviation of a series of subgroups.
u	The number of nonconformities per unit in a sample that may contain more than one unit.
$\bar{u}$	The average number of nonconformities per unit in samples not necessarily of the same size.

UCL	The upper control limit; UCL_X, UCL_R, UCL_p, etc., are, respectively, the upper control limits for averages, ranges, proportion nonconforming, etc.
USL	The upper engineering specification limit.
X	An individual value, upon which other subgroup statistics are based.
$\overline{X}$	The average of values in a subgroup.
$\overline{\overline{X}}$	The average of subgroup averages (weighted if necessary by sample size).
$\tilde{X}$	The median of values in a subgroup.
$\overline{\tilde{X}}$	The average of subgroup medians; the estimated process median.
Z	The number of standard deviation units from the process average to a value of interest, such as an engineering specification.
σ (sigma)	The standard deviation of the distribution of individual values of a process characteristic.
$\hat{\sigma}$ (sigma hat)	An estimate of the standard deviation of a process characteristic.
$\sigma_{\overline{X}}$, σ_R, σ_p, etc.	The standard deviation of a statistic (e.g., $\overline{X}$, R, p, etc.) based on sample process output. For example: the standard deviation of subgroup averages (which is $\sigma / \sqrt{n}$), the standard deviation of subgroup ranges, or the standard deviation of the distribution of the proportion of nonconforming items, etc.

REFERENCES

American National Standards Institute,*Control Chart Method of Controlling Quality During Production*, ASQC Standard B3–1958/ANSI Z1.3–1958, Revised 1975.

Guide for Quality Control and Control Chart Method of Analyzing Data, ASQC Standards B1–1958 and B2–1958/ANSI Z1.1–1958 and Z1.2–1958., Revised 1975.

American Society for Testing and Materials, *Manual on Presentation of Data and Control Chart Analysis* (STP–15D), 1976.

American Supplier Institute, Inc., *Statistical Thinking for Manufacturing Process Control*, Dearborn, MI, 1986.

ASME 889 1.12 Working Group, *Interim Standard, Method for Performance Evaluation of Coordinate Measuring Machines*, ASME, United Engineering Center, 345 East 47th Street, New York, New York, 10017, 1983.

Beer, "Compensate for Quality," Valeron Corp., *Quality*, November 1983.

Box, G.E.P, and J.M. Jenkins, *Time Series Analysis, Forecasting and Control*, Holden Day, Inc., San Francisco, 1976.

Bross, Irwin D.J., *Design for Decision*, MacMillan, 1953.

Burchett, G.L., "Testing Test Equipment," *Quality Progress*, April 1984.

Burr, Irving W., *Statistical Quality Control Methods*, Marcel Decker, Inc., 1976.

Business Week, June 8, 1987.

Charbonneau, H.C., and G.L. Webster, *Industrial Quality Control*, Prentice-Hall, Inc., Engelwood Cliffs, NJ, 07632, 1978.

Cox, D.R., "Prediction by Exponentially Weighted Moving Averages and Related Methods," *Journal of the Royal Statistical Society*, 1323, pp. 414–423, 1961.

Crandall, Keith C., and Robert W. Seabloom, *Engineering Fundamentals in Measurement, Probability, Statistics, and Dimensions*, McGraw-Hill, Inc., 1970.

Deming, W. Edward, "On Some Statistical Aids Towards Economic Production," *Interfaces*, Vol. 5, No. 4, August 1975.

Quality Productivity and Competitive Position, M.I.T. Press, Cambridge, MA, 1982.

Duncan, Acheson J., *Quality Control and Industrial Statistics*, Richard D. Irwin, Inc., Fourth Edition, 1974.

Ewan, W.D., "When and How to Use CUCUM Charts," *Technometrics* 5, pp. 1–22, 1963.

Ford Motor Co., *Machine Capability Studies*, (80-01-250), 1980.

Statistical Program—Guidelines for How to Get Started, Product Quality Office, Manufacturing Staff, July 1981.

Analysis of Control Chart Patterns, Body and Assembly–Chassis SQA, 1983.

Ford Motor Co., *Continuing Process Control and Capability Improvement: A Guide to the Use of Control Charts for Improving Quality and Productivity for Company, Supplier and Dealer Activities*, Statistical Methods Office, 1984.

Freeman, H.A., "Statistical Methods for Quality Control," *Mechanical Engineering*, Vol. LIH (April 1, 1937), p. 261.

Grant, Eugene L. and Richard S. Leavenworth, *Statistical Quality Control*, McGraw-Hill, Inc., Fifth Edition, 1980.

Hunter, J. Stuart, "The Exponentially Weighted Moving Average," *Journal of Quality Technology* 18 No: 4, pp. 205–210, October 1986.

International Business Machines Corp., *Precision Measurement in the Metal Working Industry*, Syracuse University Press, Syracuse, NY, 1939, 1940, 1941, 1942.

Ishikawa, Kaoru, *Guide to Quality Control*, Asian Productivity Organization, 1976.

Johnson, N.L. and F.C. Leone, *Statistics and Experimental Design in Engineering and the Physical Sciences*, 2nd edition, John Wiley and Sons, Inc., NY, 1977.

Juran, J.M., *Quality Control Handbook*, 3rd Edition, McGraw-Hill, 1974.

Management of Quality, 4th Edition, Juran Institute, Inc., 1981.

"Product Quality–a Prescription for the West," *Management Review*, June/July 1981.

Juran, J.M., and F.M. Gryna, *Quality Planning and Analysis*, McGraw-Hill Inc., New York, NY, 1970.

Lucas, J.M., "The Design and Use of V–Mask Control Schemes", *Journal of Quality Technology*, Vol. 8, pp. 1–12, 1976.

"Combined Shewhart—CUSUM Quality Control Schemes", *Journal of Quality Technology*, Vol. 14, pp. 51–59, 1982.

"Cumulative Sum (CUSUM) Control Schemes," *Communications in Statistics—Theory and Methods*, Vol. 14, No. 11, pp. 2689–2704, 1985.

Lucas, J.M. and R.B. Crosier, "Fast Initial Response for CUSUM Quality Control Schemes: Give Your CUSUM a Head Start," *Technometrics*, Vol. 24, pp. 199–206, 1982.

Moroney, M.J., *Facts from Figures*, Penguin Books, Third Edition, 1960.

Mosteller, Frederick, Robert E.K. Rourke, and George B. Thomas, Jr., *Probability: A First Course*, Addison-Wesley, Inc., 1961.

Naisbitt, John, *Megatrends*, Warner Books, NY, 1982.

Natrella, Mary Gibbons, *Experimental Statistics*, National Bureau of Standards Handbook 91, 1963.

Ott, Ellis R., *Process Quality Control*, McGraw-Hill, Inc., NY, 1975.

Pandit, S.M., and S. Wu, *Time Series and System Analysis with Applications*, John Wiley and Sons, Inc., NY, 1983.

Peach, Paul, *Quality Control for Management*, Prentice-Hall, Inc., 1964.

Stok, T. L., *The Worker and Quality Control*, Bureau of Industrial Relation, Graduate School of Business Administration, University of Michigan, Ann Arbor, Michigan, 1965.

Quality—Its Creation and Control, The Institution of Production Engineers, 10 Chesterfield Street, London, WI, July 1958.

Western Electric Co., Inc., *Statistical Quality Control Handbook*, 1956.

Wood, D.A., "Process Capability Procedure," Ford Motor Co., presented at ASQC Automotive Division Workshop, November 3, 1983.

Woodward, R.H., and P.L. Goldsmith, *Cumulative Sum Techniques*, Published for Imperial Chemical Industries, Oliver and Boyd, London, England, 1964.

Index

A

Accuracy, 84
  See also Gage accuracy
Action on a process, 30, 76, 79, 84
Action on the output, 30
Active involvement, 313
Adjustments, 57
  to a process, 305
Aim chart
  See short run $\overline{X}$ (X bar) and R chart
Alpha risk, 77
  See also Type I error
Arithmetic mean, 53
  See also Mean
Assignable causes, 155
  See also Special causes
Attribute, 87, 113
Attribute data, 87, 233
Automatic inspection, 28
Average, 53
  of subgroup ranges, 169
  of the sample standard deviations, 213
Average moving range, 224
Average range, 127, 129, 142, 274
Average, of subgroup ranges
  See average range
Averages chart
  analyze data plots, 136

B

Bar chart, 42
  See also Histograms
Bar graph, 288, 290
Basic tools for SPC, 35
Best-fit line, 199, 201 - 202
Beta risk, 77
  See also Type II error
Bias, 91
Brainstorming, 189, 297 - 298

C

c chart, 256 - 258
Calibration, 279
Capability analysis paper, 192
Capability analysis sheet, 196, 200
Capability anlaysis
  data collection, 194
Capability criterion, 183 - 184, 186
Capability guidelines, 181 - 182
Capability index, 168
Capability indices, 175
Capability values, 168
Cause-and-effect diagrams, 35, 296
  constructing, 298
  using, 298
Cell, 44
Cell boundaries, 44, 64
Cell midpoints, 44, 64
Center
  of the process, 177
  of the specification, 183, 186
Center line, 150, 218, 220
Central Limit Theorem, 70 - 72, 79, 149
Central line
  See Center line
Central tendency, 53, 78, 199
Characteristics
  See also Quality characteristics
  correllation between , 119
  to be managed, 119
Charts for individuals, 222 - 225
Check sheets, 35, 48, 96
  common types of, 96
  defect cause, 99
  defective item, 98
  other types, 101
  process distribution, 96
Class frequency, 48
Class interval, 46
Class limit, 47
Class size, 47

P

p chart, 235 - 254
Parameter design, 19
Pareto analysis, 35, 287, 291
Pareto charts
   See also Pareto diagrams
   multiple, 292
Pareto diagrams
   constructing, 289
   secondary, 288
   using, 291
Pareto effect, 290 - 291
Pareto principle, 287
Pattern analysis, 131, 150, 161, 325
Patterns, 39, 330
   nonrandom, 248, *See also* pattern analysis
   of variation, 32
   out-of-control, 131, *See also* Process control,
     interpret for pattern analysis
PDCA cycle, 286, 309
Percent out of specification, 168, 170, 172, 199
Percentage of tolerance, 278, 280
Periodic review, 322
Pilot program, 319
Plant managers, 315
Platykurtic, 69
Plot points, 126
Plot-point percentage, 196 - 197
Population, 27, 66, 84
Preparatory steps, 118, 235
Presentation, 30
Preventative spending
   See Continuous improvement dollars; Quality
     Loss Function
Prevention, 13, 19, 29, 294
Prevention strategy, 29
   See also Prevention
Preventive spending, 11
Probability, 31, 66
Probability density function, 66
Probability distribution, 65
Probability paper, 36
Problem solving, 251, 253
Process, 26
   capable, 201, 306
   define the, 118
   history of, 325
   not capable, 306
   revised, 253
   with a high mean, 201
Process average, 68, 127, 129, 168, 224,
   240 - 241, 248

Process capability, 109, 165
   assessing, 166
   calculate, 252
   evaluate, 181, 252
   formal study, 252
   improve, 188, 253
   in non-normal distributions, 202
   interpret for, 116, 144, 214, 219, 225, 252, 256,
     258, 263
   preliminary estimate, 252
Process capability index, 175
Process control, 112
   See also Statistical control
   goal of, 109
   interpret for, 116, 131, 213, 219, 225, 244, 256,
     258, 262, See also pattern analysis; patterns,
     out-of-control
   ongoing, 143, 220
   real-time dynamic, 332
Process control system, 29
   goal of, 31
Process elements, 83, 296
Process flow diagrams, 35
Process flowchart, 293
Process location, 136
Process mean
   adjusting, 183
Process parameters, 226
Process performance, 29, 177, 179, 181, 184, 244
   See also *Cpk* index
Process potential, 175, 179, 181
   See also *Cp* index
Process potential study, 191
   See also Short-run capability
Process standard deviation, 142, 169, 186, 214,
   219, 225
Process streams, 249
Producer's risk
   See Type I error
Proportion non-conforming, 235, 237 - 238, 247,
   See also *p* chart
Purchasing, 17, 29

Q

QFD
   See Quality Function Deployment
Quality, 6, 13, 25
   visual presentation of, 320
Quality assurance, 15, 317
Quality characteristics, 67, 79, 83
Quality control, 23